THE COLLAPSE OF EAST GERMAN COMMUNISM

The Year the Wall Came Down, 1989

DAVID M. KEITHLY

PRAEGER

Westport, Connecticut
London

Library of Congress Cataloging-in-Publication Data

Keithly, David M.
The collapse of East German communism : the year the wall came down, 1989 / David M. Keithly.
p.   cm.
Includes bibliographical references.
ISBN 0-275-94261-9 (alk. paper)
1. Germany (East)—Politics and government—1989-1990.
2. Communism—Germany (East)—History.   I. Title.
DD289.K45   1992
320.9431—dc20   92-2686

British Library Cataloguing in Publication Data is available.

Copyright © 1992 by David M. Keithly

Library of Congress Catalog Card Number: 92-2686
ISBN: 0-275-94261-9

First published in 1992

Praeger Publishers, 88 Post Road West, Westport, CT 06881
An imprint of Greenwood Publishing Group, Inc.

Printed in the United States of America

The paper used in this book complies with the Permanent Paper Standard issued by the National Information Standards Organization (Z39.48-1984).

10 9 8 7 6 5 4 3 2 1

THE COLLAPSE OF EAST GERMAN COMMUNISM

To Rosi and Lothar
and
Maggie and Larry

Contents

Abbreviations

BDI	West German Federation of Industry
CAD/CAM	Computer-aided design and manufacturing
CMEA	Council for Mutual Economic Assistance or COMECON
Cocom	Coordinating Committee for East-West Trade
CPSU	Communist Party of the Soviet Union
DBD	Democratic Peasants Federation
DFD	Democratic Women's Federation
DM	West German mark
DTSB	German Gymnastics and Sports Federation
CDU	Christian Democratic Union
EC	European Community
EKD	All-German Evangelical Church organization
ENA	Evangelical News Agency
FDGB	Free German Trade Union Federation (East German only)
FDGB	East German Federation of Unions
FDJ	Free German Youth
FDP	Free Democratic party
FRG	Federal Republic of Germany (West Germany)
GDR	German Democratic Republic
KB	League of Culture
KoKo	Commercial Coordination Section
KPD	German Communist party
LDPD	Liberal Democratic party
MfS	Ministry for State Security
NÖS	New Economic System
NÖSPL	New Economic System for Planning and Managing the Economy

NVA	National People's Army
NDPD	National Democratic party
ÖSS	Economic System of Socialization
PDS	Party of Democratic Socialism
PLO	Palestine Liberation Organization
SBZ	Soviet Zone of Occupation
SDP	Social Democratic party (East German only)
SED	Socialist Unity party
SPD	Social Democratic party
SPL	State Plan Commission
VAT	Value added tax
VEB	Council of Ministers, the individual plants
VVB	Associations of People's Industries

Acknowledgments

In the course of writing this book, I have become indebted to more persons than I can mention here. My principal indebtedness is to the people of the former German Democratic Republic whose nonviolent revolution was a source of much inspiration. The original impetus for this undertaking came from my German friends, in particular, Michael and Sigrid Augenstein, Peter Schoof, Bettina Meller, and Theresia Lork, who, beginning in our university days in Freiburg, have over the years encouraged an often perplexed American observer of German affairs in more ways than they can know. I am especially indebted to Elaine Dawson whose eagle eye, commitment to excellence, and indefatigable energy contributed significantly to this project. I am indebted to David Childs for his critical comments on early drafts, and for allowing me to use part of a previously published article. I would like to express my gratitude to an anonymous reviewer for his lengthy and helpful comments on the manuscript. My thanks to Dean Charles Owen Burgess of Old Dominion University for providing funding for this project at a critical moment, notwithstanding the budgetary constraints in Virginia state universities, as well as to my colleagues Andy Terrill, Pat Rollins, and Don Zeigler for their unflinching moral support, the importance of which should not be underestimated.

I trust those I have identified above will find this work satisfactory. Of course, I alone bear the responsibility for its shortcomings.

Introduction

> Hate is a passion all tyrants are bound to arouse; but contempt is often the
> cause by which tyrannies are actually overthrown.
>
> —Aristotle

On a warm July day of the very warm summer of 1989, I sat enjoying a picnic lunch on a small hill overlooking the Soviet air assault base at Nohra in Thuringia. In the wooded area behind me lay the Buchenwald concentration camp in whose torture sheds hundreds of thousands of people from over a dozen countries found pain and death. The jailers of that abominable place demonstrated to Germans what fate awaited those who opposed the führer. To my left, just several miles down the road, lay Weimar, home to much of Germany's rich cultural heritage and a symbol of humane achievement. In many ways the paradoxes before my eyes that day were the paradoxes of Germany. Transcendence, embodied in the splendid city of Weimar, a high point of human accomplishment, on the one hand, and utter degradation, made manifest by the grisly spectacle of the concentration camp on the other. This small corner of Germany, just off the main transit route through Thuringia, seemed to me a sort of Teutonic microcosm.

Here at one and the same time was the season of light and the season of darkness. In Weimar one discovered a spring of hope; in Buchenwald only the dead winter of despair. These triumphs and tragedies, these polar twins coexisting uneasily beside one another, were components of the modern German experience.

As I watched the Soviet assault helicopters take off and land at the rate of perhaps a few dozen an hour on that cloudless summer day, I found myself musing idly about Germany's future. Whither the Vaterland? Its recent past had been so very tragic. Defeat in two world wars; in the second, massive destruction and ultimately division. Division seemed now almost in the nature of things; it was part of everyday life; it seemed somehow normal to people regularly confronted with it. And yet, it was ghastly. A border replete with barbed wire, armed guards, mine fields and self-shooting devices running through the country—normal? How durable was this situation? Could Stalinism-in-one-country succeed in the longer term against the will of the vast majority of that country's citizens? How much longer would foreign forces be massed on German soil? For its defeat in the Second World War Germany had paid with dismemberment. The world continued to pay a high price for that division. And the Soviet Union, for its part, maintained its position in Central Europe at great cost to itself. The sprawling Soviet base I found myself contemplating that day was a further expression of Germany's tragedy.

I was no stranger to the German Democratic Republic. I had traveled there many times; I had crossed the border separating West Germany from East Germany as well as the Wall between West Berlin and East Berlin on numerous occasions. I had visited many of the GDR's cities. The prior evening I had a long conversation with East German friends about the possibilities of reform in their country. A conspicuous inability to conceal frustrations and bitterness seeped into that conversation, as was usual in open exchanges. This was a manifestation of the hate Aristotle had spoken of.

Under the guidance of proletarian leaders the GDR took pride in such humane achievements as gunning down would-be escapees on the border (a shooting had taken place on the Wall as recently as February) and locking up those insolent enough to criticize the regime (dissidents were usually jailed along with common criminals and sometimes "sat" for years). In a tasteless, somewhat ghoulish ceremony sponsored by a regime renowned for indelicacies, officers of the National People's Army (NVA) were commissioned at the gates of Buchenwald, with the express purpose of conveying the message: Never again!

Never again? The inescapable conclusion was that it was not so much the idea of concentration camps that the GDR's leadership found objectionable, but rather who ran them and for what purpose. After all, beginning in 1945 the Soviets used Buchenwald to incarcerate German political prisoners.[1]

"The government is best which governs least" is a saying attributed to Thomas Jefferson. There is little or no legitimacy when state authority is excessive: this is one of the lessons of the remarkable year of 1989. And the GDR had at its command only its socialist identity to justify its existence. Beginning that summer the GDR rolled downhill with accelerating speed, and the regime would finally collapse under its own weight. Once it had become clear that the Soviet Army was not going to be used to prop up satellite regimes, the people's pent-up hatred turned to contempt. A modicum of "I told you so" satisfaction must have warmed Aristotle's breast. The people bolted in droves: projected at an annual rate those leaving in November 1989 would have amounted to one-tenth of the entire population. The leadership fell into disgrace, and as national passions were rekindled, East Germans began demanding rapid unification.

For decades the communists had held power largely through fear. Gradually in 1989 popular fear of the regime dissipated, then in a stunning switch, fear shifted to the rulers who grew livid once they became aware of their nakedness in front of those they had enslaved. That fear led quickly to the granting of almost unimaginable concessions. Thereafter, the communist leaders were caught in a vortex of anger and rebellion that dragged them down from power.

For years Western observers had wondered whether the GDR represented a new German nation under socialism. There is, of course, no need to ponder this issue any longer. In the final analysis the GDR was the nation that could not have been, and it is the purpose of this book to outline the developments leading to the debacle of its regime. According to Aristotle, it is the habit of the tyrant never to esteem those with a spirit of dignity and independence, since he arrogates to himself a monopoly of these qualities. In 1989 East Germans rejected the tyrant's prerogative, acquired their dignity, and won their independence.

In 1989 I gazed incredulously at the strangest occurrences I have ever experienced. As a chance bystander and traveller, I can say "I was there," at least part of the time. An advantage of the onlooker's evidence is that it adds a certain authenticity. With a certain closeness to events and with the varnish of interpretation partially removed, the eyewitness can provide a better idea of people as they were, of the environment as it existed and of the atmosphere as participants sensed it. Admittedly, the eyewitness treads a fine line. This book is intended to be in part an account of history in the making, and my hope is that it will have some appeal beyond specialist circles. I have attempted to combine scholarly analysis with eyewitness record, endeavoring thereby to stake out the middle ground between scholarship and journalism. Writing contemporary history is an arduous task, one beset with potential pitfalls. Sources are often lacking; available ones are usually incomplete. Who can and will speak frankly at this point in time about the events of 1989? In dealing with such a contemporary subject, the writer must be aware of the hazard of extending current models into the past. While writing this book, I asked myself repeatedly whether or not I was falling into this trap, and I have made every effort to avoid it. Moreover, taking the impersonal, distanced view expected of the scholar poses a particular challenge when writing contemporary history. If a response is called for, one might echo the words of Thomas Carlyle about historical writing: "What is all knowledge too but recorded experience, and a product of history; of which therefore, reasoning and belief, no less than action and passion, are essential materials."

I should make some mention here of method and approach. My chief analytical focus might be referred to as the "traditional" one with respect to the German question. I argue that postwar German division and the attendant unfulfilled aspirations of the German people remained a source of momentous, albeit latent, instability in Europe. That German division conferred security and equilibrium to Europe, a notion that had gained some currency on both sides of the Atlantic in the 1980s, is one most observers now reject, although with the benefit of hindsight. Since the German question consisted in fact of several questions and puzzles wrapped in an enigma, I have concentrated on that aspect which became salient and decisive: the sudden headlong clash in 1989 of German national identity and communist ideology. A treatise on the events of 1989 in the GDR must ultimately address three themes—the internal collapse of German communism, the consequences of *perestroika* and *glasnost* upon the satellite countries, and the revolution carried out by East Germans—and must provide some explanation of their interrelationship. The point of departure of the "traditional" approach was that a legitimacy deficit in the GDR constituted a cardinal political problem for that state. Put simply, political legitimacy involves popular endorsement of a government as appropriate and correct, and consequently deserving of obedience. From this fundamental problem in the GDR, others ensued. For example, a regime that did not enjoy popular approval and, to boot, was closely identified with a foreign power, was hard pressed to portray itself to its people as one preserving German heritage and traditions. Many, not least Soviet president Mikhail Gorbachev, were surprised in 1989 by the intensity of national feeling in the GDR. Acknowledging the existence of legitimacy difficulties in Moscow's German ally, Gorbachev hoped finally to cut the Gordian knot by hastening the pace of reform. Gazing through the prism of an ideology he himself would later reject, Gorbachev did not fathom how robust the forces of nationalism could be, a remarkable miscalculation with respect to East-Central Europe, where some of nationalism's most virulent manifestations have presented themselves in the modern age.

Dismissing problems, as the East German leaders glibly did with regard to identity and nationalism in their country, hardly dispels them. Several years prior to the collapse of communism in the GDR, West German president Richard von Weizsäcker drew considerable criticism in the East for making what should have been a self-evident point about the German question: "History teaches us that a question does not cease to exist simply because nobody has an answer to it." Denial of problem in fact often ensures it will return with vehemence, as was the case in 1989 throughout the East Bloc, when the clash between national identity and ideology developed with such imposing swiftness that it was sometimes difficult to comprehend what exactly was transpiring. Once East Germans were allowed a choice, once their loyalty was put to a true test, as had not been done before, national passions burst forth.

"German national identity recovered" is necessarily a prominent theme of a book analyzing the collapse of East German communism: national identity and systemic legitimacy in the GDR went hand-in-hand. In devising an analytical framework to handle legitimacy issues, I include in the first section an overview of the concept of legitimacy. I then discuss legitimacy problems in the specific German context and correlate this discussion to the long-standing German debates about "homeland," national awareness, and national identity, the purpose being to explain how various theories of legitimacy, identity, and nationality applied to Germany.

From there the first section examines the backdrop against which the 1989 revolution must be viewed. In the main, economic performance was the key source of legitimacy in the GDR and the foremost underpinning of social stability. In the 1980s, a decade the single-party state would not survive, the GDR confronted new and complex economic challenges. At the beginning of that decade, Otto Reinhold, Rector of the SED Academy for the Social Sciences, spoke of the possibility of social conflict in the event of a significant economic downturn. It would be wrong to say that indigenous economic factors were essential in the collapse of the East German regime, but they clearly were a contributing component. Whether these by themselves would have been the regime's eventual undoing is a matter of speculation. In my view, they would not have been. But the dire economic situation in other socialist countries, Poland and the Soviet Union in particular, forced the leaders there to begin with the reforms that people throughout the bloc would call for in turn. As the German scholar Karl Kaiser aptly pointed out, once Moscow accepted the results of a Polish election which brought to power a government led by the free trade union Solidarity, it was only a matter of time before political opposition would emerge in neighboring countries and other captive peoples would fling down the gauntlet before their rulers. In response to the latter's stonewalling, the citizenry stressed the eminent reasonableness of reform, and referred the local communist authorities to Soviet leader Mikhail Gorbachev. *His* arguments would be employed against them. Thus did the swelling tide of *perestroika* pour into the GDR.

Reinhold might have been correct in his conjecture that social conflict in the GDR would have been the result of a severe economic downturn. What he did not foresee, or more likely did not care to consider, was the possibility that economic dislocations elsewhere in the bloc would suffice to begin a political chain reaction. It is notable that some East German dissidents, in particular, the law professor Wolfgang Seiffert, who defected from the GDR in 1978, predicted that continuance of the economic muddle in the bloc would ultimately convince the Soviet leadership that the USSR should cut losses and relinquish the GDR as a costly outpost. Unquestionably, economics and politics were closely intertwined, and economic conditions in the East Bloc in the late 1980s drove political decisions in a twofold manner. First, severe production downturns persuaded communist leaders that there was no longer an alternative to major reforms; second, at some point Moscow decided the GDR was a strategic luxury it could ill afford. East German communists then faced the dreadful contradiction of being tacitly ordered by the Soviet Union to pursue a course of action threatening the very existence of the GDR, the instrument of Soviet power in Germany.

Popular grievances finding expression in 1989 invariably referred back to earlier party policies and actions, which is yet another reason for examining the setting of the 1989 upheaval. Grievances ran the gamut from the establishment of police terror in the early 1950s, to the collectivization of agriculture, to the myriad of economic experiments. Placards and slogans at the fall demonstrations attested to the popular outpouring of specific complaints. "We aren't guinea pigs! Enough of this experimentation!" was a recurrent rallying cry. Persistent economic difficulties, visible economic failures, misguided planning, incessant official lying, police chicanery, despotic bureaucracy—all were ills the people had endured. To understand 1989, one must understand something about these things.

The second part of this book deals with the political chain reaction, that concatenation of circumstances leading to an open challenge of the communist dictatorship with a German face. The third part examines aspects of that challenge. To say that the collapse of communism in the Soviet Union's European allies surprised nearly everyone borders on emphasizing the obvious. Once the process of disintegration began, the regimes toppled in ever shorter increments of time. In the celebrated observation of the British journalist Timothy Garton Ash: the first domino to fall, Poland, underwent a tortured process lasting ten years; Hungary, for its part, needed only ten months to cast communism into the dustbin; the GDR required ten weeks; Czechoslovakia just ten days.[2] Events outran the ability of anyone, above all the communist leaders, to grasp what was taking place around them. That fall, one day's marvels became the following day's conventional wisdom. Decision after decision was made under the enormous pressure of events. To the last, the GDR would remain a special case. Once the enormity of communist misdeeds there became clear, once the regime's corruption, the appalling arms peddling, and the official support of international terrorism came to light, the GDR degenerated into something quite less than a state without a nation. It became a state devoid of leaders. The ensuing power vacuum simply geared up the already swift tempo of events, inducing East Germans to rush headlong into the arms of West Germans, and leaving the latter with little choice but to embrace them.

Throughout, personal observations and reflections are intended to contribute to the analysis. I will always recall how, in the first week of November, I watched in amazement as throngs of people, estimated to have been as many as a million, took to the East Berlin streets to demand sweeping reform. A tremendous roar seemed to rise from the throat of the masses: "Enough!" "Free elections!" The living sea rose, wave upon wave: "We will be slaves no longer." Placards called for free speech, an end to party dictatorship, and the right to travel. The people had long since given up on the communist leadership; the latter's promises of reform were parried with calls of "Resign!" And it was the people who set the political agenda. Those few party officials who dared to appear in public were greeted with catcalls and whistles. *"Halt's Maul"* ("Shut your trap") was the curt reply of the crowd to one official's request for serious dialogue about a "new GDR."

But contempt was tempered by humor. Even as the bitter draught ran over, people displayed some lightheartedness. In a hitherto oppressive society whose cheeriest feature might well have been its mordant wit, this too seemed to run over. One placard read, "Always forward, never backward—Erich Honecker, roofer," a reference to the disgraced former party leader and his initial calling, which most East Germans quite obviously wished he would have made his life-long one. The final speaker that day, observing the five-minute time limit for speeches, concluded her remarks by snapping: "I am asking the government to do what I am doing now—stepping down."

Just before Christmas I remember watching a televised rally in Dresden for West German chancellor Helmut Kohl. The chants of "Helmut, Helmut" were astonishing enough in a country where short months before a West German politician would not have been permitted contact with average people. But even more remarkable than this, Kohl mounted the platform and stated:

> I stand here to bring the greetings of fellow citizens in West Germany, and also to express my recognition and admiration for the nonviolent revolution in the GDR. . . . My goal, when the historic moment makes it possible, is the unity of our nation.[3]

Then, on the verge of tears, Kohl declared, "God bless our German fatherland." Few eyes remained dry that day. Many pulses seemed in fact at fever pitch. With hearts both frightened and free, East Germans were flocking to Chancellor Kohl. The spring of hope had arrived. The long, gray winter of despair had ended.

NOTES

1. Martin McCauley, *The German Democratic Republic Since 1945* (New York: St. Martin's Press, 1983), 3.

2. Timothy Garton Ash, *The Magic Lantern: The Revolution of 1989* (New York: Random House, 1990), 78.

3. Quoted in Bernard Gwertzman and Michael T. Kaufman, eds., *The Collapse of Communism* (New York: Random House, 1990), 330.

Part I
Backdrop to Revolution

1

The Nature of East German Communism

THE SED STATE

For the first forty years of its existence,[1] the "other" Germany, the German Democratic Republic, was a state officially guided by the precepts of Marxism-Leninism. The guardian of this ideology was the Socialist Unity party (SED), established in the Soviet Zone of Occupation (SBZ) in 1946 with the forced merging of the German Communist party (KPD) and the Social Democratic party (SPD) in the Soviet Zone. By virtue of this fusion of the two major working-class parties, the SED professed thereafter to represent the collective interests of the German working class. At the time of its founding in October 1949 the GDR, like the other states of Eastern Europe, regarded itself as a "people's democracy" at the intermediate juncture of socialist progress, which, in the GDR's case, followed the "antifascist democratizing" period when Nazism as a political force had supposedly been eradicated and society recast in a superior mold.

Shortly after its inception the SED became a Leninist "party of the new type," a highly centralized organization under the exclusive direction of full-time party officials, the *Apparat*. These functionaries were responsible for appointing the most pivotal people in the society including judges, government officials, industrial managers, newspaper editors, university rectors, senior military officers, union leaders, and school superintendents. For purposes of appointment the party assembled lists of suitable individuals, politically screened and carefully assessed, and the process enabled the party to effect long-term, resolute cadre development. In recent years the expression *nomenklatura* has been commonly employed in referring both to this selection process as well as to the entire "priviligentsia" of party members or party-approved people reckoned well-suited to hold responsible posts and high office. By dint of its public role the *nomenklatura* had access to goods and services that only the very wealthy in Western societies have. As a group, the *nomenklatura* represented the pinnacle of society, entitled to rights, status, and prerogatives the average citizen did not enjoy, and for this reason, it was often described as a client ruling class, self-selecting and self-sustaining.[2]

The transition of the SED to a cadre party began in 1948 and was sanctioned in the 1949-50 Two-Year Plan that effected the political and economic transformation of society. The SED's official history defended societal and party restructuring during this period as an objective imperative to advance socialism and to protect democratic and antifascist achievements against the imperialist scheming of the Western powers and their German bourgeois and social-democratic partners.[3] According to the party's self-image:

> The cadres in the socialist society are personalities, especially from the working class, engaged as leaders, functionaries and specialists in all areas of the society on the basis of their political and professional qualifications and attributes, or are being prepared for positions of responsibility.[4]

Through cadre policies that inducted new members into the party fold and provided reliable party and state officials, the SED maintained its ascendancy in all public and state organizations. Cadre policies pertained to party functionaries as well as to state administrators and hence the party apparatus made all significant personnel decisions in the GDR.

The social transformation of which the conversion of the SED to a "party of the new type" was a part, had several components, chief among these the establishment of a Soviet-style state on German soil.[5] For the SED to have assumed a position analogous to that of the Communist party of the Soviet Union (CPSU) in the USSR, the former had first to attain political supremacy in the SBZ/GDR. Accordingly, centralization deepened after 1948. State involvement in the economy grew significantly and extensive economic planning was introduced. The state administration became increasingly interwoven with the party structure and mass organizations were expanded and brought under exclusive SED jurisdiction. The edifice of the GDR had thus been put in place.

POLITICAL CULTURE

Although considerable change occurred in the GDR over the past decades (of which I will not describe here), prior to the autumn of 1989, the GDR could be correctly portrayed as a totalitarian system at least in the sense that the party uniformly aspired to totalitarian control. With the exception of the churches, no other societal organizations were tolerated, and the gathering together of citizens was condoned only if this took place under party auspices. Mass organizations such as the Free German Trade Union Federation (FDGB), the Free German Youth (FDJ), the Democratic Women's Federation (DFD), the League of Culture (KB), and the German Gymnastics and Sports Federation (DTSB) had the dual function of enabling the party to retain contact with the masses while equipping it to exercise authority directly through these societal transmission belts.

In democratic societies the notion of civic culture embraces a participatory process in which individuals are oriented positively to the input structure and input procedures.[6] It was precisely this orientation that the SED endeavored to curb in the GDR. Every effort was made to suppress any semblance of public spirit or civic culture, save what was party-ordained. The nature and scope of citizen participation in communist countries has been the subject of rigorous academic controversy,[7] but there is considerable agreement that popular organization in the GDR closely corresponded to the key facet of the "mobilization model," viz., that individual involvement in politics was the product of regime-directed recruital and assemblage. The totalitarian penchant endured in the GDR until the bitter end, when adjustment to the abundance of internal and external pressures upon the country became overbearing.

In his *Politics* Aristotle examined the means a tyrant uses to maintain his authority.[8] These, Aristotle said, plumb the depths of wrongdoing, however artful they may be, and correspond to the all-encompassing aims pursued by tyrants. The first is to break the spirit of the subjects, since poor-spirited people cannot engage in plots. The second aim is to breed mutual distrust, for tyranny will not be overthrown until people begin to trust one another, then to conspire. For this reason primarily, tyrants are "at outs with the good." Good people for their part pose a threat to tyranny in a twofold sense: they consider it shameful to be governed as slaves and they refuse to betray one another. The third aim is to render the subjects incapable of action. So long as all are incapable of resisting, no credible threat to the regime arises.

In the exercise of authority the SED employed several tools in conjunction with one another. The first of these was the blunt instrument of public coercion or repression. Overt regime opponents in any walk of life were invariably dealt with harshly, even brutally. Dissidents faced imprisonment or expulsion from the country. A milder, but nonetheless effective technique of subjugation was to be found in various forms of intimidation, ranging from anguishing bureaucratic chicanery and paper wars to the tactic of *Verunsicherung*, the widely used police term referring to the promotion of uncertainty and apprehension among citizens. Standard operating procedure of GDR officialdom encompassed abundant arbitrariness.

Anyone who had occasion to travel in the GDR experienced this in some degree, although bureaucratic capriciousness vis-à-vis foreigners was relatively innocuous unless a serious crime was involved. In need once of an additional passport stamp the border guards neglected to provide, I duly reported to the office of the "competent authorities" in an East German city and proceeded to queue with a group of disheartened-looking people waiting before a closed door. After a while I became aware that not only were the officials within not processing any paperwork, but were simply prattling. Losing patience, I knocked, walked in, and pointed out that several people were waiting outside. One of the officials, presumably the woman in charge, grimaced at me, and was on the verge of blistering my ears with a choice flow of disrespectful bureaucratese when I pulled from my pocket my U.S. passport. "Ach, so! You should have said something." My passport was quickly stamped, and the now quite courteous official wished me a pleasant day. The disgruntled people outside the door continued to wait and the officials within resumed their idle chatter as I left. The classless society? Franz Kafka's *Vor dem Gesetz* came immediately to mind.

Another workaday tool for maintaining order and regime stability, has been described by Timothy Garton Ash as "civic neutralization."[9] This stratagem, whose various aspects have been analytic focal points for several observers, refers to the modus operandi of forced political disengagement.[10] According to the "mobilization model," for instance, citizens were depoliticized and separated psychologically from political affairs.[11] Philip Roeder speaks of "enforced departicipation" in Leninist societies, a concept which plainly applied to the GDR.[12] The "social atomization" argument advanced by such authors as Zbigniew Brzezinski and Victor Zaslavsky provides a plausible explanation for the prolonged absence of organized opposition in communist countries.[13] As the expression would suggest, "social atomization" denotes a process whereby citizens are prevented from organizing themselves on their own accord and initiative, in effect, becoming politically secluded from one another. The GDR's political system was one unmistakably geared to marginalize the individual.

Since scholars have examined citizen participation in the Soviet Union far more extensively than in the countries of the former East Bloc and, in consequence, some uncertainties about the East German participative process will in all likelihood remain, even the question of how many people ostensibly participated in political life in the GDR one way or another has not been adequately addressed. Since mobilization theory attaches much importance to the sheer numbers of people taking part in regime-sponsored activities, the significance of this question should not be minimized.[14] Brzezinski and Huntington assert that supervised, regime-sponsored participation must be "intense and all-embracing" for the purposes of mobilization and ultimately for the exercise of authority.[15] Accordingly, socialization and popular participation in the GDR had considerable salience. Article 21 of the 1974 Constitution stated:

> Every citizen of the German Democratic Republic is entitled to participate fully in shaping the political, economic, social and cultural life of the socialist community and the socialist state. The principle shall be applied 'Participate in working, in planning, and in governing!'[16]

East German officials made special effort to emphasize how many citizens partook in political activities. For example, the FDJ had 2,300,000 members in 1981. The 1968 Constitution of the GDR was said to have been discussed in 750,000 "family gatherings" and some 1.5 million people served as elected trade union representatives in 1973;[17] 141,000 became members of factory production councils and 240,000 were on advisory councils of state-owned consumer trade associations in the same year.[18] In the 1980s the 15 district assemblies (*Bezirkstage*) had nearly 27,000 elected representatives; the county (*Landkreise*) and city assemblies (*Stadtkreise*) comprised over 7,000; and the local councils (*Gemeindevertretungen*) over 170,000.[19] Hence, from the regional to the community level there were over 200,000 representatives.[20] The respective institutions, essentially auxiliary organs of the executive, had only a mobilization function, not a policy-making one. Regime-sanctioned participation made differences in personal motivation and conviction largely meaningless. Individual involvement in politics had no connection with what the political scientist would refer to as "system output"; taking part in semi-coerced rallies and other official functions did not furnish East Germans with any influence on state decisions.

The stability of the system ultimately hinged on a delicate symmetry between repression, civic neutralization, and the adjustment capacity of the citizenry. Out of necessity East Germans learned how to utilize relatively intricate routines of conformity and accommodation to perform everyday matters, as well as to maintain a quiescent, albeit usually untrusting, association with the authorities. Accommodation with the regime called into being the double life citizens of communist countries were forced to lead. East Germans lived according to separate codes of conduct, one public, one private. There were two modes of speech, the official and the unofficial. Most people unhesitatingly went through the motions of the collective when the need to adapt arose. The socialist personality was thus an alternating one, zealous in public if necessary, but intensely private by preference.

While average citizens were kept apolitical through exclusion from the political process, at the same time they were to be mollified by the prospect of continuously higher living standards. Ensuing from such placation through consumption was an unspoken social compact, albeit one imposed from above and scarcely concluded between equals. It would not be amiss to depict the arrangement as a central feature of the political system for over fifteen years, as will be discussed below. Material appeasement of the citizenry was, of course, to be found elsewhere in the East Bloc, the Polish counterpart being the infamous "money, meat, and promises" offered in the wake of any expression of general dissatisfaction.[21] In the GDR, though, this became a standard point of reference in policy formulation. The regime was in a position to offer tangible improvements in the living standard and, in consequence, pledges of material well-being did not go unfulfilled as they did to a great extent elsewhere in the East Bloc.[22]

Ideologically the SED avowed to be the leading force in the construction of the socialist order, piloting turbulent political waters with a precise interpretation of dynamic communal development. The SED was the fountainhead of morality, and *partiinost* (partymindedness, or party-political involvement) the highest civic virtue. Organizational principles incorporated a strict hierarchical structure; a cadre not a mass party; disallowance of any building of factions within any of the party organs; the unconditional obligation of party decisions to party members from above to below and the imperative of party members to agree to personnel selection by party organs, also from above to below.[23] "On the basis of Marxism-Leninism's creative application and further development, the party directs and leads the shaping of the developed socialist society," the Statute of the SED asserted.[24] Because the SED had to avail itself of the scientific nature of the ideology to justify its rule officially, it was keenly sensitive to ideological dogma, more so than the other fraternal Leninist parties, and thus it was small wonder the SED dealt stringently with viewpoints smacking of ideological deviationism, for these were potentially menacing to the East German state itself.

This legitimizing function of Marxism-Leninism might be summarized as follows.[25] Political parties are expressions of the interests of social classes or of groups within social classes. They are associations of the politically active representatives of classes and are designed to effect certain specified class goals. Since the politically active members of any class have a higher level of consciousness (*Bewusstheit*), it follows that parties have provided the political leadership of classes throughout history. By definition, the party of the working class has a more profound understanding of historical forces and is therefore a "progressive influence." The party affords the fabricative cement of class reality. In accordance with the scientific tenets of Marxism-Leninism, this party represents the wave of the future, one destined to lead mankind to higher levels of social development. In the GDR, the SED established its leadership during the stage of the "dictatorship of the proletariat" which followed on the heels of the "victory of the socialist revolution" on German soil and the subsequent "antifascist democratization" period in the 1940s. As Walter Ulbricht, later to become SED party chief, proclaimed in that period:

> We are bound to be deeply thankful to the people of the Soviet Union, because they made the greatest of sacrifices in destroying the fascist German imperialists, therewith creating the prerequisites with which the German people could at last construct a new, democratic order.[26]

Armed with the infallible ideology, the SED maintained its stewardship of the advanced socialist society and would lead this society to eventual communism, the great future hope of mankind.

PARTY ORGANS

At the apex of SED authority stood the Politburo, an institution modeled closely after its counterpart in the CPSU. Elected by the SED's Central Committee, the Politburo was the chief decision-making body of the party and provided the country's primary political directives. Both the Politburo and the Central Committee were relatively small bodies of the party elite consisting of 20 and 156 full members, respectively, in 1989. According to the Party Statute the Central Committee elected: (1) the Politburo to direct the work of the Central Committee between its plenary sessions; (2) the Secretariat to direct the ongoing work, principally the overseeing and execution of party decisions; (3) the general secretary of the Central Committee.[27] Central Committee members were the chief power brokers of the East German political system. Their influence derived not only from membership in the organization, but by their tenancy of crucial state offices as well. As a sort of elite political club, the Central Committee served as a recruitment forum for future top party leaders.

Furthermore, the Central Committee had assumed an important consulting and coordinating function with focus upon the technical and social aspects of specific policy areas.[28] At least partially on account of this, a large majority of Central Committee members in the 1980s had occupational backgrounds that were either economic-technical or party bureaucratic. To maintain the party's grip upon scholarship and academia, several party institutes were founded over the years and placed under Central Committee control. Chief among these were the Academy for the Social Sciences of the Central Committee of the SED and the Central Institute for Socialist Economic Leadership of the Central Committee of the SED. In addition to providing advice and consultation to the party organs, these had a certain control capacity vis-à-vis universities and technical institutes, ensuring ideological purity and bridling potential dissension.[29]

The Secretariat was in effect the directing body of the party apparatus, supervising the work of the departments (*Abteilungen*) with a combined staff of over 2,000. According to the Party Statute: "The Secretariat is charged with the routine business of the party and acts as the party executive." The Secretariat bore primary responsibility for the elevation or demotion of cadre members as well as for the occupational assignment of many. The body transmitted political directives to mass organizations, state organs, economic planning agencies, and the armed forces. Secretariat influence derived not only from this transmission function, but also from the patronage it exercised in selecting party members with the proper ideological profile to various organs and committees, including the party secretaries and the Central Committee department heads. For this reason the Secretariat exerted primary control over appointments and removal of personnel in the party bureaucracy, the main state organs, and other societal institutions. Also, the Secretariat was delegated to identify prominent issues to be included on the Politburo agenda and to provide policy alternatives where appropriate.

Determining the boundary between Politburo and Secretariat responsibility was not always possible, all the more because of the overlap in membership. Every member of the Secretariat in 1989, as had been the case for years, was a Politburo member or candidate member. In 1989 Secretariat members were: Erich Honecker (general secretary), Hermann Axen, Hans Dohlus, Werner Felfe, Kurt Hager, Joachim Herrmann, Werner Jarowinsky, Egon Krenz, Ingeburg Lange, Günter Mittag, and Günter Schabowski. Full members of the Politburo were: Axen, Dohlus, Felfe, Hager, Herrmann, Honecker, Jarowinsky, Krenz, Mittag, Schabowski, Hans-Joachim Böhme, Heinz Kessler, Günter Kleiber, Werner Krolikowski, Erich Mielke, Erich Mückenberger, Alfred Neumann, Horst Sindermann, Willi Stoph, and Harry Tisch. Lange, Werner Eberlein, Siegfried Lorenz, Gerhard Müller, Margarete Müller, Gerhard Schürer, and Werner Walde were candidate members.

THE BLOC PARTIES

Other parties closely aligned with the SED in theory represented particular interest groups in the GDR. All four, the Democratic Peasants Federation (DBD), the Christian Democratic Union (East CDU), the Liberal Democratic party (LDPD), and the National Democratic party (NDPD) were integrated into the "National Front." The DBD stood primarily for the working peasant. The CDU, at least in so far as its name conveyed, represented the interests of Christians in socialism, while the LDPD provided a political home for professionals and those with private businesses. The constituency and goals of the NDPD, which was originally established as an organization appealing chiefly to former Nazis and soldiers, had become somewhat more obscure in later years.[30] Around one-third of its members were white-collar employees and about 22 percent were tradespeople and artisans.[31] The party's long-serving chairman was a former Nazi and *Wehrmacht* officer who had been reindoctrinated while in Soviet captivity during the war.

That "the re-education of the entire population in the spirit of communism has not been completely carried through" was the official explanation for the existence of the "multi-party" state in the 1950s.[32] Accordingly, the SED communicated through these noncommunist groups with an aim to enlisting nonworking-class support for SED goals. The bloc parties were represented in most of the national and regional assemblies, but were barred from engaging in political activity in the universities, large enterprises, or the NVA.[33]

With the intensification of socialism in the 1970s, the purpose of the parties became less clear, although membership in all four increased in those years, as did the number of affiliated groups. The GDR's social structure as seen through socialist lenses did not seem to warrant the permanency of such parties, nor did the size of some constituencies, for example, self-employed artisans and independent retailers. Both the CDU and the LDPD were purported to have been middle-class parties, but their political attitudes were somewhat beguiling. Gerald Götting, the CDU chairman, often pointed out that his was not a "church party," a comment raising questions about its commitment to Christians.[34] Official statements about the intrinsic tolerance of socialist societies as evidenced in the continued existence of the bloc parties led to the conclusion that the SED came to regard them as having some role in regime legitimation.[35]

It is also likely that the parties had a place in the GDR's system of consultative authoritarianism in which the government was able to keep abreast of potential problems and to gauge popular moods through its close association with various groups. This suggests there were more ideologically backward components of East German society in the 1980s than the regime was inclined officially to admit.

Some saw in the retention of the bloc parties a certain alibi function, which referred to a procedure whereby noncommunists could reach a modus vivendi with a basically monolithic society.[36] The supposed multiplicity of parties enabled more citizens outwardly to express loyalty to the regime. Through their affiliation with the bloc parties or other organizations, those working in the small private sector were not strictly beyond the regime's control, and such affiliation in turn permitted the SED to present a united front encompassing many who were at best lukewarm supporters of the communists. The wide basis of the National Front offered the regime additional avenues for propaganda and agitation, and it is rather ironic that the GDR, the state whose chief attribute was monolithic unity, had more parties than the pluralistic Federal Republic of Germany (FRG, or West Germany).

THE STATE INSTITUTIONS

The self-determined leading role of the party contrasted vividly with the subservience of the state apparatus. Pursuant to the ministerial statutes, the paramount mission of the ministries was "to effect the decisions of the Party and the working class on the basis of The Constitution of the GDR, its laws and other legal provisions."[37] The emphasis upon class comported with Article 47 of the 1974 Constitution of the GDR: "The sovereignty of the working people, which is implemented on the basis of democratic centralism, is the fundamental principle of the state structure."[38] For nearly three decades, the GDR had a plural executive and head of state. The two principal state organs, the Council of Ministers and the Council of State, operated on collegial principles. A comfortable consensus existed between the state and party organs, and the pattern of overarching responsibilities as well as membership between party and state was an intricate one.

For the first decade of the GDR's existence, there was a singular head of state, the president of the Republic, an office that was held by only one man, Wilhelm Pieck, the cochairman of the SED, who assumed the post in 1949. Pieck's colleague as cochairman, Otto Grotewohl, served as minister-president and chairman of the Council of Ministers. When Pieck died in 1960, the presidency was supplanted by the Council of State, which consisted over the years of between twenty-one and twenty-four members. Following his election as president of this body, Ulbricht became titular head of state. Thereafter, he embellished this position, that of First Secretary of the SED, and the chairmanship of the National Defense Council, the latter making him commander-in-chief of the military forces insofar as these were not directly integrated into the unified command structure of the Warsaw Pact. In keeping with Ulbricht's avowed principle of the "unity of state leadership," the political role of the Council of State grew, reflecting the broader influence accruing to the state apparatus.[39] Ulbricht was ousted from the top party post in 1971 and replaced by Honecker, but retained his state position until his death in 1973.

In 1976 Honecker assumed the chairmanship of the Council of State, a move paralleling political developments in the Soviet Union where the party leader also became the formal head of state. Nonetheless, Honecker based his political power primarily on his party position and downgraded the importance of the Council of State in the 1970s on that ground. The October 1972 Law on the Council of Ministers and an affiliated constitutional amendment of October 1974, both designed "to enhance the status, duties, and powers of the Council of Ministers in line with the conditions of social development," altered institutional roles.[40] The influence of the Council of Ministers expanded relative to that of the Council of State, above all in the economic sphere.[41] Under the new provisions the Council of State relinquished the right to issue decrees or to act on behalf of the Parliament. As amended, the Constitution referred to the Council of Ministers as the government of the GDR:

(1)   The Council of Ministers, being an organ of the People's Chamber (*Volkskammer*), is the government of the German Democratic Republic. It directs the uniform implementation of government policy on behalf of the People's Chamber and organizes the execution of the political, economic, cultural and social tasks and the defense tasks assigned to it. It is responsible and accountable to the People's Chamber.
(2)   The Council of Ministers directs the national economy and the other spheres of public life. It ensures the planned and proportionate development of the national economy, the harmonious organization of the various fields of public life and of local activities and the implementation of socialist economic integration.[42]

Subsequently, greater autonomy and initiative would be granted to the Council of Ministers and the Planning Commission, a development reflecting an end to the economic experiments of the 1960s and an attendant greater centralization of the economy. Under Premier Willi Stoph, the Council of Ministers, increasingly involved in the direction of the economy, would become the most important state organ.

The parliament of the GDR, the *Volkskammer*, was composed of 500 delegates from the SED, the bloc parties, the FDGB, the FDJ, the KB, and the DFD. Its role as a functional legislature was at most cursory and its legislative work consisted exclusively of approving bills, nearly all of executive origin, the majority of which were passed without any discussion. The infrequent convening of the *Volkskammer* bespoke its actual parliamentary character. For example, in the legislative period 1971-76 eighteen sessions were held, and in the 1976-81 period only thirteen.[43] In some years there were as few as three sittings. There being no need for full-time parliamentarians in the GDR, all deputies were employed outside the chamber.[44] This, moreover, mirrored the regime's perception of the parliamentary representative as a "mediator between the citizen and the state in all matters of working and living conditions."[45] According to Article 56 of the 1974 Constitution: "The deputies maintain close contact with their electors. They are to heed their proposals, suggestions and criticisms and to ensure conscientious attention to them. . . . The deputies explain the policy of the socialist state to the citizens."[46] In each of its sessions beginning in 1963 the *Volkskammer* established fifteen committees consisting of between eight and fifty-one members.

The snug likemindedness between party and state institutions in the GDR can be explained by a quick glance at the personnel registers.[47] The Council of State was composed of Honecker, Sindermann, Stoph, Krenz, Felfe, Hager, Mittag, Mielke, Tisch, and M. Müller. Co-chairing the People's Presidium, and by this authority the chief *Volkskammer* officials, were Sindermann and Mückenberger. The principal parliamentary committee chairmen were Axen, Hager, Mittag, Jarowinsky, and Stoph. The leading members of the Council of Ministers were Stoph, Krolikowski, Neumann, Kleiber, Schürer, Kessler, and Mielke. The Presidium of the Council of the National Front was composed of Herrmann, Honecker, Krenz, and Tisch; the latter also chaired the FDGB.

Any overview of the SED state would be incomplete without some discussion of the Ministry for State Security (MfS), which directed the SSD, the Stasi, or secret police. The vast size of the MfS, which was sometimes referred to by officialdom as the "sword and shield" of the party, and the extent of its permeation of the GDR did not actually become clear until after the downfall of the regime. The MfS was established in February 1950 by a law providing no guidelines about duties or jurisdiction. Official descriptions later referred vaguely to the ministry as an organ of the Council of Ministers of the GDR entrusted with special legal and security responsibilities for the protection of the socialist

Personnel Register Showing Overlap between the Politburo of the Central Committee and State and Party Organs

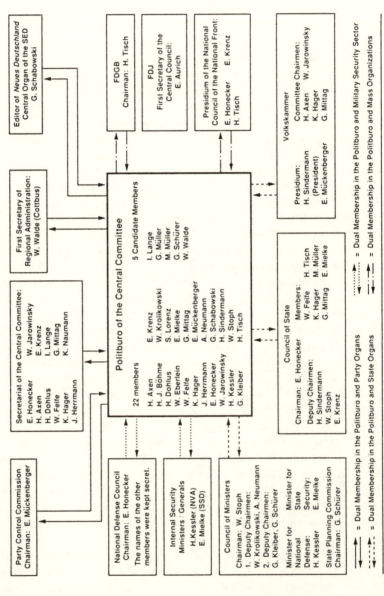

Gerd Meyer Kirsten Rohmeis, in: Die DDR, hrsg. von der Landeszentrale für politische Bildung Baden-Württemberg. Stuttgart, Reihe: Der Bürger im Staat, Heft, Heft 2 Mai 1983, S. 93.

state and society. Headed after 1957 by Mielke, who held the rank of army general, the MfS was one of the largest employers in the country, with hundreds of thousands of official and unofficial workers on its payroll, whose job it was to spy on their fellow citizens or to engage in intelligence operations abroad. The ministerial operating budget and the number of those actually affiliated with the MfS were always closely guarded secrets, but the over 250 regional and branch offices of the ministry throughout the country gave some indication of the organization's size. In safeguarding the SED state from supposed external as well as internal enemies, the ministry assembled files on millions of East Germans. Available data on the MfS impart the true meaning of the term "police state." Some observers have gone so far as to depict the MfS as the essential and distinctive institution of the GDR.

SYSTEM OPERATION

The above discussion focuses on the formal structures of the GDR. Much was and still is unknown about the real operation of the GDR's political system. Basic questions concerning, for example, the exact political powers of the general secretary and the actual procedures for making political decisions remain in part unanswered. Observers differ on the nature and amount of influence the Soviet Union exercised upon the policy-making process. Beyond saying that considerable political power was concentrated in relatively few hands, how did the GDR's leaders arrive at decisions? If one can accept that "collegial principles" were paramount in the governing of the GDR, how did such principles operate in practice? Baylis writes that

> the record of East German politics since 1956 may be viewed as one of continuing conflict, sometimes latent, sometimes overt, between policies justified by the requirements of 'politics'—that is, dogmatic ideology and traditional power considerations—and others answering to the perceived demands of economic rationality.[48]

Seldom was it clear, however, when decisions were based largely on ideological considerations and when the exigencies of the moment required more pragmatic actions. It was as laborious a task to establish a direct connection between the ideology and GDR behavior as it was to predict policies on the basis of Lenin's writings. What is more, the leaders of the GDR were so cut from the same cloth, so alike ideologically and in their relentless pursuit of what they perceived to be the interests of socialism, that it is extremely difficult to categorize individuals into various groups or schools of thought.

A complete unriddling of the imponderables is unlikely ever to occur. In a brief synopsis of the system's working, Peter Christian Ludz posited that the political will of the party translated into political directives in the following ways:[49]

- through the compulsory nature of all decisions of the party organs upon state institutions, mass organizations, and the bloc parties;
- through the *nomenklatura* system and the cadre policies;
- through the large overlap between party and state officials and the appointment of "party representatives" to state agencies and planning organs;
- through the parallel and interlocking state and party structures;
- through the security and control forces of the party that checked dissent and isolated potential opposition;
- through the propaganda and agitation instruments over which the party maintained a monopoly.

NOTES

1. The German Democratic Republic was a state for just short of forty-one years. As a result of the autumn 1989 revolution, the GDR effectively ceased being a communist dictatorship in the last weeks of that year. Free elections were held on March 18, 1990, and the GDR was a parliamentary democracy from then until October 3, 1990, when it united with the Federal Republic of Germany.

2. See *DDR Handbuch*, 3d ed., vol. 1 (Cologne: Verlag Wissenschaft und Politik, 1985), 697-701.

3. Mike Dennis, *German Democratic Republic Politics, Economics and Society* (London: Pinter, 1988), 17.

4. *Wörterbuch des marxistisch-leninistischen Soziologie*, 2d ed. (East Berlin: Dietz, 1977), 325.

5. Martin McCauley, *Marxism-Leninism in the German Democratic Republic* (London: Macmillan, 1979), 57-58.

6. Gabriel A. Almond and G. Bingham Powell, Jr., *Comparative Politics: A Developmental Approach* (Boston: Little, Brown, 1966), esp. chap. 2.

7. See Donna Bahry and Brian D. Silver, "Soviet Citizen Participation on the Eve of Democratization," *The American Political Science Review* 84, no. 3 (September 1990): 821-48; Wayne DiFranceisco and Zvi Gitelman, "Soviet Political Culture and Covert Participation in Policy Implementation," *The American Political Science Review* 78, no. 1 (March 1989): 603-21.

8. Aristotle, *The Politics of Aristotle* (London: Oxford University Press, 1974), 246.

9. Timothy Garton Ash developed the notion of civic neutralization with regard to Polish communism, but it has applicability to most communist countries. See Timothy Garton Ash, *Polish Revolution: Solidarity* (New York: Scribner's, 1983), 14-17.

10. See, for example, Zbigniew Brzezinski and Samuel Huntington, *Political Power: USA/USSR* (New York: Viking, 1965).

11. Bahry and Silver, "Soviet Citizen Participation on the Eve of Democratization," 821-24.

12. Philip Roeder, "Modernization and Participation in the Leninist Development Strategy," *The American Political Science Review* 83, no. 2 (June 1990): 859-84.

13. Victor Zaslavsky, *The Neo-Stalinist State: Class, Ethnicity, and Consensus in Soviet Society* (Armonk: Sharpe, 1982); Bahry and Silver, "Soviet Citizen Participation on the Eve of Democratization," 823.

14. Mere numbers say little about the form of political involvement, of course. Some analysts have attempted to identify categories of political activism, but there is disagreement on how to conceptualize these. See Bahry and Silver, *Soviet Citizen Participation on the Eve of Democratization*, 824. DiFranceisco and Gitelman identify three forms of participation in Leninist societies: "formalistic-ritualistic," "citizen-initiated contacts with officials" and "contacts over implementation."

15. Brzezinski and Huntington, *Political Power USA/USSR*, 92.

16. *The Constitution of the German Democratic Republic* (East Berlin: Staatsverlag der DDR, 1974), 20.

17. Arnold J. Heidenheimer and Donald Kommers, *The Governments of Germany*, 4th ed. (New York: Harper and Row, 1975), 304.

18. Ibid.

19. Mike Dennis, *German Democratic Republic*, 98-99.

20. Ibid., 97.

21. Ash, *Polish Revolution*, 14-17.

22. See for example, Mike Dennis, *German Democratic Republic*, 76.

23. *Statut der Sozialistischen Einheitspartei Deutschlands* (East Berlin: Dietz, 1988), 30-32.

24. Ibid., 6.

25. *DDR Handbuch*, vol. 2, 1,187.

26. Walter Ulbricht, "Hallsche Sozialdemokraten und Kommunisten für die Einheit der Arbeiterklasse," *Die Entwicklung des deutschen volksdemokratischen Staates 1945-58* (East Berlin: Dietz, 1959), 41.

27. *Statut der Sozialistischen Einheitspartei Deutschlands*, 38-41.

28. Heidenheimer and Kommers, *The Governments of Germany*, 301.

29. *DDR Handbuch*, vol. 1, 34-36; also, *Das Wissenschaftssystem in der DDR*, 2d ed. (Frankfurt: Campus Verlag, 1979).

30. McCauley, *Marxism-Leninism*, 58.

31. Dennis, *German Democratic Republic*, 90.

32. Rodrich Kuhlbach and Helmut Weber, *Parteien im Blocksystem der DDR* (Cologne: Verlag Wissenschaft und Politik, 1969), 34.

33. Dennis, *German Democratic Republic*, 91.

34. David Childs, *The GDR Moscow's German Ally*, 2d ed. (London: Unwin Hyman, 1988), 338.

35. *DDR Handbuch*, vol. 2, 928-29.

36. Heidenheimer and Kommers, *The Governments of Germany*, 294.

37. Childs, *The GDR*, 127.

38. "Statut des Ministeriums der Justiz," *Gesetzblatt* 1, March 3, 1976, 185.

39. *The Constitution of the German Democratic Republic*, 35.

40. Hartmut Zimmermann, "The GDR in the 1970s," *Problems of Communism* 27, no. 2 (March-April 1978): 9.

41. Heidenheimer and Kommers, *The Governments of Germany*, 299.

42. Dietrich Müller-Römer, *Die Neue Verfassung der DDR* (Cologne: Verlag Wissenschaft und Politik, 1974), 53.

43. *The Constitution of the German Democratic Republic*, 45.

44. *Handbuch der DDR*, vol. 2, 1,443.

45. For profiles of *Volkskammer* deputies, see Dennis, *German Democratic Republic*, 93-100.

46. *Handbuch der DDR*, Vol. 2, 1440.

47. *The Constitution of the German Democratic Republic*, 37. See Dennis, *German Democratic Republic*, 110-11; *Handbuch der DDR*, vol. 2, 1,005-10.

48. Thomas A. Baylis, *The Technical Intelligentsia and the East German Elite* (Berkeley: University of California Press, 1974), 221.

49. *DDR Handbuch*, vol. 2, 1,188-89.

2
Legitimacy Deficit

THE LEGITIMACY OF POLITICAL SYSTEMS

Efforts to identify the nature, sources and effects of public attitudes toward political institutions and leaders have given rise to considerable amounts of scholarly literature. The complexities of systemic legitimacy are evidenced by the host of concepts employed in efforts to analyze it. A catalogue of terms would include "support,"[1] "system affect,"[2] "political allegiance,"[3] and "political community."[4] Analysts seem to agree that identifying the "objects" of political attitude is opportune to the examination of the public outlook. Accordingly, Gabriel Almond and Sidney Verba distinguish between the "output affect," people's expectations about the way they will be handled by officialdom, and "input affect," their understanding of and position toward participatory processes. David Easton differentiates between citizen perspectives toward the political community, the regime, and public officials, respectively.[5] William Gamson speaks of four specific "objects of political trust": officials, the regime's philosophy, political institutions, and the political community.[6] He reasons that assessment of the intensity of citizen feeling toward each of these objects enables the observer to measure the overall level of support for a particular regime. At least a general sense of loyalty on the part of rank-and-file citizens is essential to successful governing, and a regime enjoying an adequate amount of legitimacy can operate within more or less defined parameters, requiring certain sacrifices and imposing deprivations, in the knowledge that citizens will not withdraw support and will go along.

In short, those who wield power must establish their right to do so. This is not a pious wish, or a peculiarly democratic canon, but a general political necessity. Every ruling group that presumes to gather prerogatives for itself, or to inflict deprivations on others, must identify itself with a principle acceptable to the community as justification for the exercise of power. Such doctrinal tenets are known as "principles of legitimacy" and their function is to establish authority as distinct from naked power. A rule is based on authority when most of those who are supposed to obey do so willingly and need not be coerced.[7]

In the view of Max Weber rulers and governmental systems that are devoid of legitimacy will be at an impasse to wield power effectively, much less to achieve long-term stability.[8] Law and order can at times be maintained through fear and coercion alone, but such a situation is seldom durable, he argued. A functional society depends upon a modicum of trust between rulers and ruled, whereby a regime is accepted by the latter as correct and the rightness of the former's position is generally acknowledged. A more contemporary assessment expresses this notion in the following way:

> The inculcation of a sense of legitimacy is probably the single most effective device for regulating the flow of diffuse support in favor both of the authorities and of the regime. A member may be willing to obey the authorities and conform to the requirements of the regime for many different reasons. But the most stable support will derive from the conviction on the part of the member that it is right and proper for him to accept and obey the authorities and to abide by the requirements of the regime. It reflects the fact that in some vague or explicit way he sees these objects as conforming to his own moral principles, his own sense of what is right and proper in the political sphere.[9]

Similarly, Michael Hudson suggests that for a regime to avoid legitimacy problems it must succeed in convincing the masses that it is genuinely national, joins in the nation's history, protects traditions, acts in accordance with society's values, and safeguards common interests.[10] Only regimes able to convey such an impression in the public mind are likely to attain the legitimacy instrumental to the effectual exercise of authority, and it is incumbent upon rulers to convince the ruled that they (the rulers) merit credence and confidence. Legitimacy requires a certain ability on the part of the system to generate popular conviction that existing political institutions are at least appropriate for the respective society. Regimes remain legitimate insofar as their citizens consider them suitable and entitled to support, Ted Gurr suggests, adding that citizen obedience can be summoned up on the grounds of custom, self-interest, expediency or fear.[11] Seldom if ever is only a single factor involved, of course, and even in those societies where retribution for disobedience is heavy and fear the chief motivating force, the latter is invariably applied in some combination with other factors. Totalitarian societies, those where the greatest amount of popular fear was present, were disposed by their nature to employ government's coercive power to transform social and economic relations, beliefs, and values, with the express aim of harmonizing interests and values.[12]

LEGITIMACY AND THE GDR

Recognition of the signal difference between the GDR and its East Bloc neighbors, namely, the lack of national tradition, is crucial to understanding the consequences of the whirlwind of events striking the country in 1989. Legitimacy was the central problem of government in a fabricated nation vindicating separate statehood with the utopian tenets of authoritarian socialism. By contrast, Poland and Hungary, devoid of socialism, remained Poland and Hungary, nations with long histories and traditions. Intense national feelings in Poland sustained the existence of a Polish nation even during those many decades when there was no Polish state. Bereft of Marxism-Leninism, the GDR, for its part, forfeited the official purpose of its existence, becoming once again the eastern half of the German question. How was a second German state alongside an indisputably successful and affluent Federal Republic of Germany to be justified? This question increasingly entered the minds of East Germans as winds of change began to blow across the Soviet Bloc.

Historically, the problem of East German legitimacy had two facets, one international, the other domestic. For over fifteen years the GDR was internationally isolated, recognized only by communist "fraternal states" and often referred to disparagingly in the West as the "Soviet Zone of Occupation," or simply SBZ. Relations between the Germanys had reached such a low point in the 1950s that the FRG officially regarded any recognition of the GDR as an unfriendly act, and consequently instituted a "recognition embargo" against the other Germany. International isolation of the GDR effectively ended in 1972 with the signing of the Basic Treaty (*Grundvertrag*) between the two Germanys which allowed unlimited third-party recognition of the GDR.

Domestic legitimacy, the acceptance of the regime by its own people, was an issue that lingered on. Notwithstanding the regime's intense ideological indoctrination efforts, Marxism-Leninism, by the regime's own implicit admission, did not by itself suffice to create a national consciousness and the SED strove uninterruptedly to make itself more acceptable through its domestic policies. Lacking a true self-identity, the citizenry maintained a close cultural and historical affinity with a capitalist, Western state. Designs to eradicate such feelings of kinship by the SED were largely in vain. There is considerable evidence, in fact, that regime efforts to foster identification with a separate socialist *nation*, for example, by emphasizing supposedly progressive aspects of German history, insofar as these had any effect, only strengthened East Germans' feelings of "Germanness." The SED's chief long-term predicament thus inherently derived from the division of the country. The GDR was a relatively new state, arisen out of the ashes of the Third Reich, and its national traditions were indubitably German. However hard the regime may have tried, the GDR was never able to escape the effects of the common German past. However outwardly different the GDR was from the FRG, however persistent the SED was in accentuating those differences and in demarcating the GDR from the Western neighbor, the GDR remained a product of common experiences and was shaped by these.

Weber indicated that the legitimacy of an order can be established by tradition, by positive emotional attitudes, by rational belief in its absolute value, or by recognition of its legality. In modern societies, he said, "the most usual basis of legitimacy is the belief in legality, the readiness to conform with rules which are formally correct and have been imposed by accepted procedure."[13]

SED efforts to develop a legitimacy grounded in Weber's notions of legality and "accepted procedure" were largely unavailing. According to the procedural concept, governmental actions are legitimate if they reflect the outcome of a process of altercation and compromise in which most or all interested groups have participated.[14] The more established and versatile political institutions and structures are, the more they contribute to regime legitimacy, thereby nurturing the general and independent belief in the validity of structure and norms.[15]

Any consideration of the "right rules of the game" in GDR society could not sidestep the question: whose rules? Those set by the party were merely the rules of the game, not necessarily the right rules to the great majority of East Germans. Authority and legitimacy, while largely coinciding in democracies, were quite different things in the GDR. From such a discrepancy ensued the inclination of citizens to think in terms of a "we-they" dichotomy, with "they" usually referring to those directly affiliated with the regime. And the "we-they" dichotomy cut both ways. Operating on the assumption that "everyone not for us is against us" the party elite had no tolerance of dissent or opposition.

According to the premise of democracy theory that governmental actions are rendered legitimate to the extent they embody the will of the people, the GDR was in plain words politically deficient. "Who asks us?" East Germans cynically quipped. The spirit of this remark was later to be captured in the rallying cry of the 1989 demonstrations: *"Wir sind das Volk"* ("We are the people"). In other words, *we* are now going to be consulted about the *right* rules of the game.

SOURCES OF LEGITIMACY

What resources might a regime draw upon to convince the citizenry that its governance is proper and deserving of support?[16] Let us consider in turn three types of legitimacy: personal, ideological, and structural.[17] In the first case a strong, charismatic personality engenders legitimacy for a particular regime. In the second, general commitment to principles, highly valued goals, and/or to a *Weltanschauung* can provide legitimacy. The third, the most abiding source and the one most closely resembling Weber's right rules of the game, entails broad public deference to the political process, adjudicative functions, and decision making. Structural legitimacy is for the most part characteristic of developed, industrialized societies and evolves only after the populace acquires considerable trust in governmental institutions.

Easton states that in regimes "where the behavior and personalities of the occupants of authority role are of dominating importance," the basis of legitimacy may be highly personal.[18] He suggests that a leader engendering considerable legitimacy through his person might transgress prescribed forms and pay little attention to usual arrangements. This notion of personal legitimacy closely resembles Weber's idea of charisma. Charismatic authority to Weber had a mystical quality, clothing a leader with power to captivate people. But few if any GDR leaders enjoyed such personal appeal; as steadfast Leninists nearly all abhorred spontaneity of any sort. They were apparatchiks who owed their positions exclusively to the party. Interestingly enough, demeanor and presentation became contentious matters in the Gorbachev era. Disdaining bourgeois popularism, Honecker and his entourage looked increasingly askance at Soviet leader Mikhail Gorbachev's popular style, so offset by their own solemn public aspect. Weber's observation that the charismatic leader is most likely to be found in political systems experiencing significant change is notable in this context. Charisma simply had no place in the GDR and only in the formative years was there much accentuation of a personage, that of Josef Stalin.

According to Easton, ideologies may be interpreted from a manipulative or instrumental point of view "as categories of thought to corral the energies of men; from an expressive point of view we may see them as ideals capable of rousing and inspiring men to action thought to be related to their achievement."[19] In the GDR ideology was to have assumed a paramount legitimizing function; that is, it was not seen as a temporary expedient preceding the development of a more structured legitimacy. Instead, ideology represented an end in itself, the key to understanding the past, the method for explaining the present and the framework for a vision of the future. Officially, Marxism-Leninism provided a guide for managing all political issues. Elevated to what David Apter describes as "political religion," ideology formed a basis for public policy.[20] To its adherents Marxism-Leninism was a systematic statement of the highest values and ideals. As with religion, Marxist-Leninist ideology has a vision as the end product of values. This vision is one of peace, the peace of self-alienated people restored to themselves.[21] The eschatological moral theology of Marxism-Leninism promises secular salvation: the emergence of the just, classless society devoid of conflict from which springs the puritanical new human being.[22] Any political system, Apter suggests, that begins to ritualize its leadership and traditionalize its consummatory values by making these into an effective link between innovation and the past, practices "political religion" to some extent.[23] These consummatory values would ultimately legitimize the regime's purposes and instill in citizens a sense of socialist community. A critical assertion made by a leading East German dissident Rudolf Bahro mimics this notion.

The politburo dictatorship is a grotesque exaggeration of the bureaucratic principle, in as much as the party apparatus subordinate to it is at the same time both church hierarchy and superstate. The whole structure is quasi-theocratic. For the core of its political power . . . is power over minds, with the constant tendency toward inquisition. . . . With their pretense to know the laws of history and the true interests of the masses, any political decision, no matter how costly it might be in economic terms, can be justified.[24]

The population's willing support of governmental power in the GDR was dubious throughout its history, although certain welfare-state features of the society—health care, public education, and government support of the arts—gained widespread public approval. But in contrast even to other socialist states, Poland or the USSR, say, no affection for a motherland existed. More conspicuously, certain attributes of the society, such as the lack of civil liberties, the arbitrariness of state authority, incursions into personal privacy, the chicaneries of officialdom, the dreariness of everyday life, and the sometimes merciless "rat race" in metropolitan areas were acutely resented. The legitimacy the regime commanded was unsubstantial, sporadic, and lacking solid institutional underpinning.

TRICKY NATIONALITY ISSUES

Some Western observers submitted that early hostility toward the regime emanating from widely held impressions of its imposition from abroad and from above, began evolving first to passive acceptance, then to a sort of positive loyalty in the 1970s. Loyalty resulted largely from the absence of any alternative, but this did amount to more than mere resigned accommodation, went the argument. A few observers even went so far as to depict what they perceived to be the gradual development of separate East and West German nationalities.[25] Such a development was in part attributed to the SED's campaign in the 1970s to create a new, separate East German consciousness. Most analysts subscribed to the notion that East Germans were more "traditionally German," a distinction not usually to be interpreted positively when voiced by European neighbors, West or East. Feelings of belonging to a pan-German whole were plainly stronger in East than in West Germany, whose citizens often undertook to subordinate national aspirations to the European idea, and East Germans identified with West Germans much more so than the reverse. Although ambiguities on national issues abounded, and both Germanys suffered the consequences of what might be termed "truncated nation-building," in the 1980s it appeared both states were behaving more in accordance with perceived national interests.

Nationality issues were less salient in the FRG where people had the opportunity to associate with a larger European entity and national institutions were gradually being replaced by Western European ones. On the other hand, daunting and elusive difficulties of popular national awareness troubled the SED. Polls, when taken at all, indicated that some three-quarters of the East German population in the 1970s considered themselves German and their homeland Germany.[26] And in 1975 an official questionnaire revealed that less than one in three East Germans regarded the FRG as a separate country. The persevering feeling of Germanness in the GDR presented the regime with such acute national identity quandaries that the SED seemed at times uneasy about the very name of the country, as well as the awkward designation of its inhabitants, "citizens of the German Democratic Republic." The official appellation, "Citizenship—GDR Nationality—German," was not completely satisfactory, above all, because it did not convey the proper sense of distance from the FRG. It also had the undesirable connotation from the regime's standpoint of lending support to the official West German position on the presence of "two states, one nation" in Germany, something the SED under Honecker's stewardship disputed. One Western observer hypothesized the SED had in fact been trifling with the possibility of renaming the country, a pretty sure indication of fundamental self-identity problems. "Maybe something like the People's Republic of Prussia," he said. "I'm half-convinced it will happen."[27]

No country can free itself of its geography or history, and it was evident that the SED desired to preserve some aspects of the German heritage. The kind of national features the party wanted the GDR to possess wasn't always easy to discern, though. Aside from a careful selection of positive threads of German history to adorn the socialist fabric, there appeared to have been no determinate criteria employed for designing the GDR's national character. What is more, official histories changed over time. In 1983, the centenary year of Karl Marx, the GDR officially celebrated the five-hundredth anniversary of the birth of Martin Luther, by no stretch of the imagination a socialist. The SED had in fact shifted from denouncing Luther as an apologist for feudalism to depicting him as a pioneer in the social struggle and a progressive in early modern times. Luther thereafter overshadowed Thomas Müntzer, the prior champion of the GDR in that period, as a leading proponent of liberation, and hence a precursor of socialism. Extraordinary historical interpretations, part and parcel of the sometimes tortured effort to establish separate East German traditions and culture, invited facetious remarks like the one about the "People's Republic of Prussia." In a 1970 speech to the 14th Plenum of the Central Committee, Stoph confidently heralded that Beethoven's musical genius belonged wholly to the "Socialist German national culture" and not to "imperialist Bonn."[28]

Although the SED's grip on the society was as strong as ever through much of the 1980s, shadowy omens portended that positive loyalty and a sense of separate national identity remained elusive. The year 1989 brought growing indications of SED misgiving. The evasive response in January by the Soviet foreign minister, Eduard Shevardnadze, to questions about the future of the Berlin Wall evoked a sharp rebuke from East Berlin when the official media issued a contemptuous rejoinder, emphasizing Honecker's pronouncement in 1988 that "the Wall will remain in place until the circumstances that led to its construction have been eliminated." In Honecker's estimation, this could well have been one hundred years in the future. His remark was strangely reminiscent of Stalin's sarcastic hammer-blow retorts about the need for walls to keep out imperialists, drug-traffickers, and spies. A prime SED fear about reform programs was that these would at some point test East Germans' loyalty. In 1982 Jeane Kirkpatrick posed a central question about East Bloc regimes:

> (H)ave they managed to reform human consciousness? Have they managed to educate . . . citizens so that they would freely choose to behave according to the norms of Soviet culture if the constraints of coercion were removed? The answer is of course we do not know.[29]

Neither did the SED.

HONECKER'S CONSUMERISM

Popular support in industrial societies depends in great measure upon living standards, and in recognition of this, the GDR exhibited an increasing tendency to base legitimacy on rank-and-file citizen endorsement of the regime's economic accomplishments in sustaining economic growth and satisfying demand for goods and services.[30] The FRG, a country also wanting of national symbols and many of the usual underpinnings of legitimacy, followed the same path, though with two significant differences. First, economic performance there was far superior; second, governmental actions were legitimized by virtue of the fact that they embodied the will of the people.

In the East Bloc the GDR had become the undisputed economic powerhouse, with wages and living standards to match. Through improvements in material conditions the regime hoped to glean popular approval, and whatever popularity the SED could claim stemmed largely from relative prosperity. That living standards should have assumed such a prominent place in the economic planning of a regime continuously wrestling with legitimacy problems certainly was not coincidental. Official publications teemed with facts and figures about economic successes and over-fulfillment of plan quotas.

Although the GDR's consumer sector was neglected in the 1950s and 1960s, under Honecker's leadership the SED demonstrated growing awareness of the importance of foodstuff and product availability to general contentment. Accordingly, the consumer portion of GNP increased significantly during Honecker's tenure as general secretary. Honecker appeared to harbor few illusions about the efficacy of utopian schemes or quixotic appeals to insure citizen loyalty, as Ulbricht had been inclined to do. Honecker's efforts to win hearts and minds were geared to a lower common denominator. As soon as he ascended to power, Honecker let it be understood that the regime would assign top priority to satisfying people's basic material needs. Honecker as a rule avoided idealism and ideological innovation; for example, the technological-scientific panaceas for the GDR's problems that Ulbricht toyed with were simply discarded.[31] His administration demonstrated little interest in earlier high-minded guidelines concerning the "correct socialist life-style."[32] Such guidelines were in fact provided by Ulbricht in "The Ten Commandments of Socialist Morality," a discourse criticizing consumerism and materialism as manifestations of capitalist decadence and thus incompatible with socialist ideals. The idealistic Ten Commandments were included in the SED program of the Sixth (1963) and Ninth (1976) Party Congresses, but in the Honecker era they were at most objects of mere lip service.

For the individual, material incentives would take the form of higher wages, a larger array of consumer goods, and greater purchasing power. One of Honecker's first steps as party chief was to announce a grandiose new housing program that kept workers busy almost around the clock for a few years. By 1975 some 600,000 units had been either newly constructed or renovated.[33] In the period 1971 through 1982 functional housing in the GDR was supplemented with 1,794,300 dwellings of which 1,207,100 were new apartments, 142,000 were new detached houses and the rest made available by renovation.[34] By comparison, though, approximately 5.7 million new residences were constructed in the FRG in the same time frame, and on average these were 34 percent larger than those of the GDR.[35]

Housing remained the core of SED social policies. The Five-Year Plan, 1981-85, made available 940,000 additional residences, 600,000 through new construction. Projected costs were 50 billion marks, approximately 19 percent of total investment.[36] Rising energy and raw material costs pushed the actual outlays higher, forcing the planning authorities to reallocate funds and to increase public debt.

Emphasis upon material well-being in the Honecker era, however, invited direct comparisons between the GDR and the affluent West, a largely unanticipated side effect. Policy reorientation prompted the use of the FRG as the yardstick by which both average citizens and the SED evaluated achievement. The irony of the attachment to West German standards was in fact quite profound: the FRG was at one and the same time the principal ideological enemy and the standard-setter, whose level of wealth the GDR would one day attain. Such was the great promise of communism.

By the same token, lackluster growth aroused cynicism and demoralization. All too often, it seemed, the SED was unable to deliver on its economic promises. But what is more, comparisons encouraged appraisals of the country's political institutions according to Western democratic standards, and in consequence unfavorable popular assessments incurred political overtones. As the GDR became more open to the West through direct contacts, family visits, and the media, East Germans cast an increasingly critical eye upon their leaders, the institutions of their state, and above all the economy. In the matter of genuine participation, GDR institutions simply did not pass muster. The fraternal proximity of an affluent, liberal democracy gave greater currency to democratic ideas and was a constant reminder of the great disparity between official claims about "real socialist democracy" and the reality of everyday life in the GDR.

"MAIN TASK"

Honecker's goals translated into the "main task" policies of the 1970s, whose fundaments, as put forth in the Eighth Party Congress in 1976, became leading indexes of economic performance. Clearly, the regime's new attitude reflected a more sober, mundane policy approach. Officially, main task called for "the further enhancement of the material and cultural living standard of the people on the basis of a rapidly accelerating tempo of socialist production, increased efficiency, enhanced scientific technological progress, and the growth of labor productivity."[37] It stressed greater production efficiency as a prerequisite for the improvement of working and living conditions. Main task served as an economic lodestar, but more than this it marked a new course in social policy and ideological tenor, attesting to a recognition on the regime's part that rising popular expectations would have to be resolutely addressed. "In the main task, the position of the workers' needs in the socialist society is defined as fundamental," said Honecker, "and the workers' needs are distinguished as the decisive basis for economic management and planning."[38] There can be little doubt that the Politburo saw a crucial link between popular complacence and adequate supplies of goods. At the Ninth SED Party Congress, Politburo member Werner Krolikowski referred to the "irrevocable political course of turning toward the masses, toward their immediate interests and requirements."[39]

Centrally planned economies tend to have both high rates of labor force participation and relatively large percentages of national product going to investment. Rapid growth in the 1970s partially cushioned the impact of investment bias, but with the slowdown in economic expansion after 1983 the GDR faced some hard choices. Economic data indicated that funds earmarked for investment were at times rechanneled into the consumer sector to cover anticipated shortfalls there. Troubles in Poland in the 1970s, not to mention the upheaval in the early 1980s, seem to have shocked the GDR leadership into realizing that prolonged forced investment at the expense of consumption was a formula for popular disgruntlement, even political instability. Thus, heavy state subsidization amounting to perhaps one-quarter of the entire state budget was steadily provided in several areas including food, housing, and public transportation.[40] Already large rent subsidization on dwellings grew during the 1980s. In many urban areas the rent paid on older buildings in 1983 had not changed since 1938.[41] Even in the largest cities families seldom paid more than one mark per square meter of living space.

Retention of this subsidization even in lean years signified the importance the SED attached to the tacit social compact and main task policies. Policy statements disclosed unremitting official attention to "real" situations and needs. Increasingly absent from party pronouncements in the Honecker years were references to lofty future objectives, "advanced stages of socialism," "the organic linkage of the achievements of the scientific-technological revolution with the merits of socialism." The jargon of the Honecker administration, laced as it was with words like "real," "actual," and "reality," denoted absorption with the here-and-now, with current social processes. The term "actually existing socialism" (*der real existierende Sozialismus*), that was to become the watchword of Honecker's regime and the subject of innumerable parodies, captured the spirit of main task, whose ultimate objective was to bolster regime legitimacy in a way that lofty paroles had no chance of doing. But what was the average East German to think when the capitalist FRG continued to outpace the GDR economically? What claim to legitimacy could the SED make when it faltered in achieving the quite straightforward economic goals it had set for itself?

Notwithstanding substantial increases in imports of technology from the West, and in spite of the allocation of substantial resources to innovation and research, the technological gap between the Germanys continued to widen after 1971, suggesting that the GDR was not maintaining the standards it had set. Five years into Honecker's tenure in office (1976) Western figures indicated that GDR industrial output per employee as compared with the FRG had declined to 65 percent, down from 72 percent in 1967.[42] West Germans were in fact achieving what SED leaders were hesitant even to promise their people. It is notable that as far back as 1947, before the establishment of separate German states, then chairman of the Social Democratic Party (SPD), Kurt Schumacher, developed the so-called magnet theory for overcoming German division. "One must create social and economic facts," Schumacher said, "that bespeak the superiority of the Western Zones over the Eastern Zone." There was, he went on,

> no other way to achieve German unification than to employ the economic
> magnetization of the West; this drawing power of the West must be so strong that
> the possession of the power apparatus is not a means to thwart it. This is certainly
> a difficult and presumably a long path.[43]

As the economic hiatus between the Germanies widened, the FRG's allurement gradually grew and Western Europe's wealth in fact generated considerable drawing power.

NOTES

1. Talcott Parsons, "Introduction," in Max Weber, *The Theory of Economic and Social Organization* (translated by A. M. Henderson and Talcott Parsons; edited with an introduction by Talcott Parsons) (New York: Oxford University Press, 1947), 58-61.

2. Gabriel A. Almond and Sidney Verba, *The Civic Culture* (Boston: Little, Brown, 1965), 30.

3. Karl Deutsch, "Social Mobilization and Political Development," *American Political Science Review* 55, no. 3 (September 1961): 493-514. Ralf Dahrendorf, *Essays in the Theory of Society* (Stanford: Stanford University Press, 1968).

4. Seymour Martin Lipset, *Political Man* (Garden City, N.Y.: Doubleday, 1960), 184-85, 232-35; Herbert J. Spiro, *World Politics: The Global System* (Homewood, Ill.: Dorsey, 1966).

5. David Easton, *A Systems Analysis of Political Life* (Chicago: University of Chicago Press, 1979), 285-87.

6. William Gamson, *Power and Discontent* (Homewood, Ill.: The Dorsey Press, 1968), 2-19, 74-81.

7. Philip Selznick, *The Organizational Weapon* (New York: McGraw-Hill, 1952), 242.

8. Weber, *The Theory of Social and Economic Organization*, 124-26.

9. David Easton, *A Systems Analysis of Political Life* (Chicago: University of Chicago Press, 1979), 278.

10. Michael Hudson, *Arab Politics The Search for Legitimacy* (New Haven, Conn.: Yale University Press, 1977), 2.

11. Ted Robert Gurr, *Why Men Rebel* (Princeton: Princeton University Press, 1970), 183-85.

12. Dennis H. Wrong, *Power, Its Forms, Bases and Uses* (New York: Harper and Row, 1979), 46-47, 172-78; Ronald Wintrobe, "The Tinpot and the Totalitarian: An Economic Theory of Dictatorship," *American Political Science Review* 84, no. 3 (September 1990): 849-72.

13. Weber, *Theory of Social and Economic Organization*, 130-32.

14. Samuel Huntington, *Political Order in Changing Societies* (New Haven, Conn.: Yale University Press, 1968), 27.

15. Easton, *A Systems Analysis of Political Life*, 287.

16. Gurr, *Why Men Rebel*, 185.

17. Easton, *A Systems Analysis of Political Life*, 302-3.

18. Ibid., 302-3.

19. Ibid., 290.

20. David Apter, *The Politics of Modernization* (Chicago: University of Chicago Press, 1965), 266.

21. Robert C. Tucker, *Philosophy and Myth in Karl Marx* (Cambridge: Cambridge University Press, 1972).

22. James E. Dougherty and Robert L. Pfaltzgraff, Jr., *Contending Theories of International Relations*, 2d ed. (New York: Harper and Row, 1981), 215.

23. Ibid., 305-6.

24. Quoted in Childs, *The GDR*, 100.

25. For an example, see: Jonathan Steele, *Socialism with a German Face: The State that Came in from the Cold* (London: Jonathan Cape, 1977); see also Gebhard Schweigler, *National Consciousness in Divided Germany* (London: Sage, 1975), esp. 277-81.

26. Robert Gerald Livingston, "East Berlin between Moscow and Bonn," *Foreign Affairs* 50, no. 2 (January 1972): 304-5.

27. *The Wall Street Journal*, October 21, 1983.

28. Arnold J. Heidenheimer and Donald Kommers, *The Governments of Germany*, 4th ed. (New York: Harper and Row, 1975), 292.

29. Jeane Kirkpatrick, *Dictatorships and Double Standards: Rationalism and Realism in Politics* (New York: Simon and Schuster, 1982), 123.

30. Thomas Baylis, "East Germany: In Quest of Legitimacy," *Problems of Communism* 21, no. 2 (March-April 1972): 47.

31. Lawrence L. Whetten, *Germany East and West* (New York: New York University Press, 1980), 147. See also: "Political Aspects of the Development, Change, and Application of the Concept of Scientific-Technological Revolution in the GDR," *Deutschland Archiv*, Special Volume 1976, 17-22.

32. Hartmut Zimmermann, "The GDR in the 1970s," *Problems of Communism* 27, no. 2 (March-April 1978): 5.

33. A. James McAdams, *East Germany and Detente* (Cambridge: Cambridge University Press), 137.

34. *DDR Handbuch*, vol. 1, 154.

35. Ibid.

36. *DDR Handbuch*, vol. 1, 159.

37. Quoted in Zimmermann, "The GDR in the 1970s," 18.

38. Erich Honecker, *Die Rolle der Arbeiterklasse und ihrer Partei in der sozialistischen Gesellschaft* (East Berlin: Dietz, 1974), 170.

39. Quoted in Zimmermann, "The GDR in the 1970s," 19.

40. Subsidy amounts could not always be precisely assessed. See Manfred Melzer, "The GDR Housing Construction Program: Problems and Successes," *East Central Europe* 11, nos. 1-2 (1984): 78-96.

41. *DDR Handbuch*, vol. 1, 157.

42. "Social Product of the GDR and of the Federal Republic of Germany in Comparison," *Wochenbericht* (Deutsches Institut für Wirtschaftsforschung), June 9, 1977.

43. *Die Zeit*, February 9, 1990.

3

The Debate on the Nation

THE GERMAN PROBLEM

What is the German fatherland? What are the qualities of national identity in a divided nation? In the 1960s the renowned German historian Gerhard Ritter noted that West Germans were enthusiastically making a bold leap from Germanism to Europeanism. Not unexpectedly perhaps, Germans wished an abrupt change from exaggerated and badly abused patriotism to a cool and skeptically neutral detachment from the concept of fatherland.[1] Later, in the mid-1980s another leading historian, Hans-Peter Schwarz, would describe German yearning for such a shift in a book entitled *Die gezähmten Deutschen Von der Machtbessenheit zur Machtvergessenheit* (*The Tamed Germans: From Obsession with Power to Oblivion of Power*).[2] Writing over twenty years apart, both expressed considerable regret about this attitude, not because of the inexpediency of a European consciousness per se, but for quite another reason. A European identity was proving illusory: for the foreseeable future Europe would remain a collection of states and nationalisms. For better or for worse, Europeans maintained close affinities with their own ethnic groups, and identified principally with their respective nations. But largely because of the unfortunate experience with extreme nationalism, many Germans had developed an aversion to the idea of the nation as a binding community. The likely results of the arrested drive toward Europeanism would be intense disappointment, even disillusionment, Ritter predicted.

Only through heightened public awareness of the national past, he suggested, would there be any hope of building a sound German state. Accordingly, national histories had to be more than narratives; these had to raise basic questions of German political existence, place German issues in some sort of historical perspective, and clarify German problems in historical terms. Some scholars agreed with Ritter; others deflated his arguments bitterly, labeling them apologies for the excesses of nationalism.

In the ensuing years numerous theories of identity, nationality, and nationhood were advanced in Germany, most of them in the West, but some in the GDR as well. Ritter and other historians were responsible in part for inspiring and energizing debates on the nation, and subsequent discussions showed that historians too could be people of considerable passion. Perspectives were often radically different, and the vigorous debates, as intended, often awakened interest in various corners. But German unification was remote and hypothetical, benevolently so from the standpoint of Germany's neighbors. That the status quo in Europe was locked in for some time to come was a universally recognized fact. Rendered to the back burner, the German question had become largely conjectural, and discussions of the nation theoretical. So many uncertainties were associated with examinations of German national consciousness that these by necessity remained on a fairly high level of generalization, although stalemate on national issues seemed to stir greater historical interest by the 1970s.

Debate and discussion prior to 1989 aid us in understanding the events of that year. When the possibility of unification became a real one, ideas about the nation depended to a large extent upon perceptions of Germany's past, and those with strong sentiments often provided considerable insight into what happened in Germany in 1989. This chapter will examine how various German theories and analyses of nationality, identity, and nationhood applied to the German states. These can be considered under four headings: *Staatsnation* (nation-state), *Kulturnation* (cultural nation), *Staatsbewusstsein* (state consciousness), and *Bewusstseinsnation* (national consciousness). The first, the "state-nation," or nation-state, refers to a national group enjoying a single government, as Germany did from 1871 to 1945. With division of the country, and the subsequent establishment of two states in 1949, Germany ceased being a *Staatsnation*. The difficult recent past appeared to some to be fostering a growing popular indifference to a German homeland, even the outright rejection by many intellectuals of the idea of the nation as an historically uniting community. The second term refers to the cultural unity of a nation (for example the German culture uniting the myriad of German states prior to political unification, or the cultural ties linking Austria and Germany). The third, related closely to the first, pertains to the identification of a people with a particular state. In 1949 the FRG and the GDR established their own separate political systems, but whether the relative success of the respective systems promoted new sources of citizen identification remained an open question. The fourth term, related to the first two, refers to a consciousness of nationhood, that is, the way in which, and the extent to which Germans, East and West, identified with a single nation. Did they have only a language and culture in common, or did they cling to deeper feelings of kinship? This was one of the great imponderables of the German question after 1949. Lack of reliable polls and data rendered any endeavor to assess national consciousness in the GDR, as Gebhard Schweigler aptly put it, "a hazardous intellectual enterprise."[3]

Discussion and debate with respect to the German question were often a blend of normative and empirical analyses. Observers provided not only their perceptions of German consciousness and national identity, but often interjected their beliefs about the form that consciousness and identity should take. As an example, many of those indifferent to or opposing German unification avowed that Germany constituted only a *Kulturnation.* Association beyond this would not only be unacceptable to Germany's neighbors, but would in all likelihood be detrimental to the Germans themselves. Furthermore, participants in debates on the nation not infrequently exchanged charges of harboring hidden agendas. Because they encouraged Germans to reflect upon their nationality and to keep alive a sense of German community, Ritter and those concurring with him, were attacked, primarily from the political left, for their supposedly nationalistic and anachronistic viewpoints. Ritter's hidden agenda, according to some allegations, was a neo-nationalist one, whose objective it was to reestablish the former German *Staatsnation.*

Ritter denied this was his goal, and claimed to have no particular political agenda. His purpose, as he described it, was to discourage Germans from turning their backs on their national past, to promote careful consideration of the basic problems of political life in Germany, and to encourage critical examination of the German national character. He professed to be doing no more than providing an historical and philosophical context for basic political issues. The motive of his 1948 book, *Europe and the German Question*, he explained, was the keenly felt need to reply to the torrent of attacks against German history and institutions. In a later book, entitled *The German Problem*, published in 1965, Ritter argued that the sense of Europeanism in Germany was not only an effort to escape a difficult past, but also represented the sort of anti-nationalism typifying German philosophical oscillation, the time-honored inclination toward drastic alterations in the espousal of ideas. Contemporary seesawing, said Ritter in the 1960s, received considerable encouragement from the assaults, both domestic and foreign, upon German history and society in the wake of the defeat of the Third Reich. The atrophying of historical identity and the loss of Germany's organic permanence, he insisted, would prevent the reconstitution of a German state, at least one resting upon the confidence of its people.

A politician who echoed this theme in the early 1960s was Eugen Gerstenmeier, president of the West German *Bundestag*, or lower house of parliament. He argued that if Germans were to survive as a nation, they had to know who they were and what they wanted. He wrote:

The task of our national consciousness today does not lie in stylizing unclear emotional states, but it must provide the spiritual and character basis of the self-creation in the form of a state of our people, of the unity of the nation and of its orientation in the world-historical struggle of our time. Whether we will be able to create and make effective such an orientation of our own, for which we consciously accept responsibility, will decide the question whether we will remain a nation capable of a history.[4]

One of Ritter's chief opponents among German academics of stature was the Hamburg historian Fritz Fischer, whose voluminous and controversial writings of the 1960s set the stage for what would later become the so-called *Historikerstreit*, the great debate among leading German historians about the German nation and national identity. The *Historikerstreit* ultimately dealt with such basic issues as the concept of the fatherland, the idea of the German nation, elements of national identity, and the role of the German nation as a unifying community. Fischer's 1961 book entitled *Germany's War Aims in the First World War* and a later treatise, *War of Illusions*, published in 1969, set the tone for a reevaluation of the German nation that would extend far beyond academic circles. In portraying Imperial Germany as predatory and aggressive, and in attempting to establish Germany's war guilt in 1914, Fischer was implicitly disparaging the achievements of Bismarck and the character of the state he founded. On the premise that Germany unilaterally planned, and thus bore primary responsibility for having caused World War I, the "Fischer thesis" as it became widely known, necessitated considerable soul-searching in a nation specializing in it. As David Gress pointed out, the Fischer thesis implanted into postwar German historiography significant amounts of moralizing.[5] For if Germany had so often been an aggressor in recent history, then it stood to reason there was something morally deficient about the German nation. Perhaps the Nazi period was not an historical aberration after all. Fischer's writings would become powerful ammunition for scholars who saw moral deficiencies in the Germany of the 1960s, and for those who searched for the roots of Nazism in German history, culture, and national character. Some of Fischer's students, who comprised what was frequently referred to as the Fischer School carried his historical arguments further by depicting threads of continuity between Bismarck's Reich and Hitler's.

As popular writers and the media took stock of his primary themes, Fischer's arguments had effects that reached beyond academic circles, and implications extending past historical controversies. It is largely a matter of judgment whether the principal arguments of the "Fischer School" were accepted too uncritically by fellow academics and other observers. In the view of many, a logical result of the postulate that German society for the past century was socially flawed, aggressive, even morally deficient, was that the reemergence of a German nation-state was politically unwelcome. In this sense, those probing the broader ramifications of Fischer's writings often endorsed precisely what Ritter had cautioned against: an aloofness from the fatherland idea and a rejection of the unifying force of German history. The battle lines were drawn, as it were, not only between historians, but between many others, between those opposed to a *Staatsnation* composed of both the GDR and the FRG, to those favoring unification, between adherents to the *Kulturnation* to those insisting that German national identity transcended this.

Ideas about nationhood and German identity did not always coincide with political fault lines, nor did they fit neatly into left or right, liberal or conservative categories. Some on the political left accepted Fischer's arguments about past German regimes, but drew quite different conclusions. Others who found a measure of common ground with many conservatives on the matter of nationhood, formed a group commonly known as "leftist nationalists." The phenomenon of nationalism from the left that appeared in the late 1970s ensued from a leftist movement urging the establishment of a bloc-free *Staatsnation*.

DEUTSCHLANDPOLITIK

The 1980s subsequently brought abundant new ideas about nation, homeland, and fatherland from all locations on the political spectrum. From peripheral groups working to change the current order, new nationalist tones were being heard which crystallized within the peace groups and the alternative Greens into a sort of populist nationalism envisaging a nonaligned, bloc-free, and unified Germany. Two leading spokesmen of this new nationalist program, Peter Brandt and Herbert Ammon, described themselves as "leftist patriots" and unreservedly promoted nationalism from the left. Unencumbered by traditional rightist-nationalist and autocratic baggage, left-wing patriotism found sympathetic listeners among people long troubled by an identity crisis.

A less radical expression of national sentiment was found in the "Europeanization of Europe" concept whose leading proponent was the Social Democratic publicist, Peter Bender. In his widely read book *Das Ende des ideologischen Zeitalters Die Europäisierung Europas* (*The End of the Ideological Epoch: The Europeanization of Europe*), appearing in 1981, Bender advanced the argument that Europe had ceased being divided ideologically. European division was merely "political," and could be overcome in the longer term by Europeans if the latter were prepared to distance themselves from the superpowers who, Bender said, were prolonging the division of the continent. In the mid-1980s Bender's theories acquired fresh accents. In a contentious discourse entitled "The Superpower Squeeze" published in 1986 by *Foreign Policy* magazine, he termed the situation of the Europeans "bewildering," and argued that the threat to Europe lay largely, if not exclusively, in the tension arising between the superpowers. He grudgingly acknowledged the United States as a past protector on the one hand, but assailed it as a source of danger in the power struggle with the USSR on the other, and even suggested that Washington used the goal of German unity as a "pretext" for continuing to control the European continent militarily.[6]

Gaining considerable currency in the FRG, Bender's theories came to enjoy substantial support within the ranks of the SPD. Bender's overriding but unpronounced objective was to get the superpowers out of Europe. His writings provided an intellectual underpinning for the proposition that the superpowers were responsible for Europe's division, as well as for the contention that both the United States and the Soviet Union were essentially influence-hungry great powers in the traditional mode, virtually indistinguishable from a moral standpoint from each other. While for some, "Europeanization" meant only that Europeans should gain greater influence within the Western Alliance, thereby acquiring greater control of their affairs, the logical inference for others was that Germany should distance itself from the West and steer a middle course between the blocs, a plan of action known as the *Sonderweg*, the "special" or "third," way, which was supplemented by a vague "Third Road" ideology. Third Roadism foresaw a society that was neither capitalist nor socialist, finding its own path forward. As might be presumed, such notions appealed to some who felt acutely frustrated by their country's situation. Among proponents there was considerable agreement about the desirability of avoiding not only the material disadvantages of capitalism such as consumerism and bouts of unemployment, but the less tangible drawbacks as well, "soullessness," selfishness, individualism, the lack of community spirit.[7]

On one issue the views of "leftist nationalists" diverged sharply from those of Bender and like-thinking Social Democrats such as Oskar Lafontaine and Erhard Eppler. Whereas the "new patriots" encouraged Germans to develop their sense of identity (*Nationalbewusstsein*), and actively explored possibilities for achieving national unification, Bender proposed that the FRG cease pursuing unity and renounce reunification as a policy goal. "The two Germanys are no longer enemies," Bender wrote, "and in fact are becoming partners who detect common interests and the advantages of common endeavors." Bender saw in the SED not a totalitarian communist clique so much as a misguided, leftist party. Many Social Democrats would in fact later be accused of having been averted, even beguiled, particularly in the 1980s, by the unspoken postulate that Marxism-Leninism was in some way progressive and rooted in their own legacy. Even if not always so intended, the grave reservations about the pursuit of German reunification expressed by the left wing of the SPD, which became increasingly influential within the party in the 1980s, represented appeasement of the SED. A 1983 policy statement read: "Whoever here, now and in all seriousness declares the German question 'open' not only destroys the fragile base of Ostpolitik but also the very foundation of European postwar politics." This a mere six years before the GDR collapsed.

One of the most prolific writers on German affairs was the University of Kiel law professor Wolfgang Seiffert, who emigrated from the GDR in 1978. Until his defection, Seiffert had been a professor of law at the Humbolt University in

East Berlin and a top advisor to the SED Central Committee. No radical, Seiffert presented cogent, firsthand insights into the workings of the SED and the thinking of its leading officials. Harking back to Gerhard Ritter, Seiffert pointed to the need for Germans to think more about their identity and their nation. National feelings and a sense of "Germanness," remained strong in the GDR and showed few signs of abating, Seiffert observed. West Germans had a moral as well as a constitutional obligation to support the aspirations of the 17 million people living in the "other" Germany who considered West Germans their fellow countrymen, he insisted. In a contributing article to a popular and controversial book entitled *Die deutsche Einheit kommt bestimmt* (*German Unity Is Certainly Coming*), edited by the leftist writer Wolfgang Venohr and published in 1982, Seiffert, along with fellow authors, explored possibilities for the first steps toward reunification. Beyond this, Seiffert inferentially admonished Germans not to ignore national issues, for the day was coming, as the book title suggested, when different circumstances would push the German question to the top of the world agenda. Then German problems would become actual, and Germans would face the totality of national issues.

Seiffert's 1986 book, *Das Ganze Deutschland Perspektiven der Wiedervereinigung* (*Germany as a Whole: Perspectives of Reunification*), was a frank and articulate pronouncement of the traditional approach to the German question. Germany's division was not only an unjust arrangement in that it denied the right of self-determination to those held captive in the East, he asserted, but constituted a source of insecurity and political instability in Europe because it was based on the denial of freedom and self-determination. Such denial, he reasoned, fostered conflict. In a bold chapter entitled "The Unavoidability of Being a Nation of Germans," Seiffert attacked those displaying a chill or cynically neutral detachment from the fatherland.[8] The time of European identity had not yet come, and hence Europe could not offer a true substitute for a homeland. Europe remained a loose community of nations, and had undergone a cruel division that resulted in East-Central Europe falling into the Soviet orbit. Although nations continuously squabbled, and petty nationalisms contributed mightily to Europe's disunity, at the same time nations were protectors of claims to freedom and national self-determination, he said. To illustrate this point, Seiffert cited the cases of the Baltic states and Poland. The latter was particularly instructive in that the nation had survived, notwithstanding the disappearance of the Polish state owing to great power partition. For over a century Poland had ceased being a nation-state, but remained a *Kulturnation* with a keen sense of national consciousness. Germans would be well-advised to see the parallels with their own situation, Seiffert indicated, but too many Germans either would not acknowledge these or failed to see them.

Since World War II, Polish nationalism formed a bulwark against both Russian imperialism and totalitarian encroachment. German nationalism assumed a similar function in the GDR. If not upon German nationhood, Seiffert asked rhetorically, upon what could popular demands for self-determination and freedom in the GDR be based? Certainly not Marxism-Leninism. The SED regime was predicated on the denial of freedom, and the nationhood of the SED state was spurious. Many "Europe enthusiasts" and those West Germans advocating a final renunciation of German reunification were inattentive to the constructive properties of nationalism which were manifest in Poland and other areas of the East Bloc. Renunciation of unification eliminated the chief foundation for popular assertions of freedom in the GDR, played into SED and Soviet hands, and was tantamount to endorsing liberty and self-determination only for West Germany, said Seiffert. National self-determination and the attainment of popular aspirations, ultimately the struggle for freedom against dictatorship, was the essence of the German question, the argument went. The distinction between the term "national," that is, the usually healthy identification with one's country, and the term "nationalistic," involving extreme patriotic feelings, was a crucial one, Seiffert pointed out. National affinities had quite positive features, while nationalism could be, and often was, hazardous. Seiffert advocated an active Deutschlandpolitik, whose professed goal would be the eventual realization of national self-determination for all Germans. Given the continued existence of national consciousness in both Germanys, but particularly in the GDR, he said, the preconditions for such a policy existed.

But at the same time he warned of the dangers of a "new" (read: leftist) nationalism in the FRG. In the FRG the danger was that a leftist national polity might eventually endeavor to satisfy national aspirations through leftist formulas, then venture to conclude a kind of "Faustian bargain" with the Soviet leadership to "solve" the vexed German question. What Seiffert shuddered at, and thought not improbable sometime in the future, was a neutralist, rather anti-Western Germany.

Its genesis he saw in developments within the SPD and in the emergence of the Greens, and he singled out for criticism those SPD members, who, as leaders of the political opposition after 1982, grappled for new positions in relations with the GDR, and devised vague ideas about a "second Ostpolitik." In Seiffert's view, many Social Democrats were not only on the wrong course, but were using intra-German issues for domestic political purposes. To grasp the essence of the issue, one must understand its background, and the considerable political and emotional investment all German political parties had made in the Ostpolitik, the term generally used to describe relations with the East Bloc and the Soviet Union. The SPD, in coalition with the Free Democratic party (FDP), took considerable pride in formulating and effecting new policies toward the GDR and the East Bloc in the early 1970s. Although these policies met with considerable opposition at first, by the end of the decade a consensus on the Ostpolitik had emerged in the FRG. When the SPD-led coalition foundered in 1982, the new coalition led by the conservative Christian Democrats pursued basically the same policies vis-à-vis the GDR. Alois Mertes, a senior foreign ministry official and member of the conservative CDU, provided the following frame of reference with respect to the national problem:

> What's troubling for us in West Germany is that many Americans show so little understanding of the moral and political substance of the "German question."
>
> As long as Germany is divided by a most inhuman and barbed wire barrier, it remains the human and national duty of West Germany to insure the cohesion of the German people by developing relations with East Germany. At the simplest level, we hope to alleviate the family or personal situations of hundreds of thousands of human beings by making possible travel, family reunions and the like. But this practical aspect of the problem is not its most important side. It is not a question of territory or borders but of national self-determination and individual human rights on both sides of the German border.[9]

Unable to oppose with any sort of credibility those policies it had worked to put into effect, the SPD searched for new avenues in intra-German detente, and some Social Democrats hoped, almost quixotically, for a breakthrough in relations which normally moved forward in small, often minute, steps. In the opposition and impeded by inner divisions, the latter a perennial problem of out-of-office parties freed of the daily business of governing, the SPD frequently exhibited frustration and disappointment. Assuming a role not usually discharged by an opposition party, the SPD began negotiating directly with the SED, establishing the joint Commission on Fundamental Values in 1982, which would later issue three joint position papers, on common security, on a chemical-weapons-free zone in Central Europe, and on the "principles of dialogue." Since these were not agreements between governments, not at least on the West German side, the papers were no more than resolutions or statements of principle. That the SED was the ruling *Staatspartei* in the GDR was a conveniently ignored detail, and in its participation in the Commission the SPD displayed a considerable amount of ideological relativism. The Social Democrats were pursuing a sort of shadow Deutschlandpolitik, while the SED for its part was negotiating with both the governing coalition in the FRG as well as with the major opposition party. SPD actions were legally dubious and politically unwise, Seiffert said, above all, because relations with the GDR were becoming increasingly politicized as these became the stuff of domestic politics in the FRG.

What is more, Seiffert exhorted, the "left-wing nationalists," and proponents of the "Europeanization of Europe" such as Bender and Lafontaine were harboring illusions about what Germans could reasonably hope to achieve on their own. For all their differences, several of the groups believed that Germany should increasingly go it alone, that somehow Germans could settle the German question by their own devices. It was simply foolish to think, Seiffert maintained, that Germans largely by themselves could, in Bender's words, "relieve Europe of the German question." The "equidistance" between the United States and the Soviet Union that Bender favored was in fact only a mild variant of the unabashed anti-Westernism of the far left and the Greens.

In any event, renewed interest in the homeland and nation reflected changing perspectives. By the 1980s symbols of nationhood and notions of fatherland in the FRG, and in an increasing measure in the GDR, ceased to carry the ominous burden they once did. Conservatives in the FRG, recognizing the importance of national symbols, and reassured by decades of stable democracy, became much less hesitant to speak up on national issues. Uneasiness about Reagan's America, which gave many Germans occasion to question some of the tenets of "Atlanticism," and growing dissatisfaction with the progress of Western European integration, were motivating factors as well. In the national election campaign of 1983, the SPD adopted as its chief slogan, "In the German Interest," a move some observers found quite remarkable.

The conservative journal *Die Politische Meinung* regularly published articles after 1980 on such topics as "Democracy and Fatherland," "Fatherland and Nation Today," "The Divided Brothers," and the "Nation and Democracy," examining national values, investigating national consciousness, posing central questions about the German nation. In a 1986 article, Karl Carstens, former president of the FRG and a target of scathing periodic attacks from the left because of a shadowy past, deplored what he perceived to be a lack of affinity with the German homeland on the part of younger Germans. In many young German minds, Carstens suggested, a regrettable psychological connection had been drawn between the German nation and the National Socialist past, with the result that positive German values and traditions were either belittled or in some cases completely ignored.[10] Germans in the 1980s, Carstens contended, must ask themselves key questions, such as "What do we mean when we speak of the German fatherland?" "What should be the nature of German national consciousness?"

Not pretending to have definitive answers, Carstens left the reader with a few observations and recommendations. Suppression of national consciousness, not to mention a refusal to think about nation and fatherland, were not solutions. Such attitudes in fact contributed to existing problems, he said. Neither did the Europeanization process obviate the need on the part of West Germans to reflect on national issues, or to seek solutions to the German question. European unification could only be seen as a long-term goal, and a veritable European identity would not replace national identities for generations to come. Finally, he said, West Germans had cause to look favorably upon the FRG, a country offering its citizens stability and freedom in relative affluence. West Germans could justifiably be proud of their state, and should revere it as being in the best German social and political traditions.

In a similar vein, Hartmut Schiedermair, a professor of international law in Cologne, and Michael Stürmer, an historian at the University of Erlangen, took to task leading leftist intellectuals for politicizing discussions of the nation in what they considered a most regrettable fashion. At the forefront were Jürgen Habermas, a sociologist at the University of Marburg, expelled from the SPD for his extreme views, and Günter Grass, one of the best-known West German writers of fiction, both of whom tended to equate love of country with virulent nationalism, jingoism, even militarism. Outspoken opponents of NATO, they condemned patriotic manifestations in Europe as "militaristic NATO philosophies." Habermas argued that Germans had to face the stark choice between national identity and freedom, since these in his view were incompatible on many points. Nationalism in Germany had a dismal tradition, he said, and the revival of national sympathies entailed considerable risks of a return to undemocratic patterns. Schiedermair observed that Habermas failed to make any distinction between national consciousness on the one hand, and the extreme forms of nationalism that had brought such grief to Germany and Europe in the twentieth century on the other.[11] Grass, for his part, who often displayed strong emotions about the subject, appeared incapable of distinguishing between simple patriotism and immoderate nationalism. Discussion of the German fatherland would frequently elicit references to Auschwitz and the concentration camps from Grass. To him, national awareness smacked of right-wing authoritarianism, and raised suspicions in his mind about hidden nationalist agendas. Prone to oversimplification, and voicing his unreserved loathing for quests for a German identity, Grass condemned efforts to achieve reunification, and in 1989 became an outspoken opponent of German unity.

Schiedermair and Stürmer found such reasoning objectionable, and they frowned upon the lack of proportion. Both agreed that West Germans could take pride in their post-war political achievements. There was little basis for believing West German democracy was not stable, much less that Germans would once again collapse into savage barbarism. The anxieties Habermas, Grass, and several leftist historians involved in the *Historikerstreit* harbored about German national awareness were largely without foundation, said Schiedermair. For Stürmer, it was not national awareness that was worrisome, as Habermas argued, as much as its absence. National heritage sustained bonds of commonwealth, and the democratic achievements of the West German state would be best preserved by a binding sense of community and through public interest in the German past.[12]

Heightened interest in the German nation was not confined to the FRG. Greater self-confidence among officialdom in the GDR, which seemed to be on a sort of international political roll in the early 1980s, increased attentiveness to the national heritage. The SED recognized that national symbols furnished opportunities for citizen identification that an abstract ideology was unable to provide. Accordingly, many official views underwent significant change, and the GDR made ever greater historical claims about "progressive" elements and figures in German history. To some Western observers, such as Hermann Rudolph, the GDR's historical assertions represented a tacit admission that the socialist state could not offer a sound national identity. As a consequence, said Rudolph, the SED had increasingly to rely upon the German national past to nurture feelings of community and to give an impulse to nation-building. But he found official assertions about the "progressive continuity" in modern German history, from the peasants' war in the sixteenth century to the establishment of the GDR, for instance, as largely inconsistent and arbitrary, and therefore doing nothing in the way of combating a popular perception of the regime, especially among its own citizens, as capricious at best. The fanciful threads of historical continuity the SED sketched were, if anything, intensifying such attitudes. Although most East Germans had adapted themselves to their situation, accepting the GDR as a state as such, Rudolph wrote in 1986, this outlook had not (or not yet) evolved into a separate national consciousness. A perceptible national awareness transcending the inner-German border lingered on, Rudolph concluded.[13]

Rudolph saw another not unrelated reason for growing official preoccupation with the national past in the GDR. For years Western observers had been pointing out the intense "privateness" in the GDR. Günter Gaus, a former West German diplomatic representative to East Berlin, and a man not without some admiration for East German society, described the latter in his writings as a Nischengesellschaft, or "niche society" in which the vast majority of people retreated to the private sphere, where they could live their "real" lives.[14] Families tended to be close-knit, and circles of friends intimate by necessity. What Gaus found positive—the maintenance of a more personal, traditional lifestyle and the preservation of past values—the SED did not. Such a retreat into the private sphere undermined the collective spirit that was a canon of Leninism. Western observers for the most part agreed that the niche structure was a form of accommodation with the regime, if not a manifestation of popular resignation. The SED bid to promote the advent of a socialist identity, was made with a eye to eradicating the "niche society" and eliminating the vestiges of an all-German consciousness.

Those with firsthand experience of the GDR frequently detected a certain popular attachment to the nation in the traditional sense, not in any convoluted socialist sense.

East German dissidents who had emigrated to the West, such as Reiner Kunze and Günter Kunert, would periodically allude to the robust feelings of "Germanness" in the GDR. Kunze granted that ideological indoctrination from the earliest years in people's lives might have been having some effect upon popular attitudes and opinions, but suggested the SED was far from achieving its proclaimed goal of instilling in its people a sense of the "socialist national culture of the GDR."[15]

In their works, both Kunze and Kunert communicated experiences of national as well as personal tragedy, and in so doing imparted their own German sensitivities. In his poems depicting Berlin's crumbling buildings, Kunert recast bricks and pavements into impressions of collective remembrance.[16] His message is clear: The breaks in continuity with Germany's past compounded the political division of the country. Berlin, devoid of its internal reality and adrift somewhat like a dream city, represented a rootless Germany, wanting of a national past capable of binding the nation together. The images in his writings bring to mind Ritter's counsels in the 1960s.

Most West Germans regarded the quest for German identity, as well as the exchanges associated with it, as altogether healthy developments. The discussions of national identity in the FRG in which many groups participated (artists, journalists, politicians, academics, and even ordinary citizens) were often thoughtful, even lively. In part the discussions reflected the effort, whether conscious or unconscious, to rediscover German roots, Kunert suggested. The many West German citizens' movements that sprang up beginning in the late 1970s were evidence of a new national awareness and a popular desire—for the first time on the part of many—for civic involvement. Rudolph referred to the West German citizens' groups, in which the peace movement and the Greens had their origin, as *Suchbewegungen* (quest movements), analogous in some ways on a popular level to the intellectuals' search for meaning in a divided land.[17] Such developments in the FRG contrasted sharply with the network of social "niches" in the GDR, a pattern involving apathy and withdrawal, that was by most accounts becoming more ingrained.

The candid reflections and debates on the nation that took place in the FRG would have been impossible in the GDR, a state not renowned for candor or spontaneity. New official SED interest in the German past beginning around 1977 constituted in large part an effort to mold and shape what, in the regime's assessment, were improper popular attitudes. It was an acknowledgment that a stable socialist state could not be built if all organic continuity with the past was severed, but at the same time, it was a reaction *against* to a greater extent than it was a search *for*.

Here was the rub. Equating "nation" with "nationalism," for the better part of the 1970s, the SED condemned both as repugnant features of the past. In the early 1970s the idea of a *"Volksnation"* (a nation of a people) was dropped, and the regime subsequently embraced the concept of the *"Klassennation"* (class nation), with particular emphasis given to "class." Was the official interpretation of nationhood about to come full circle in the 1980s? Was the SED in the process of reverting to a "national-patriotic" course? A sort of leftist nationalism in the GDR? In the 1980s the SED set about to a far greater extent than previously to distinguish between nation and national on the one hand, and nationalism on the other, promulgating entirely new historical renditions emphasizing progressive elements in German history. The regime was devising new state-supporting myths and regime legitimacy was clearly to be based on an historical whole without limitation with respect to class.

GERMAN ANGST

> The crime of genocide, summed up in the image of Auschwitz, inexcusable from whatever angle you view it, weighs heavily on the conscience of this unified state.
>
> Never before in their history had the Germans brought down upon themselves such terrifying shame. Until then, they were no better and no worse than other peoples. But the megalomania born of their complexes led them to reject the possibility of being a cultural nation within a federation and to insist instead on the creation of a unified state in the form of a Reich—by any and all means. This state laid the foundation for Auschwitz.[18]

Made in early 1990, with Germany unifying but still divided, this statement by Günter Grass was summary testimony of a leading opponent of a revitalized German nation-state. Although Grass claimed to believe passionately in a *Kulturnation*, he and no few leftist intellectuals maintained that freedom and security would be served not by a German political union, but rather by two separate German states, joined, if at all, by very loose confederative structures.

What was the basis for such an argument? The short answer, by Grass's own admission, is the pat German word that has found its way into the English language: angst. Grass seemed unable to think of German nationhood separate from war and the concentration camps. Mere deliberations of national identity and national awareness conjured up images of Auschwitz in his mind. Grass, along with other "Third Roaders," the East German writers Stefan Heym and Christa Wolf are examples, distrusted and even feared popular national feelings. Recalling their wartime experiences, Heym and Grass recounted the suffering extreme nationalism had brought to their country. Indeed, German ambitions, dilemmas, misfortunes, and errors in this century seemed to Grass to be fused in one almost unimaginable horror: Auschwitz. Angst vis-à-vis the German nation-state assumed extreme dimensions in his colleague, Heinrich Böll, who died in 1987. Böll's dread of the state bordered on the paranoiac, and seemed fraught with disdain for constitutional democracy. The conjunction of trepidation and self-pity, the latter huge in Böll's case and aptly described by one observer as *Leidensdrang* (the need to suffer), was for Böll the upshot of life in West German society.[19] As the writer Peter Schneider ruefully and derisively remarked, angst had somehow become an indispensable emotion among Germans. Feelings had reached such a point, Schneider once quipped, that "whoever has no fear in Germany is an idiot or has no imagination."

The theme of suffering is infused into Grass's writings also, as is at least modicum of the same self-pity. And the sense of alienation is prominent, put into words with Grass's more than occasional coarseness. In a reference to the uniting Germany of 1990, Grass said: "I am already a traitor to this fatherland. Any fatherland of mine must be more diverse, more colorful, more neighborly—a fatherland that has grown, through suffering, wiser and more open to Europe."[20]

Grass took pride in being a "rootless cosmopolitan," a term employed by the right in the 1930s to stigmatize leftist intellectuals. Rather than securing freedom and furthering self-determination, a single German nation-state in his view would constitute a "monster" with the potential of bringing misery to Germany and her neighbors. In substantiating his positions, Grass drew historical parallels that were dubious, often rash, and contrived for maximum rhetorical effect. "Reich" for Grass meant "Third Reich," and he conveniently disregarded the prior two. The foundation for Auschwitz was laid by the "unified German state," he claimed, but did not take the trouble to specify which one. "The unified German state" assisted in providing "an appallingly firm foundation for the radical ideology of National Socialism." Did he mean to suggest the German states of the past century were pretty much the same?

Grass somewhat disingenuously accused many of his interlocutors in discussions of national issues of thinking in either-or patterns. "As a writer to whom the German language means the ability to transcend borders, I find, whenever I analyze political statements critically, that I come up against this dread either-or, all-or-nothing principle," Grass wrote, "yet we do have a third possibility for answering the German Question." Be that as it may, the contention that national unification provided a firm foundation for Nazism did not appear an oversimplification for Grass, nor were the following alternatives, as he enumerated them, indicative of thinking in either-or terms—continued German division with a refinement of the *Kulturnation* or the probable revival of nationalist extremism. Grass had for years expressed his grave concern that a unified German nation would produce "waves of hate," and he continues to do so.

Contending that he was "mindful of history" in his views about the German nation, Grass occupied himself with a number of the broader questions pertaining to the *Historikerstreit*. In the FRG's leading leftist academics he found political allies on occasion, and his sentiments coincided on several points with those of revisionist historians. Critics of Fischer and Imanuel Geiss, intimated that these historians nurtured an unvoiced political agenda not unlike Grass's. Continuity in German history, from the German Reich under Prussian rule, to the precarious Weimar Republic, to the brutal Third Reich is a principal, albeit implied, theme of Fischer's writings, and especially those of Geiss, his star pupil. Fischer, Geiss and Hans-Ulrich Wehler all perceived flaws in German society which eventually led to catastrophe. In arguing that German leaders in the years prior to World War I planned a military campaign against Germany's neighbors with the purpose of dominating the European continent, Fischer afforded evidence of the ideology of expansionism, laying the intellectual groundwork for later historians who determined that the roots of Nazism were to be found in certain economic and social conditions in Germany. Geiss, an historian, like Grass and Böll, writers of fiction, found certain attributes of the German nation innately reproachable and morally unsuitable.

For many German artists and writers, most of whom had strong feelings about national identity and homeland, their country was a paradigm of a world torn by conflict and calamity. Wolf Biermann is probably the best-known example of the alienated artist, scorning communism and capitalism with equal fervor, a German who could not find a home in either the GDR or the FRG, whose works radiate feelings of double alienation. His verses seem to transfer his personal estrangement to the nation, and he indicates Germany may have lost her identity altogether. In a sense his poems are reminiscent of Heinrich Heine's satire of the last century.

Biermann was by no means alone in his concern about the potential loss of German identity. In Uwe Johnson's fiction of the 1960s, scarred urban landscapes are the setting for the pursuit of an elusive national personality. The bizarre ritual of crossing intra-German borders, and a yearning for the elimination of barriers are themes of his writings. Peter Schneider, whose satire is also suggestive of Heine, frequently took a more politicized view. Schneider derided many West German policies, and largely blamed the FRG's first chancellor, Konrad Adenauer, and his CDU for the division of Germany.[21] Whereas East German leaders had little leeway and no real choice on national matters, Adenauer, Schneider argued, in acquiescing to the Western allies on major issues, forced Stalin's hand in the Eastern Zone. Although less critical of East German leaders in light of the dearth of options available to them, he suggested that Germany's early political elite, both West and East, was insufficiently patriotic. As it was, he argued, Germany's "state identity" (*staatliche Identität*) was determined by foreign powers. The German people were divided against their will, and the price the FRG paid for Western integration was high.

Schneider's writings contain anti-American overtones, and his "Third Way" politics come dangerously close to equating the superpowers morally and socially. For him, Germany's postwar national identity was improperly cast precisely because it was externally determined. Foreigners forced the Germans apart, and were responsible for the emergence of two very different German lifestyles. The policies of neither German state advanced the cause of unity, as they should have, and consequently, the two German states were becoming socially more diverse. Oblivious to national purpose, the FRG continued the course of Western integration at the expense of the fatherland and national unity. Still more deplorable, the GDR appeared to be cultivating some of the most unpalatable features of former German states, like the tradition of unquestioning obedience and rigid authoritarianism (*Obrigkeitsstaat*). Such was the fatherland's sad situation.

Schneider's *Deutsche Ängste* (*German Fears*), published in 1988, is a collection of short essays concerned largely with German identity. Unlike Grass, Schneider harbored few misgivings about manifestations of national consciousness; he seems in fact to have shared the conviction of many that the

German nation should be an historically bound and binding community. The United States and the Soviet Union had divided Germany politically, he claimed, and on occasion he referred sardonically to the inner-German border as the "Soviet-American border." Germans were in the process of losing their identity, and they could begin to recover it, in his view, through a new *Nationalbewusstsein*, pursuit of the "Third Way," and assertiveness vis-à-vis the superpowers. The GDR and the FRG were drifting apart, and a rootless nation awash like a phantom vessel on the strands of time was evolving from political division. Germans, he implied, should overcome their fears and find the courage at last to alter the conditions of their nation.

In a re-unified state, according to Schneider, Germans would have the best chance of recovering their lost identity. His ultimate goal resembled that of the "leftist patriots," but differed markedly from that of, say, Grass or Heym. Grass, for his part, feared German nationalism above all else, while Schneider seemed most concerned about continued division of the country and the attendant loss of national identity. Each, like Biermann, was alienated in his own special way. In postwar German writing alienation and angst often went hand-in-hand, becoming mingled at times with self-pity.

NOTES

1. Gerhard Ritter, *The German Problem* (Columbus: Ohio State University Press, 1965), preface.

2. Hans-Peter Schwarz, *Die gezähmten Deutschen Von der Machtbessenheit zur Machtvergessenheit* (Stuttgart: Deutsche Verlags-Anstalt, 1985).

3. Gebhard Schweigler, *National Consciousness in Divided Germany* (London: Sage Publications, 1975), 107.

4. Quoted in Schweigler, *National Consciousness*, 10.

5. David Gress, *Peace and Survival* (Stanford: Hoover Institute Press, 1985), 55.

6. Peter Bender, "The Superpower Squeeze," *Foreign Policy* 65 (Winter 1986-87): 100.

7. George Schöpflin, "The End of Communism in Eastern Europe," *International Affairs* 66, no. 1 (1990): 12.

8. Wolfgang Seiffert, *Das Ganze Deutschland Perspektiven der Wiedervereinigung* (Munich: Piper, 1986), 23-34.

9. Quoted in Dennis L. Bark and David R. Gress, *Democracy and its Discontents 1963-1988*, vol. 2 of *A History of West Germany* (Oxford: Basil Blackwell, 1989), 460-61.

10. Karl Carstens, "Demokratie und Vaterland," *Die Politische Meinung*, 31, no. 229 (November-December 1986): 34-41.

11. Hartmut Schiedermair, "Deutschland als Ganzes," *Die Politische Meinung* 32, no. 233 (July-August 1987): 4-12.

12. Michael Stürmer, "Nation und Demokratie," *Die Politische Meinung* 32, no. 230 (January-February 1987): 15-27.

13. Hermann Rudolph, "Die Getrennten Brüder," *Die Politische Meinung*, 31, no. 227 (July-August 1986): 24.

14. Günter Gaus, *Wo Deutschland liegt Eine Ortsbestimmung* (Hamburg: Hoffmann und Campe, 1983), 156-233.

15. Reiner Kunze, "Panzer und Feldhasen," *Die Politische Meinung* 31, no. 224 (January-February 1986): 69.

16. *The Independent* (London), 13 November 1989.

17. Rudolph, "Die Getrennten Brüder," 30-31.

18. Günter Grass, *Two States—One Nation?* (San Diego: Harcourt Brace Jovanovich, 1990), 6.

19. Quoted in Gress, *Peace and Survival*, 135.

20. Grass, *Two States—One Nation*, 3-4.

21. Peter Schneider, *Deutsche Ängste* (Darmstadt: Luchterhand, 1988), 19-27.

4
Economic Difficulties in the GDR

CENTRAL PLANNING

The two most basic functions of any economy, the designation of authority over factors of production, and the furnishing of information about what production is to take place with what disposable resources, were performed in the GDR almost entirely by administrative fiat. Democratic centralism, the governing maxim of the SED, aimed to minimize the effect of market forces upon the utilization of factors of production, while heavy party involvement in virtually every aspect of the economy assured the primacy of politics over economics. Commitment to central planning was included in Article 9 of the 1974 Constitution of the GDR:

(3)   The German Democratic Republic bases itself on the principle of the management and planning of the national economy and other social spheres. The national economy of the German Democratic Republic is socialist planned economy. Central state management and planning of the basic issues of social development are combined with the individual responsibility of the local organs of state and enterprises and with the initiative of the working people.

(4)   The currency and financial systems are prescribed by the socialist state. Laws govern the raising of taxes and imposts.

(5)   Foreign economic relations, including foreign trade and foreign exchange economy, are the monopoly of the state.[1]

Article 12 specified:

(1)   Mineral resources, mines, power stations, barrages and large bodies of water, the natural resources of the continental shelf, the industrial enterprises,

banks and insurance companies, nationally-owned farms, traffic routes, the means of transport of the railways, ocean shipping and civil aviation, post and telecommunication installations, are nationally owned property. Private ownership thereof is inadmissible.[2]

Course corrections in the GDR, with an attendant waxing and waning of centralization, bore witness to the problems associated with central planning. In the period 1949-61 the GDR became one of the most centrally planned and administratively organized states of the world. In 1952 the old German states of Thuringia, Saxony-Anhalt, Saxony, Mecklenburg, and Brandenburg were dissolved and fifteen centrally administered *Birzirke* with little formal and less effective authority replaced them. By 1960, some 95 percent of agricultural holdings had been collectivized and thereby brought into the "socialist sector" either in the form of collective farms (*Landwirtschaftliche Produktionsgenossenschaft*, or LPG), or state farms (*Volkseigenes Gut*).[3] In ensuing years central direction of agriculture increased, and the vast majority of collective farms were converted from the Type I organization with only the arable land completely socialist and some private ownership of buildings, livestock, and equipment, to the Type III organization in which virtually everything on the farm was in state hands. Eventually, 98 percent of the collective farms were to become Type III organizations, a development which, in conjunction with the augmentation of individual farm size, effectively placed the entire farming sector under state control.[4]

In the late 1950s the economy began to stall, the consequence of the severe shorter-term dislocations brought on by agricultural collectivization, and the longer-term problem of the staggering burden of industrial centralization. Abandonment of the overly ambitious Seven-Year Plan in 1959, which decreed by law that the GDR was to surpass the FRG economically, in favor of a more modest transitional plan, attested to official recognition of the troubles. The year 1963 brought an end to the first distinct phase of the GDR's economic history with the adoption of the New Economic System for Planning and Managing the Economy (NÖSPL), often referred to simply as the New Economic System (NÖS), which would in 1965 evolve into the Economic System of Socialism (ÖSS). The latter, according to official explanations, embraced the notion that economic planning should be "supplemented by" social planning based on wider "prognoses" of societal development.[5] Planning was to be the shared duty of the State Plan Commission (SPK), the Council of Ministers, the individual plants (VEB), the Associations of People's Industries (VVB), and regional councils. The concentration of investment and research in the structurally determinant branches of the national economy reflected an acknowledgment that prior economic planning schemes had been far too ambitious. Only certain select sectors were to be officially targeted for the attainment of "world standards of technology and profitability" (i.e., would be internationally competitive).[6] The

VEB organization was given primary responsibility for managing the specified target sectors such as steel, shipbuilding, and potash production.

The Economic System of Socialism represented an application of theories devised by the Soviet economist Yevsey Libermann of the Kharkov Engineering and Economics Institute several years prior that aimed to decentralize control of production in the socialist states and introduce market-oriented concepts of profit, price, cost accounting, and interest. Such decentralization necessitated the relaxation of political control, a controversial issue at the time which in part explained the hesitancy to initiate the plan in bloc states, as well as the backpedaling that would later occur in the Soviet Union. Libermann summarized the operation of his new system in the following manner:

> It is necessary to find a sufficiently simple and at the same time reasonable solution for one of the main tasks that has been put forward by the program of the Communist Party of the Soviet Union: to develop a system of planning and evaluating the performance of enterprises in such a way as to mobilize their self-interest in the highest possible planning targets, in introducing new techniques, in improving the quality of products—in a word, in the highest possible efficiency of production.[7]

Throughout the industrial sector in the GDR considerable tinkering took place, and the rapidity of the adoption of the reform program bespoke a certain urgency in dealing with the country's economic ills. By its own admission, the Economic System of Socialism aspired to eliminate the ill-devised components of long-range central planning and to foster greater enterprise flexibility, allowing rapid adjustment to changing market conditions. Notions of profitability were introduced; bonuses were to be paid only to the employees of plants demonstrating sizeable increases in efficiency, and an effort was made to link wages to economic performance, although how precisely the latter was to be measured remained a mystery of socialist accounting methodology. Financial institutions were to assume an entrepreneurial role, whereby state banks were to be "obstinate business partners demanding effective use of financial resources."[8] Firms were to be charged interest on capital with a view to more sensible capital fund utilization. Nonetheless, the problem of insufficient financial discipline lingered. Soft budgeting remained the order of the day. A veritable unforgiving credit regime proved impossible to establish, above all, because of the political clout of the various management and planning authority tiers. The fox continued to guard the chicken coop.

Two predicaments appear to have hastened the collapse of the reform experiment. The first, largely an administrative matter, pertained to ambiguities of authority. Partial and uneven decentralization increased uncertainties in some cases about the allocation of policy-making responsibility. The second was that the targeting of certain industries resulted in economic imbalances and dislocations, with an attendant stagnation of entire sectors. One-sided promotion caused outright failure of some basic manufacturers upon whom selected industries depended, a wholly unforeseen ripple effect that reverberated through the economy. Planners acknowledged the impact to be so far-reaching that some target sectors faced bottlenecks.

In addition to these domestic determinants of the retreat from reform, there were two transnational ones as well, both involving the political climate in the East Bloc. Nikita Khrushchev's ouster as general-secretary of the CPSU in the fall of 1964 brought with it a revitalization of economic centralization in the Soviet Union. More significantly, the "socialism with a human face" experiment in Czechoslovakia in 1968 discredited any liberalization schemes requiring a sacrifice of political control in the eyes of SED chief Ulbricht and the party elite. The disturbances and strikes in Poland in the fall of 1970 that toppled party chief Wladyslaw Gomulka was an additional premonitory sign of the possible consequences of political relaxation. Ulbricht came to fear the "infection" of his own people with ideas about reform even more than he did economic slowdown.

In a pointed about-face in December 1970, the SED Central Committee quietly terminated the economic reform efforts and swung the economy around almost full circle. The move marked the beginning of the third historical phase in the GDR, one characterized by a renewal of centralized planning with a subsequent elimination of the pseudo price system and credit regimen of the New Economic System. The party figures most closely associated with the reforms, Ulbricht, Stoph, and Mittag were all demoted in the wake of the turnaround. Ulbricht was toppled as SED chief. Stoph, hitherto chairman of the Council of Ministers, was assigned a position on the Council of State. Mittag was replaced as Central Committee economic planning secretary. Later in the 1970s, with vexed questions of overcentralization reemerging, Stoph and Mittag, those SED leaders with the most economic expertise, were restored to their former positions. Mittag for his part would become closely associated with the much heralded *Kombinate*.

Thereafter, and for nearly two decades, the SPK, the Ministerial Council's organ for planning and control, directed the recentralized economic decision-making process in the GDR. The Commission had almost complete responsibility for internal resource allocation, for the foreign trade sector, for providing long-term prognoses, for identifying those sectors of the economy to be "promoted," even for setting domestic living standard levels.[9] Shorter-term economic goals were set by an annual plan, and longer-term ones by the five-year plans, with the SPK bearing primary responsibility for devising both. Growth targets, annual and multi-year, were subdivided by sector and decreed by the SPK to the respective economic ministries.

INDUSTRIES OF THE GDR—UNITE!

Beneath the ministries in the politico-economic hierarchy were the so-called *Kombinate* (combines), the large aggregations of industrial enterprises merging administrative and economic functions. In an administrative reorganization in the late 1970s the VVBs, which had been granted considerable independence and had assumed important planning duties under the reform procedures, were phased out or reorganized into larger units. Plants in associated product sectors were amalgamated into various industrial groups and placed directly under the GDR's dozen industrial ministries. The typical *Kombinat* would consist of more than ten factories, often dispersed, with a workforce of perhaps as many as 20,000. The *Kombinate*, thereafter the principal enterprises of the centrally managed industrial sector, were integrated vertically, to allow producers in particular areas to pool their resources, and horizontally, to bring research and development units into close proximity to the producers. Many observers accredit the GDR's relative economic success in the 1980s to the organization of the *Kombinate* that encouraged better utilization of technological innovation and permitted some flexibility to cope with changing market conditions. Each *Kombinat* had a research center of its own, and some advantages of economies of scale accrued to the industrial group, the result of the sheer size of operation. By East Bloc standards, the directors of the approximately 130 *Kombinate* enjoyed considerable managerial authority within the organization, which somewhat decentralized the macro-economic decision-making process, while the organizational structure greatly simplified the chain of command. The chief bureaucratic rationale for the new line-up was that management would bear extensive responsibility for the entire product cycle from research stages to overseas marketing.[10]

Nonetheless, the *Kombinate* faced many of the usual difficulties of the planned economy. National ministries, not a management board, appointed the enterprise directors. Although ministries were merely to set targets and provide guidelines, leaving the management considerable leeway, authority remained ill-defined and ministerial meddling was not infrequent. Major technological innovation and product upgrade required ministerial sanctioning. Individual enterprises did not compete with one another for domestic or foreign markets, and, most hampering of all, prices and wages were determined by the central planning authorities. Prices provided management with little information about scarcity of resources, and price distortion was a major hindrance to intelligent decision making. The correlation between wages and economic performance remained indistinct. Nor was there opportunity to adjust the size of the labor force or to shift human resources according to changing conditions. One observer suggests that a principal task of the enterprise director was to interpret "SED goals as they apply to the life of the enterprise."[11] An odd managerial task.

Smaller factories and local service companies, some 8,000 altogether,[12] formed the second tier of the GDR's enterprise structure. These for the most part were directed separately from the *Kombinate* by the County Council for Local Industry which, in turn, was subordinate to the respective ministry. Arguably, it was in this second economic tier that state heavy-handedness was most detrimental. The national ministries specified plan targets and drafted production schemes based upon estimated resource inputs required to meet economic objectives. Local managers had no flexibility even within their own enterprises to respond to changing demand, nor were they in a position to incorporate technical innovation into the production process. Managers were limited to making "proposals" for output targets, which higher authorities could ignore when they chose to. The ministries submitted their plans to the SPK, whereupon the Council of Ministers determined the annual "material balance" for the entire economy and developed aggregate economic schedules based on these.

INHERENT DILEMMAS

The purpose of this overview of economic issues is to explain how certain economic problems fit into a broader context and to describe the role of economic factors in the upheaval of 1989. It is important to understand that the GDR's economy was not merely a poorly managed version of a market economy, one that with a few reforms and a bit of mending might have performed adequately. Command economies are very different from market economies, and these differences were too often minimized. For example, Western authors were given to speaking of profits, credit, prices, and taxes in the GDR as if these had functions analogous to the ones they do in a market economy.[13] Such parallels can be misleading. In the East German setting these terms had for the most part quite another meaning.

One of the lessons of 1989 must be that festering problems often involved more than single issues; they were intrinsic, part and parcel of economic and political failure. Furthermore, one should judge the SED regime by its own standards. Throughout the GDR's history economic issues prevailed in the media, in political statements, and in scholarship. The Marx-in-Wonderland world of East German newspapers and television was inundated with successful production figures and glowing reports of economic achievements. In the main, the shortcomings of the GDR's command economy might be described as having had the following principal dimensions.[14]

No Scarcity Pricing

This was the most profound difference between the GDR's economy and the market variety. If markets function, prices act as signals to consumers as well as producers. The price system works in an economy only where it allocates resources and is the chief determinant of consumer behavior. The absence of scarcity pricing precludes an efficiency calculus to establish investment priorities. Markets in the GDR seldom connected supply with demand to enable the economy to provide what consumers most wished to purchase. Economic priorities were not set by markets, but by political authorities. Devoid of the crucial market information provided by the price system, planners were unable to shift resources to meet constantly changing demand, which is the basic reason command economies have found it difficult to be internationally competitive. Such is the practiced hand of market capitalism that existing demand does not go long unsatisfied.

Managers in the GDR were given too little incentive to economize on scarce resources, and as a consequence, enterprise consumption appetites tended to be enormous. The setting of prices by administrative fiat was undertaken with specific political goals in mind, for example, to maintain full employment, to reduce the costs to the consumer of basic foodstuffs and public transportation, to keep visible inflation down. Prices seldom reflected the costs of production and cost variables were determined arbitrarily. Notwithstanding official resolve to channel resources into more profitable sectors, especially to the export sector, reconsignment often proved difficult because of great built-in rigidities. So long as it was in power, the SED was unwilling to relinquish control of prices.

Low Capital Productivity

This is, of course, closely related to the above. Capital productivity is the ratio between investment in stock in trade and the net worth of goods and services generated by these assets. Significant inefficiencies resulted, for example, when planning authorities overestimated anticipated return on investment. Without market-determined prices to indicate which industries were operating most efficiently, capital productivity problems arose. The GDR often had to rely upon external sources of capital to make up for investment shortfall.

Raw Materials Wastage

Consumption of raw materials in the GDR was excessively high by Western standards. Evidence would suggest that industrial fuel consumption was among the highest in the East Bloc.[15] With little incentive to conserve, enterprises squandered artificially low-priced commodities. Absent a functional efficiency calculus in any sector, the economy was unable to shift resources away from unproductive enterprises. In fact, the greatest wastage was often found among inefficient producers who had shown some promise in the past. In light of their former successes, they were allocated disproportionately greater amounts of resources by the central planners.

Technology Lag

Retarded technological innovation exacerbated the low investment problem. Since virtually all decisions for the incorporation of scientific and technological innovation were made in some form or another by the central planners, renovation generally was slow, and necessary upgrading of plant and equipment suffered delays. Basic research was not as a rule conducted by enterprises themselves or affiliated institutes able to incorporate technology into production, but rather by detached research organizations under party control by dint of central planning authority funding. Moreover, sheltered state monopolies and enterprises effectively shielded from foreign competition were provided with few inducements to increase productivity through technology upgrade.

THE VISAGE OF FAILURE

Necessarily, the GDR was not immune from economic problems elsewhere, and the Soviet reform programs of the 1980s had to be viewed against the backdrop of deepening domestic crisis in the USSR. Although the GDR could boast the strongest economy among the East Bloc states in the 1980s, this merely meant it topped a list of mediocre economic performers. The full extent of the GDR's economic deterioration, concealed as far as possible by SED authorities, was often underestimated in the West. Figures, when available, seldom conveyed the enormity of problems in certain areas.

Even a relatively superficial glimpse at the GDR revealed all was not well. Cities were drab and relentlessly dirty, especially in the winter when urban areas were sometimes immersed in yellow smog generated by the burning of lignite (brown coal). Low rents, induced by huge state subsidies, provided powerful disincentives to renovate older buildings, with the result that city centers were usually in advanced stages of decay. Roads, especially in urban areas, were pitted and for the most part unreconditioned since World War II. The few existing highways, whose maintenance the West helped finance, were rarely in good repair. Congestion was not infrequent, although the GDR was among the least motorized countries in Europe. In 1989 only around 4 million automobiles were registered in the GDR, a country with a population of nearly 17 million.

Railroads were neglected and worn-out, despite, perhaps because of, heavy industrial reliance upon rail transportation. Track and rolling stock were severely damaged in the war, and rebuilding had never been completed. Passenger trains were notoriously slow and on many lines never achieved pre-war speeds. Only a small fraction of the lines were electrified, in spite of planning authority commitment to rail system electrification as an energy-saving device. The railroads depended on diesel locomotives, many of them of Soviet manufacture and energy inefficient.

A palpable offshoot of the skewed growth characteristic of central planning was the sparsity in the GDR of basic services essential to a modern economy. An example was the telephone system. In the 1980s barely 6 percent of GDR households had telephones, and even commercial enterprises had difficulties acquiring linkups. An inadequate telephone network precluded computer utilization and advanced data processing which depend upon telephone lines for transmission.

Price distortions in the GDR would have struck the uninitiated observer as nothing short of remarkable. For instance, an average apartment in an East German city would seldom cost more than 60 marks a month, since SED policies had decreed that families should pay no more than 4 percent of their income for housing. A ride across town on the tram might have cost as little as 10 pfennig. A two-pound loaf of bread could be purchased for one mark or less. At the same time an automobile, and a modest East German one at that, with a two-cycle engine and approximately 25 horsepower, cost over 20,000 marks, and this with a twelve-year waiting list. A Western manufactured car would fetch over 100,000 marks. Even the humble Wartburg, a locally produced car, when equipped with a Volkswagen engine made under license, bore a 30,000-mark price tag. A color television might sell for as much as 6,000 marks, a large percentage of an average yearly salary. A new washing machine could not be bought for less than 3,000 marks. Clothes and other household appliances had comparable prices. Furniture on display in shops could seldom be purchased straight from the showroom floor, but only ordered, with subsequent long and indefinite waiting times. Acquiring a driver's license took as much as five years because of the inordinate wait for a place in driver education school.

The length of a waiting list for product delivery or the span of time people spent queuing had to be added to merchandise prices, of course. Shopping for meats, fresh vegetables, and fruits usually entailed standing in line. Tropical fruits of any sort were rare and treasured items. Obtaining spare parts for an automobile virtually always meant painstaking searches, necessitated long drives (assuming the automobile in question was running), and might well have required payment in foreign, that is, Western, currency. This assumed no pilfering, which was another means toward the same end. Real costs of goods were thus seldom reflected in the actual price, but had to be measured by the "externalities"—the length of the queue, the years on a waiting list, the time spent in a prolonged search. Official prices were often mere details, actual costs of goods and services to the individual and to society were invariably higher and often unmeasurable. It was sometimes difficult for Westerners to grasp the machinations and frustrations running in the blood of daily life in the GDR. For those wishing to see, the experience was numbing: and this in the most prosperous of communist countries.

Beyond the burdens upon the individual were the aggregate social and economic costs. An implicit arrangement between employer and employee often permitted people to take off several hours a day for shopping. Friday afternoons were usually a time when office shutters were closed up and people went about to forage. In a factory the resultant absenteeism might have brought on costly downtime, work stoppage, or machinery shutdown. Employers agreed to such an arrangement not only because most understood the need for it, but also because many of them engaged in the same practices on a grander scale. In a society with huge price distortions, sensible management decision making was difficult, and a reversion to primitive business transactions was almost preordained. Stocking commodities was far preferable to holding the local currency, and consequently firms hoarded materials and fuels, either for the firm's own use later on in the event shortages arose (they often did), or to be exchanged for something needed on relatively short notice. A collective farm might have squirreled away supplies of oil, for instance, or a machine tool factory might have stored large quantities of building materials. These provisions would then be bartered with other firms to acquire needed goods or materials. Such procedures, of course, would exacerbate existing shortages.

People with time on their hands joined queues without knowing exactly what was being marketed. It mattered little: a line of people was a sure indication of a product in demand. If the purchaser could not use the product, it could be readily swapped for something desired. Western visitors to the GDR often noticed the great numbers of cars with small trailers attached. Such a trailer was in fact a prized possession in the GDR since it allowed the owner to take advantage of bulky items, like household appliances, or great quantities of goods, like building materials, when these suddenly appeared on the market. Acquisitions might have been either for one's own use or for swapping.

Beneath this stratum of troubles lay yet further problems of the byzantine methods of command economy bookkeeping. Bitterfeld, the small city with the far too apt name and the largest chemical complex in the once-GDR, became a symbol of command economy stultification. In 1990 senior officials of the plant began to allege that the Bitterfeld region was deliberately poisoned by the central planning authorities to raise money for the state. According to the allegations, the SPK extracted hundreds of millions of marks from the enterprise through fines for dumping toxic wastes into the local rivers and creeks. "The SPK milked the chemical industry like a cow," said a former executive.[16] The management made repeated requests for treatment plants, only to have these denied. "They wanted the money. They preferred the funds in order to spend them on other things," remarked the executive, pointing an accusing finger at the party elite.[17] According to some reports, the fines could have in fact paid for the antipollution technology four or five times, had the planning authorities with responsibility for fund appropriation for the treatment facilities been willing to make the initial investment. The Ministry and the SPK had been regularly informed about the chemical industry's dangerous emissions and the possible remedies for these. They chose to ignore the appeals as well as the warnings. Since a firm's performance was measured by overall output and fulfillment of plan quotas, the Bitterfeld chemical complex continued to be "successful." Hearsay about similar occurrences was not uncommon in the GDR before the toppling of the SED. But how were such stories to be corroborated in the SED state, and what could have been done anyway? "Who is to guard the guardians?" is one of the oldest political quandaries.

THE TWO-CURRENCY PROBLEM

Benjamin Disraeli once remarked "the only thing to have driven more men mad than love is the currency question." The GDR was plagued with the typical problems of a nonconvertible currency. An outgrowth of the GDR's location and partial opening to the West was the emergence of a de facto two-currency standard, with the West German mark (DM) the much-preferred means of exchange. By the 1970s some goods and materials became obtainable only by payment in West marks. Although the official exchange rate was set at one to one, East Germans were usually prepared to pay at least four East marks for one West mark, and illicit currency trading became widespread.

In the hope of countering black-marketeering, but also to raise foreign exchange, the regime opened the so-called Intershops in the early 1960s, where Western goods or very high quality products made under license in the GDR were marketed at quite attractive prices. Westerners would avail themselves of the Intershops to make purchases for gift-giving in the GDR, it was reasoned, and subsequently would shun exchanging money on black markets. The Intershops were a success insofar as they furnished the GDR with a ready supply of foreign currency. It was estimated that these establishments had over DM 700 million in average annual merchandise sales beginning in the 1970s.[18] For several years, though, the Intershops were not open to East Germans, nor was foreign currency possession allowed. Then the authorities, partially in response to citizen gripes but also with an eye to the chronic hard currency shortages in the GDR, passed the Foreign Currency Law of 1973 which let East Germans hold West marks in amounts up to DM 500 and to use them to make purchases in the Intershops. As expected, spending in the Intershops skyrocketed, although the new procedures had consequences very different from those intended. Designed in part to quell citizen resentment, the 1973 law had the opposite effect of widening social differences and stimulating the emergence of a privileged class of individuals—those with handy sources of hard currency. Such inequity caused considerable resentment among people without West German funds, a circumstance hardly contributing to the harmony of a society where the connection between performance and reward was nebulous anyway. Higher living standards deriving from the ability to purchase Western goods hinged largely on one's good fortune of having family ties or friendships. Ensuing envy and pique were targeted primarily against the regime, which was, after all, largely to blame. The Intershop became the subject of the notoriously cynical GDR humor that was at one and the same time an outlet for citizen frustration, and thinly disguised criticism of the regime. Intershops, according to popular wisdom, had the earmarks of pornographic book shops, that bane of the decadent West. There were no window displays, but once inside all was revealed![19] A 1979 ruling required East Germans to exchange their Western currency at state banks for coupons used for purchases in the Intershops, the rationale being that such a move would deter black marketeers. The law had little effect and did not appear even to have been uniformly enforced, so "Intershop socialism" functioned for the most part as before. Intershops remained popular, and money-changing at black market rates did not abate. Presumably, many West marks acquired on the black market found their way into Intershop cash registers. Wary of foreign exchange losses and fearing civil unrest as well, the SED probably never seriously considered closure of the Intershops.

With access to ministry stores carrying Western goods, high-ranking party officials had little personal need of the Intershops, but rank-and-file party members, for their part, arguably had the worst of all worlds. They could not avail themselves of the special shopping and medical services reserved for the party elite, and they were officially discouraged from maintaining the sort of Western contacts that were a source of hard currency for many average citizens. As a result, the two-currency standard fostered certain irregularities in state institutions, notwithstanding a long German tradition of bureaucratic correctness.[20] Although difficult to prove, rumors abounded in the GDR about the influence in many offices of "Western currency gifts."[21]

Foreign currency oiled the wheels of the GDR's economy. Without adequate amounts of it, planning authorities could not procure the Western technology and machinery needed for continued economic growth, the popular standard for gauging overall system performance. Factory managers outfitted with West marks could obtain needed materials or spare parts on short notice. Those without foreign currency assets, and by law firms could spend monies only with prior planning authority approval, faced bottlenecks and production downtime as a result of shortages. Beginning in the 1970s, dependence upon Western suppliers steadily increased.

People with valuable skills—carpenters, painters, plumbers, electricians, automobile mechanics—frequently moonlighted and not infrequently wanted remuneration for their work in hard currency. Understandably, those who could not or would not moonlight did not take kindly to the financial adjustments. DM payment usually ensured prompt, quality work, and the acquisition of some services, telephone installation and repair among others, took some doing without West marks. In a country with an extensive second economy, tolerated by authorities vaunting full employment, the second currency provided powerful incentives to work on the sly, even to engage in illicit business. Pent-up resentment, the upshot of bad money and scarcities, was evident in another bit of GDR humor whose deeper meaning requires no elaboration: "They pretend to pay us and we pretend to work."

But the SED chose to accept the difficulties and risks affiliated with a dual medium of exchange. In fact, hard currency procurement remained a priority item in economic planning for over fifteen years, while accompanying social and political problems were at most secondary considerations. Certain socioeconomic issues were almost painfully awkward, witness the operation of the so-called *Exquisit* and *Delikat* shops. In the hope of assuaging consumer resentment, the planning authorities decreed the opening in the mid-1970s of the *Delikat* stores to complement the already existing *Exquisit* marts, special shops where imported goods could be purchased with the local currency. Hard currency, it was to be shown, was not always be needed to buy choice merchandise.[22] But here the central planners came face-to-face with yet more unpleasant economic realities. Given unfavorable real exchange rates, large amounts of local currency were needed to buy imported goods, with the result that the prices in the *Exquisit* and *Delikat* were exorbitant. Cans of tropical fruit might cost as much as 40 marks, and whisky over 100. Backlash was quick in coming. Far from enabling the average wage earner to enjoy imported goods, these establishments disclosed the weaknesses and intrinsic unfairness of the command economy. The operation of these shops was widely regarded as more of an affront than anything else. The daunting prices belied regime claims about the strength of the GDR's mark, furnishing a down-to-earth, everyday example of the underlying fragility of the GDR's economy and its consequent inability to compete internationally. With a glance at the pricing labels one could discern realistic exchange rates, as opposed to those set arbitrarily by the planning authorities.

THE INDUSTRIAL SOUTH

The heavy concentration of industry in the southern regions of the GDR brought with it an equally heavy concentration of urban industrial problems. The metropolitan areas of Dresden, Leipzig, Halle, Karl-Marx-Stadt, and Zwickau all reflected the grim reality of "actually existing socialism." That there was some connection between economic conditions there and political upheaval is an almost inescapable conclusion. It was not entirely coincidental that Leipzig and Dresden became hotbeds of dissent.

Uncertainties about the proper consignment of policy authority, stock part of command economies, were most pronounced in the large *Kombinate* of the south.

The perplexing configuration of relationships among the Council of Ministers, the intermediate planning levels, and the production enterprises caused considerable displeasure in these thickly-spread industrialized regions, especially among industrial managers tending to attribute many of the country's economic difficulties to excessive centralization of authority. A fair number wanted greater decision-making latitude and would have preferred less input from far-off Berlin, although the depth of feeling did not become clear until late 1989 when all could speak openly.

Moreover, friction between Saxony and Berlin had historic roots, and it was by no means only the industrial managers who considered the central planning organs obtrusive. Throughout the urbanized south, neglected infrastructure had widespread and telling effects. Sporadic energy shortages were one facet of failing infrastructure. The transportation system often proved ill-equipped to supply manufacturing enterprises and to dispatch finished products. Production facilities sometimes operated at reduced capacity as a result of supply delays. The trouble and expense of transporting food supplies from other areas on inadequate roads and rail lines induced the planning authorities to decree that southern areas should be self-sufficient in food. But agricultural production in a region pinched by land scarcity was insufficient for this, with the consequence that the supply and the selection of foodstuffs tended to be better in the north.

There was also the environmental issue. Studies done at universities in the GDR had been indicating for years that Leipzig was one of the most polluted cities in Europe.[23] Lung cancer and respiratory diseases were closely linked to befoulment of the air. Acid rain caused considerable damage, especially in the forests of Thuringia. The toll sulfur dioxide and other gas emissions took upon buildings was visible in every urban area. Toxic automobile emissions in cities plagued by overcrowding exacerbated matters.[24]

In addition to holding the central planning authorities largely responsible for these troubles, many residents felt that the GDR's most productive regions were being exploited, with too much going out and too little coming in. Grounds for such charges were easily found. for example, in the alarming deterioration of downtown Leipzig. "The city is falling apart and the planners do nothing," was a common gripe.[25] For years, in fact, the Leipzig party boss, Horst Schumann, had been an SED scourge who unflinchingly complained to East Berlin about what he perceived to be planning muddle and outright unfairness.[26] To Mittag's chagrin, Schumann at one point rejected central plan production targets, returning them for revision.

NOTES

1. *The Constitution of the German Democratic Republic*, 14-15.
2. Ibid., 15.

3. *Statistical Pocket Book of the German Democratic Republic 1978* (East Berlin: Staatsverlag der DDR, 1978), 52-53.

4. David Childs, *The GDR*, 2d. ed. (London: Unwin Hyman, 1988), 155.

5. Hartmut Zimmermann, "The GDR in the 1970s," *Problems of Communism* 27, no. 2 (March-April 1978), 7.

6. *DDR Handbuch*, vol. 2, 1489-90.

7. Quoted in Arthur Hanhardt, *The German Democratic Republic* (Baltimore: Johns Hopkins University Press, 1968), 90.

8. Günter Mittag, *Probleme der Wirtschaftspolitik der Partei bei der Gestaltung der entwickelten gesellschaftlichen Systems des Sozialismus in der DDR* (East Berlin: Dietz, 1968), 38-39.

9. *DDR Handbuch*, vol. 2, 993-94.

10. *The Economist*, February 22, 1986.

11. C. Bradley Scharf, *Politics and Change in East Germany* (Boulder Colo: Westview/Pinter, 1984), 67.

12. *Deutschland Nachrichten* (German Information Center), November 2, 1990.

13. See for example, Scharf, *Politics and Change in East Germany*, 65-70.

14. Manfred Melzer, "The GDR Economic Policy Caught Between Pressure for Efficiency and Lack of Ideas," in *The East European Economies in the 1970s*, ed. Alec Nove, Hans-Herrmann Hohmann, and Gertrud Seidenstecker (London: Butterworths, 1982), 45-90.

15. *The Economist*, June 25, 1988.

16. *New York Times*, September 9, 1990.

17. Ibid.

18. *Handbuch der DDR*, vol. 2, 672.

19. Childs, *The GDR*, 146.

20. Gerd Meyer, "Perspektiven des Sozialismus," in Gerd Meyer and Jürgen Schröder, *DDR Heute Wandlungstendenzen und Widersprüche einer sozialistischen Industriegesellschaft* (Tübingen: Günter Narr, 1988), 24-26.

21. Zimmermann, "The GDR in the 1970s," 38.

22. *Handbuch der DDR*, vol. 1, 369.

23. Hannsjörg Buck and Bernd Spindler, "Luftbelastung in der DDR durch Schadstoffemissionen," *Deutschlandarchiv* 15, no. 9 (1982): 943-58.

24. Reiner Raestrup and Thomas Weymar, "'Schuld ist allein der Kapitalismus': Umweltprobleme und ihre Bewältigung in der DDR," *Deutschland Archiv* 15, no. 8 (1982): 832-44.

25. *Der Spiegel*, October 16, 1989.

26. Ibid.

5

The West German Connection

THE BASIC TREATY

With the signing of the Basic Treaty on December 21, 1972, the German states agreed to ease tensions and foster cooperation, and undertook to negotiate subsequent accords to this end. Marking a significant reordering of relations between the Germanys, this watershed settlement formed the cornerstone of political association for the next sixteen years. As the texture of the relationship changed, and as the two states faced the daily tasks of managing their relations and implementing the provisions of the agreements, new and sometimes unanticipated issues arose. Negotiations necessitated continuous, high-level governmental contacts, and as a result the inter-German dialogue would develop a certain dynamic of its own over time.

According to Article 1, the two states agreed to develop "normal, good-neighborly relations on the basis of equality." Article 2 specified that the parties consented to recognize the Charter of the United Nations "as the basis for their conduct." Under Article 3, the renunciation of force provision, the parties agreed to settle their differences without resort to force. Under Article 4 neither state would assert any claim to represent the other abroad, as the FRG had done for nearly two decades. In Article 5 both states pledged themselves to work for peaceful relations between European states, for the reduction of armed forces and for disarmament. Also, they agreed to respect one another's internal and external sovereignty and independence. Article 7 provided for cooperation in the fields of economics, science and technology, traffic, law, postage and telephones, health services, culture, sports, and the environment.[1]

In several ways the conclusion of the Basic Treaty represented a significant diplomatic breakthrough for the GDR. In an accord with its western neighbor it had attained official acceptance of its existence and a guarantee that successive relations would be conducted on equal terms. Bonn's recognition of the GDR as a separate state opened the way for third party recognition without prejudice, hitherto a contentious issue, as well as for the entry of both German states into the United Nations. Recognition of the GDR thereafter presented no legal or political problem even for NATO members, most of whom subsequently established normal relations. The GDR had come a long way, a fact Honecker often took pains to emphasize, as for example, at the country's October anniversary celebrations when he was in the habit of providing the exact number of states having accorded full diplomatic recognition to the GDR. On October 7, 1984 a beaming Honecker announced that the count stood at 132, a deviation from the printed text of his speech in light of the very recent addition of the Ivory Coast to those states recognizing the GDR.

The successful conclusion of the Basic Treaty entailed compromise on both sides, however, and the GDR failed to achieve several key objectives. First, the GDR had to accept the Quadripartite Agreement on Berlin acknowledging the "original" rights there of the three Western allies, France, Great Britain and the United States, and permitting "ties" between the FRG and West Berlin, in effect, sanctioning the West German social order in half of the city. Somewhat to the SED's discomfiture, West Berlin did not become an "independent political entity" unsheltered by the West. Second, the GDR failed to attain its maximum position on nationhood, and acquiesced, however grudgingly, to the West German concept of a "special relationship" that precluded the mutual recognition of separate nations. As a consequence, relations between the Germanys were not elevated to the customary interstate level under international law. Under the Basic Treaty each state consented to dispatch permanent representatives (instead of ambassadors) to the other's capital to head permanent missions there. Third, and stemming from the second, Bonn did not concede a separate GDR citizenship, but instead insisted upon a single German citizenship. Of the myriad of litigious issues between the German states, this one, conspicuously unresolved, was probably the most sensitive. The FRG based German citizenship on a 1913 law, while the GDR cited its own 1967 law establishing GDR citizenship. While the GDR, according to the treaty protocol, "proceeds from the assumption that the Treaty will facilitate a regulation of questions of nationality," the official position of the FRG by contrast was that: "Questions of nationality have not been regulated by the Treaty."[2]

Refusal on Bonn's part to recognize a separate citizenship was a refined, yet trenchant move. Under Article 4 of the Basic Treaty Bonn renounced its claim to be the sole national spokesman for Germans (*Alleinvertretungsanspruch*). Since only German citizenship existed in the official view, nothing legally prevented the FRG from issuing documentation and providing succor to all ethnic Germans, including those in Romania, Poland, and the Soviet Union, who could avail themselves of the opportunity of West German refuge. Any East German upon request had immediate access to a West German passport in like manner, and hence the Basic Treaty codified a fraternal "special relationship." Retention of a single citizenship would later have implications that could not have been foreseen at the time of the accord's negotiation.

Following the conclusion of the Basic Treaty, the special relationship afforded the GDR an odd benefit in the operation of the celebrated social safety valve. The presence of an ethnically identical society just across the border routinely encouraged disgruntled East Germans to petition to leave the country. With its definitive political and legal interest in all Germans, the FRG was willing to "buy free" political prisoners, ridding East Berlin of its worst troublemakers and procuring hard currency for it in the bargain. The social safety valve functioned relatively smoothly from the SED's vantage point for over a decade, but began to come apart at the seams in the late 1980s when flocks of East Germans began demanding to emigrate, primarily because of the regime's aversion to reform. Then, after openings began to appear in the East Bloc's physical barriers in 1989, the SED could no longer sustain enough pressure in the valve to assure its proper functioning. An affluent and liberal German state, where citizenship was automatic, attracted many East Germans, many more in fact than the GDR could afford to lose.

An earlier unexpected property of the valve presented itself in the hue and cry of expelled members of the East German intelligentsia. As a matter of policy the SED isolated and expelled dissidents, confidently assuming that intellectuals detached from their audience and native soil would die on the vine, so to speak, as was the case with many expelled Soviet dissident intellectuals.[3] In fact, the very opposite occurred. Affinities between the Germanys were too close, the communications network too highly developed, for exiles to be hushed and made irrelevant. The SED had inadvertently created a whole class of expellees, bitter and clamorous, some of whom, the song-writer Biermann, the playwright Kunze, and the Marxist intellectual Bahro, commanded considerable attention in the West. Finding ready forums there, they unflinchingly attacked the SED, serving as constant reminders of the true nature of the regime to all who cared to listen.

The most immediate and perceptible result of the Basic Treaty between the Germanys, however, was that it made possible a nearly threefold annual increase in the number of West German visitors to the GDR. In 1970 1,254,084 visits were reported; by 1973 this sum had already reached 2,278,891; by 1975 it was 3,123,941; then in 1980, in the wake of required exchange hikes, it fell back to 2,276,273.[4] The numbers of East Germans below pension age permitted to travel to the West remained very modest, but personal contacts between the Germanys were growing by leaps and bounds. The borders of the GDR became more porous and the Basic Treaty established an enduring modus vivendi between the German states. For the nearly sixteen years it was in force the agreement fostered a businesslike relationship, but one whose central feature was an odd ambivalence. Time after time both sides would encounter notable contradictions and dilemmas.

DILEMMAS FOR THE FRG

What was the Basic Treaty's chief rationale from the standpoint of its West German architects? What did Bonn actually hope to accomplish in the longer term through this modus vivendi with the GDR? In short, Bonn sought to effect an eventual thaw in East-West relations which, in turn, would better the lot of the people having to live under communist rule. Following some initial footwork in Moscow, Bonn endeavored to deal with the East Bloc states on an individual level, treating each on the basis of equality and with comity. If the respective regimes showed signs of introducing programs of gradual reform, the FRG made clear it would respond generously with different sorts of aid, chiefly financial.

It was reasoned that improved East Bloc economic performance, in part the result of financial assistance from the West, would slowly enhance political stability and lift regime confidence throughout the East Bloc and the Soviet Union. Greater security would encourage Moscow to ease its clutches on the satellites little by little, while inducing East Bloc leaders to treat their people better, and eventually to carry through reforms. Visionary West German politicians such as Willy Brandt and Egon Bahr anticipated the day when East Berlin's communists would be sufficiently confident and their regime adequately secure that border fortifications between the Germanys would become superfluous.

The longer-term efficacy of Bonn's policies, however, rested upon the critical assumption about social change that modernization and enhanced efficiency of command economies nurture political liberalization over time.[5] Although Bonn's strategy was innovative and well-meaning, in hindsight the basic underpinnings of the postulate proved fallacious with respect to the GDR. Financial aid did not, as a matter of course, advance the position of the advocates of reform in the GDR. Although some East German managers and planners did recommend scientific innovation, the introduction of new technologies, more diverse sources of information and more extensive consultation, a subsequent relaxation of state control did not ensue. The trend was rather in the opposite direction as centralization of the East German economy in several areas increased and bureaucratic heavy-handedness persisted, even as inter-German detente acquired a certain intensity. And the regime chronicle on human rights spoke for itself. The glaring lack of evidence of much liberalization in the GDR generated frustration and considerable handwringing in the FRG. What, though, was the alternative to these policies toward the GDR?

This is not to imply that the SED squandered its aid and foreign currency, at least not to the extent other communist regimes, such as Romania and Poland, did. That sad tale has been told elsewhere. With Western help some modernization of the economy did occur, and in the case of the *Kombinat* reorganization, East Berlin carried out very reserved economic reform. This change took place quite apart from any tempering of repression, let alone the introduction of participatory reform. The "liberalizers" whose hands were supposed to be strengthened by economic aid and political assurances did not move to the center stage, nor did it seem that many SED minds were changed by subtle inducements.

But Bonn by its own admission was in no hurry. Its designs to overcome Europe's division were frequently described as "policies of small steps." As the trade and transfer payment figures provided below suggest, these policies of small steps shifted to a rather brisk economic stride in the GDR's direction over the years. That loans and trade fostered conditions "binding the nation together" became Bonn's resolute position, one taken by three different West German administrations, and about which there was considerable domestic consensus.

Notions of *Wandel durch Annäherung* (change through rapprochement), the guiding principle of inter-German detente as designated by one of its leading architects, called into being a comprehensive policy toward the GDR whose tenets can be summarized in several sentences. Given the realities of German division, it was argued, dialogue and practical cooperation with the GDR had to be encouraged. From fruitful negotiation would come treaties providing assistance to the people of a house divided. By virtue of a common nationality with the people of the GDR, West Germans had a special responsibility for the GDR. Similarly, all Germans had a responsibility to work toward the alleviation of the East-West conflict in Europe. Finally, all states were to aspire to effect greater openness, striving to abolish those frontiers that separated peoples.

By the late 1960s Bonn as a matter of policy no longer sought to change the political system of the GDR, but instead focused on the improvement of the human condition and the easing of the human misery affiliated with division of the country, aims often characterized as *menschliche Erleichterung*, or human amelioration. The gradual alteration of the circumstances of German division and the betterment of everyday life in the GDR were to be policy ends in themselves. Cooperation between the German states on a host of issues was seen as the most effective way to accomplish these ends, since confrontation, as experience had already taught, had a direct and adverse impact upon the people of the GDR. When the SED leaders felt pressured or threatened from outside, they invariably reacted by increasing repression at home. "We have no intention of harming or destabilizing the GDR," as a cabinet member succinctly put it in 1985, expounding what had emerged as a principal axiom of the FRG's Deutschlandpolitik. The more secure and predictable the government of the GDR, Bonn officials repeatedly argued, the better they could pursue "a policy on behalf of the people of the GDR."[6] The problem was that the people were not in a position to express their views of the policy pursued on their behalf. Hence, the first dilemma for Bonn: If SED interests and those of East German citizens did not coincide on all points, weren't West German policies periodically carried out against the people's wishes? Compounding the dilemma was the typical popular response to the very modest liberalization that greater stability and attendant regime confidence produced. Incremental easing of oppression brought to the surface a measure of latent, pent-up dissatisfaction and anger, manifested in fresh waves of requests to emigrate to the West, other modes of protest being simply too dangerous. This in turn induced the GDR authorities to respond with new rounds of repression, setting in motion the cruel treadmill that in part stymied Bonn's policies and caused yet more handwringing in the West.

The workaday normality of inter-German relations in the 1980s prompted SED leaders to become more confident, less introverted, and outwardly more self-assured. Here, Bonn confronted its next dilemma. The employment of economic policy instruments raised the long-standing question: To what extent should democracies engage in economic relations with dictatorships in the knowledge such relationships will improve an undemocratic regime's performance? Didn't transfer payments to the GDR raise the general living standard, but at the same time help consolidate communist rule? Trade might have benefited average citizens, but it bolstered the command economy as well. The SED regime used Western financial assistance not for purposes of reform, but as a substitute for it. Bonn's eager expressions of good faith, which boosted the SED leadership's self-confidence, arguably did little for ordinary East Germans, most of whom privately sneered at the *Bonzen* ("the bosses").

An example, one of many, illustrates the point. In the course of some fifteen years, Bonn bought free approximately 150,000 dissidents and political prisoners, in most cases sparing these people lengthy jail sentences and continued persecution (in accordance with "human amelioration"), but in so doing, also removed a smarting thorn from East Berlin's side (regime stabilization). In light of the harsh facts in Central Europe and the frustrations attendant to relations with the GDR, it was not difficult to understand why Bonn officials couldn't as a rule furnish completely satisfactory answers to two basic questions: What is the principal objective of your Deutschlandpolitik? Are you helping the people of the GDR or the regime?

The quandaries of an unfortunate and difficult past loom large for Germans. The question, Who is to be brought to book for years of socialist dictatorship? places the cardinal dilemma of Bonn's Deutschlandpolitik in contemporary perspective. After the autumn of 1989, West German politicians cringed at the mere thought of the red carpet treatment accorded to Honecker during his official visit to the FRG in 1987. Hadn't this solemn old man been for over eighteen years the leader of that sham commonly known as "actually existing socialism"? Wasn't this the man who, along with the party elite, creamed off tens of millions from the public coffers? Wasn't this the man who sheltered notorious terrorists wanted in the West for murder? Wasn't this the man whose brutal regime Bonn helped stabilize?

DILEMMAS FOR THE SED

Often billed as a "grand bargain" of Ostpolitik, the Basic Treaty's "two state, one nation" formula allowing the two Germanys to normalize relations with one another, represented in fact little more than an official acknowledgment of political realities in the early 1970s on Bonn's part. The accord's West German architects called attention to this from the beginning. That the *Kulturnation* with common features such as language, kinship, history, and social traditions still existed was indisputable, for which reason there appeared to be more uniting Germans than dividing them, however hard the SED leaders tried to rid themselves of the nationality problem. German national awareness posed a standing challenge to the GDR so long as the latter lacked popular institutions and stable social foundations.[7] However great the shift in the relative strength of the Germanys over the years, the GDR remained the smaller, less affluent German state, without a popularly elected government, whose right to speak on behalf of some 17 million Germans had not been democratically established.

To accentuate fundamental differences of social organization with an aim to sidetracking national consciousness, the SED adopted a defensive strategy vis-à-vis Bonn in the 1970s, reinvigorating the friend-foe approach and promulgating the finality of Germany's division. By focusing on the distinctiveness of the GDR, it was thought, separate development of the socialist German state could be effectively justified. By closing the German question once and for all, East Berlin would no longer have to compete with Bonn on nationhood matters, but could narrow the encounter to the political sphere. Through demarcation policies the SED would at one and the same time vaunt the superior qualities of socialism and demonstrate the separateness of an East German nation-state. "History has decided the German question," Honecker declared in 1971 on the occasion of the Eighth Party Congress, defining what appeared to be the new policy guideline.

The idea of the socialist German nation with its fresh nuances and deeper implications thereafter became a favored theme of party discussions, and Politburo members were disposed to provide comments. Hermann Axen, musing on the Basic Treaty in 1973, remarked: "There is no German question at all, rather there are two sovereign, socially opposed, and independent German states and nations."[8] SED efforts to discount traditional ideas of nationhood did have their own logic in that popular identification with socialist political-institutional forms and not with a larger national culture, if this could be achieved, would have furthered regime legitimacy, and thus been in the GDR's self-interest. Axen's explanation at the time set forth the SED's reasoning: "Nations are above all the result of basic economic and social development processes as well as historical class struggles."[9] Reference to the "German socialist nation" in the title of Axen's 1973 book indicated the importance the SED attached to the notion of complete and final divergence of the two German paths. The new approach to the national question was also in evidence when the word "German" was deleted from several official terms and the national hymn, written by Johannes Becker in 1943 while in Soviet exile, was dropped.[10] The stanza, "Arisen out of the ruin and headed for the future, let us serve Germany, our united fatherland," did not conform with the SED's new concept of nationhood.

Warily on the lookout for manifestations of the prickly nationality issue, the SED hoped doggedly never to find any. In his 1972 treatise on the struggle against imperialism, Politburo member Albert Norden, brushing away all notions of commonality between the German states, bore witness to fresh demarcation efforts. Attributes of a common culture, he said, "no longer exist, because the principal culture is always the culture of the ruling class."[11] It followed, the argument went, that since the FRG remained a bourgeois state, while the GDR was a socialist workers' state and by definition a higher form of social organization, the Germanys were, quite plainly, separate and distinct nations. But Norden's denial of all commonalities between the Germanys whether "territorial, historical, cultural or in national feeling" revealed the lurking difficulties the SED encountered in coming to grips with the nationality issue.[12] Was the SED leadership completely comfortable with its own assertions about the *Kulturnation*? Did it feel secure enough to disclaim the "Germanness" of the GDR on this scale? The answer to both questions was clearly negative.

In a December 1974 Central Committee meeting Honecker defined the point of departure for the recent constitutional amendment on nationality, presumably to clarify the official position for the comrades. "Our socialist state is called the German Democratic Republic because the vast majority of its citizens are German. Citizenship—GDR, Nationality—German. That is the way things are."[13] By rejuvenating some vague concept of German nationhood, Honecker soft-pedaled the prior diminishing of the GDR's cultural affinities with the FRG. Short years later he would endeavor to rekindle national feeling and to enlist it for the cause of socialism. Had Honecker concluded that East Germans might take offense at Norden's extreme position, or could Honecker's own German sensitivities have been the chief motivating factor?

What is certain is that the various elements of the national issue were not merely to be edited out as the censor might have done with unpalatable bits of news. Contemporary reviews indicated the issue of necessity retained a salience in SED thought. In the 1970s books on the subject continued to appear, the most authoritative by A. Kosing, whose study begins with a lengthy statement of the rationale for the "defensive strategy" vis-à-vis the FRG.[14] "The problem of the nation has become the field of significant ideological struggle for us," he wrote, attesting to the party's enduring "friend-foe" schemes. At the same time, he intimated official acknowledgment that the extreme position of disclaimer was tantamount to the gainsaying of a heritage instrumental to regime legitimation. How else is the following statement to be explained? "Evidence of the relative ethnic homogeneity of the socialist nation in the GDR and the capitalist nation in the FRG is to be found in their common historical origin but not in any uniformity of the opposing social structures."[15] Noteworthy is that the SED began distinguishing between "nation" and "nationality," something Norden and Axen previously neglected to do. Kosing for his part stressed this distinction. "It is not in ethnic character or in nationality that the socialist nation in the GDR and the capitalist nation in the FRG differ, but in their social foundations and components. This is a matter of qualitatively different historical types of nation."[16] Refinement of the SED's position several years after the signing of the Basic Treaty had the added advantage of permitting the GDR to identify more closely with the German past. Was the SED in fact laying the groundwork for the eventual founding of the People's Republic of Prussia?[17]

The multiple dilemmas the SED faced in the era of inter-German detente thus take shape. Intrinsic to the ideologically motivated defensive strategy, was postulated estrangement (*Entfremdung*) from the state that was to become the GDR's second leading trading partner and upon whose economy the GDR became increasingly dependent. The SED was determined to maintain ideological vigilance against socialism's enemies, and to shield the population in the face of greater personal contacts with the West. Yet, in the coming years the GDR strove to deepen its economic association with Western European countries, the FRG in particular. Whether or not the economic relationship enabled the FRG to apply more pressure upon the GDR is actually another issue.[18] But like it or not, the SED had to contend with some basic realities of economic production. Accessibility and openness were prerequisites for the expansion of trade, for the more extensive use of Western technology, and for greater economic efficiency. Not a few East German industrial managers countenanced a freer exchange of information and the decentralization of decision making for this reason. But the political vulnerabilities of the regime, both real and perceived, held sway, and the restrictive posture that translated into an iron grip on authority was maintained. Thus, the closure-openness dilemma.

What is more, establishment of normal interstate relations under international law with the FRG, a much publicized SED purpose, was scarcely facilitated by the latter's attitude.[19] Accentuation of the East German state's "separateness" required posturing that in turn nurtured strains and made confrontation unavoidable at times. By inducing tensions instead of reducing them, the SED often worked against, not for, normalization of relations. It is somewhat ironic that the defensive strategy bespoke the inter-German relationship's special nature, whose existence the SED vehemently denied. Although estrangement is by no means uncommon in international politics, explicit demarcation of separate and independent states is pointless.[20] If the two German states had so few commonalities, why the defensive strategy? What was the SED really defending against? In the final analysis was it not against German nationhood, whose "progressive" elements the GDR increasingly claimed as its own? Seldom has history proffered such brazen attempts to square a circle. Thus, the myth-making dilemma, whose magnitude Otto Reinhold stressed in mid-1989. The GDR, he said, "is imaginable only as an anti-fascist and socialist alternative to the Federal Republic (of Germany). What right to exist would a capitalist GDR have alongside a capitalist Federal Republic?" Indeed.

Laden as these were with ambiguities, East Berlin's policies were not always easy to assess; observers had to differentiate carefully between information and noise, between substance and pretense. While Bonn spoke of *Wandel durch Annäherung*, East Berlin for its part spoke of *friedliche Koexistenz*, or peaceful coexistence, a condition involving merely a suspension of hostilities between two basically hostile and incompatible systems. According to the SED's official definition, "Peaceful coexistence is never to mean class peace between exploiters and exploited. Peaceful coexistence means neither the maintenance of the socioeconomic status quo nor an ideological coexistence. . . . Peaceful coexistence should create favorable conditions for the victory of the socialist revolution in the nonsocialist countries."[21] As one observer suggested, the distinction in most SED minds between peaceful coexistence and cold war was largely cosmetic.[22]

"Socialism's struggles" were to go on, in Africa, for example, where East German political and military commitment had become extensive. But what was to be the pith of the class conflict with the enemy in Europe? The SED obscurely and inconsistently defined the parameters of the truce with the FRG. Official statements characteristically provided precious little illumination, for example, "The dialectic of detente and class struggle consists of the fact that the goals of detente and the class goals of the international working class to obtain social progress are intimately related." The difficulties associated with equivocal policies became even more pronounced in the 1980s once SED leaders had acquired a vested interest in the maintenance of good relations with the West. In maneuvering to limit damage to detente, East Berlin found itself uncomfortably caught between Bonn and Moscow.

In light of the GDR's geostrategic situation, the sincerity of SED expressions of a determination to avoid large-scale war could not have been in doubt. In the 1980s, forced by events to scrutinize the relationship with Bonn, GDR leaders championed "the rebirth of detente," "a coalition of reason," even "a partnership in peace" with the FRG. Interestingly enough, Honecker adopted a West German government slogan, Make peace with less and less weaponry (*Frieden schaffen mit immer weniger Waffen*).[23] And in the efforts to preserve detente's achievements, the national issue invariably resurfaced. In October 1983, *Neues Deutschland* published a letter from Honecker, by that time more at ease with matters of national consciousness, to West German Chancellor Helmut Kohl, saying he was supporting the demand for a nuclear weapons-free zone in Central Europe "in the name of the German people."[24]

Yet, incapable of ensuring its permanence as a state upon the fundament of national legitimation or without abstruse entreaty to Marxism-Leninism, the GDR found itself in the delicate position of expressing unqualified support for "humanity's great historic alternative," the Soviet Union, while portraying the foundations of the East German state as set in positive German traditions. Displays of devotion to Moscow, above all pretentious ones, did not endear East Berlin to its own people, many of whom were inclined to consider any sort of emotional attachment to the Soviet state incompatible with German values.

To enunciate critical differences between the German states and to highlight the superiority of the socialist rendition, the SED relied on a battering ram of propaganda against the FRG and the West. Perhaps the bluntest instruments of the propaganda campaign were the party organ, *Neues Deutschland,* and the prime-time television program, *Der Schwarze Kanal,* whose chief commentator was the SED's media dean, Karl-Edward von Schnitzler. Both persistently strove to promote polarization of the German states, while exhibiting a corresponding tendency to politicize social conditions.[25]

Though East Germans tended to dismiss outright the half-truths and make-believe of postulated estrangement, the vivid politicization of social and international issues, occurred at the behest of a regime that actively pursued "civic neutralization," (i.e., depoliticizing its people to forestall the emergence of any channels of interest articulation or independent political actors). Honecker's politburo gravitated inadvertently to politicizing the society it had wished to depoliticize, thereby uncomfortably entangling itself in cross-purposes. Yet another dilemma.

As might have been expected, the most discernible outcome of this greater politicization of issues, domestic and foreign, was heightened popular cynicism. The regular flow of information to the GDR from the West enabled even the most ordinary East Germans empirically to verify what they were being told in their own country. Every schoolchild acquired some inkling of the immensity of the SED's lies. In a confession made after the SED regime's toppling, Joachim Herrmann, once Central Committee secretary for propaganda, provided an insight into the working of the propaganda machine.

> Success-propaganda was law. Greater mindfulness would indicate that the opposite was accomplished, hence unbelief propagated. The contradiction between reality and what was said in the media was total. In the belief we were doing something for the GDR, instead we did something that was damaging. I regret not having directed attention to this essential contradiction.[26]

Another depiction of this bitter harvest from the perspective of the average citizen was furnished by the Polish dissident and Solidarity member Jacek Kuron in an October 1981 interview, "If there were to be an announcement that the government had laid a golden egg, people would say: first of all, not golden; secondly, not an egg; and thirdly, it didn't lay it but stole it."[27]

TRADE AND TRANSFER PAYMENTS

By the 1980s the FRG was influencing its eastern neighbor in profound and complex ways which must be viewed on different but interacting levels. No discussion of the inter-German relationship that emerged after the mid-1970s could be complete, though, without at least a summary overview of economic issues, since all analysts would concur that politics, economics, and security are interwoven. There is perhaps no better example of how economic power in the course of things translated into political power than that of the inter-German relationship.

The FRG always carefully distinguished between inter-German trade (which it described as "intra-German trade") and foreign trade. Numerous advantages accrued to the GDR from its singular status. Its imports and exports were charged a low value added tax (VAT). East German farm produce was not subject to the special Community agricultural tariff. Trade between the Germanys, which had been almost completely liberalized by the late 1970s, was exempt from European Community (EC) tariffs, and thus the GDR enjoyed partial access to the Common Market, although notions of secret membership in the EC were somewhat misleading.[28]

East German trade deficits with the FRG were covered by the "swing," a credit arrangement allowing for interest-free overdraft up to a specified and quite high amount. As particular of the special economic relationship, the FRG maintained the creditworthiness of the GDR in the West, in spite of the fact that East German per capita foreign debt approached that of Poland. On at least two occasions West German commercial banks injected considerable amounts of liquidity into the East German economy by providing government-guaranteed loans in amounts close to a billion Western marks.

In any given year, large amounts of rock-ribbed currency were transferred to the East German state and its citizens. In 1988 alone, for example, the FRG paid DM 525 million in highway user fees for the Berlin transit routes. Another DM 200 million was paid for postal services. On average the GDR received DM 450 million annually for the minimum currency exchange required of visitors. East German citizens obtained on average as much as DM 1 billion in direct cash transfers from relatives and friends. Another DM 1 billion worth of gifts was shipped or brought in yearly and some DM 200 million worth of gifts arrived via "Genex," an East German mail order service accepting only hard currency. On top of this came hard-to-quantify amounts for "humanitarian services," a euphemism for the liberation of political prisoners by purchase, estimated to have entailed an annual payment of more than DM 500 million. Political prisoners were rumored to have fetched DM 20,000 to DM 40,000 a head, but exact numbers were always kept secret. Then came the transfers from Western religious organizations. Total transfer payments likely approached DM 5 billion per annum.[29] Total intra-German trade volume in the 1980s exceeded DM 15 billion yearly. By the mid-1970s the FRG had already become the largest trading partner of the GDR after the Soviet Union.

These payments and transfers represented indispensable sources of foreign exchange for the GDR, assisting it in attaining a place among the world's leading industrial powers. From a domestic standpoint Western largess acted as a cushion against the inadequate quality and quantity of consumer goods, a matter of no small consequence. A significant amount of industrial imports from the West consisted of goods the GDR did not produce and could not acquire through CMEA (Council for Mutual Economic Assistance or COMECON) trade. In several key industrial sectors, especially where quality of output was more important than quantity, semi-finished products and technology were obtainable only through inter-German trade.

For this reason, trade with the West provided crucial insertions into the unwieldy East German supply system that sometimes caused delayed materials deliveries and subsequent production downtime. By relying on Western suppliers for certain materials and spare parts, the *Kombinate* could nip in the bud the periodic shortfall problems that otherwise would have resulted in production bottlenecks. Such deliveries, which included in some cases emergency transfers, significantly enhanced the GDR's reliability as an industrial supplier, allowing it to be competitive in some Western markets and to fulfill the large and growing Soviet demand for imported goods.

NOTES

1. *DDR Handbuch*, vol. 1, 579-80.

2. Quoted in Dennis L. Bark and David R. Gress, *Democracy and its Discontents 1963-1988* (Oxford: Basil Blackwell, 1989), 216.

3. Lawrence Whetten, *Germany East and West* (New York: New York University Press, 1980), 153.

4. *DDR Handbuch*, vol. 1, 634.

5. Timothy Garton Ash, *Polish Revolution* (New York: Scribner's, 1983), 319.

6. *Süddeutsche Zeitung*, January 16, 1989.

7. Hartmut Zimmermann, "The GDR in the 1970s," *Problems of Communism* 27, no. 2 (March-April 1978): 12.

8. Quoted in James McAdams, *East Germany and Detente* (Cambridge: Cambridge University Press, 1985), 143.

9. Hermann Axen, *Zur Entwicklung der Sozialistischen Nation in der DDR* (East Berlin: Dietz, 1973), 16.

10. Gebhard Schweigler, "German Questions or the Shrinking of Germany" in *The Two German States and European Security*, ed. F. Stephen Larrabee (New York: St. Martin's Press, 1989), 103.

11. *DDR Handbuch*, vol. 2, 926.

12. McAdams, *East Germany and Detente*, 143.

13. *Neues Deutschland*, December 13, 1974.

14. Quoted in *DDR Handbuch*, vol. 2, 926.

15. Ibid.

16. Ibid.

17. Schweigler, "German Questions or the Shrinking of Germany," 103.

18. McAdams poses this question in an article entitled, "The Origins of a New Inter-German Relationship." He argues that "the strength of the East German economy means that West Germany's ability to apply economic pressure on its neighbor is not as great as it was in the past." See McAdams in Larrabee, *The Two German States and European Security*, 60.

19. *Neues Deutschland*, October 14, 1980.

20. Wolfgang Pfeiler, "Intra-German Relations in a Period of East-West Tensions," CISA Working Paper No. 50, Center for International and Strategic Affairs (June 1985), 26.

21. *DDR Handbuch*, vol. 1, 482.

22. Bark and Gress, *Democracy and its Discontents*, 205.

23. Quoted in Pfeiler, "Intra-German Relations in a Period of East-West Tensions," 24.

24. *Neues Deutschland*, October 10, 1983.

25. Zimmermann, "The GDR in the 1970s," 13.

26. *Der Spiegel*, April 16, 1990.

27. Quoted in Ash, *Polish Revolution*, 283.

28. Angela Stent, "Soviet Policy in the German Democratic Republic," in *Soviet Policy in Eastern Europe*, ed. Sarah Meiklejohn Terry (New Haven: Yale University Press, 1984), 52.

29. *The Economist*, October 7, 1989.

Part II
Upheaval and Revolution

6
Winds of Change

SOVIET *PERESTROIKA*

"New thinking" in the Soviet Union brought new external pressure to bear upon the GDR. As the main trading partner of the Soviet Union, it was increasingly charged with assisting "economic restructuring," or *perestroika*. Modernization was to be effected through the mobilization of hidden reserves in the socialist system and the "utilization of the achievements of the scientific-technological revolution," the latter much ballyhooed in the GDR.[1] Having concentrated for a number of years on such key technologies as automation, robotics, computer-aided design and manufacturing (CAD/CAM), data processing, and chemicals, the GDR was in a strong position to jump-start the lagging Soviet economy, it was reasoned. Accordingly, the GDR was pressed to enlarge its critical economic role as chief hard currency producer of the East Bloc, a laboratory for basic research and, above all, a conduit for greater amounts of sorely needed technology to refurbish Soviet industries. Such an agenda was not entirely agreeable to an SED leadership facing domestic economic problems that demanded attention.

Equally, if not more unnerving from the SED's perspective, Soviet leaders began communicating their growing conviction that links between economic reform and political liberalization were inherent and fundamental. Uncompromising in its repudiation of the existence of such an interrelationship, the SED regarded deliberation on political reform as unnecessary, indeed troublesome. Out of a sense of duty more than anything else, SED spokesmen would occasionally pay lip service to the merits of moderate economic "restructuring," while resisting any broader definition of reform involving *societal* modification. Anticipating that discussion would continue, the GDR began to take precautions, endeavoring to ensure *perestroika* would remain just that: talk.

As late as 1989 observers still surmised that the Kremlin would not resolutely urge the GDR to contemplate radical reform unless the East German economy proved unable to fulfill the expanding requirements of Soviet *perestroika*.[2] What this argument appears to have overlooked, however, was that the GDR, confronted with potentially serious economic woes, found itself in an increasingly less favorable position to aid the Soviet Union. Irrespective of this, the Kremlin began leaning on Honecker and his Politburo, lest the Soviet Union not receive the assistance without which the entire reform course might have been in jeopardy. Soviet leaders began to prod the SED's old guard to effect a greater opening of the society, to encourage more economic competition, and to begin freeing markets. Although Gorbachev was subject to ever stiffer criticism in his own country for being overly cautious on economic and political change, he was willing to tolerate, even to abet, an energetic pace of reform in the bloc countries, as the year 1989 was to show.

In the face of the growing reform debate, the SED blew hot and cold. Its smooth high-mindedness prompted condescension vis-à-vis the Soviet Union, discernible in the now infamous wisecrack of the party's chief ideologist, Kurt Hager, "If your neighbor would re-wallpaper his apartment, would you also feel compelled to re-paper your apartment?"[3] In incidental acknowledgments of the need for partial Soviet economic reform, scarcely veiled hauteur on the part of the SED shown through. According to the official line, proposed reforms in the Soviet Union had long since become routine in the GDR, a tenable claim only to the extent that the GDR's economy was modern by East Bloc standards and benefited from a higher overall technology level. The SED's postulate about recurring reform commanded for the most part only slight credence in the Kremlin, and assertions about routine and ongoing changes in the GDR were often subscribed to more in the West than in the East. The continuous routine reforms the party hierarchy alluded to could in fact be described as structural modernization in only one respect: the so-called "socialist intensification" of the economy that moved it partially away from a smokestack behemoth of yesteryear to one with a modest high tech orientation in such areas as robotics, machine tools, microelectronics, and CAD/CAM. In discussions of reform, SED spokesmen sidestepped the term *perestroika*, preferring the more subdued *Reformpolitik* to characterize the GDR's economic development strategy they advanced as a socialist model.

What the SED was portraying as a steady evolution in the GDR over the years had little in common with what Gorbachev had in mind, let alone more radical reformers in the Soviet Union and other East Bloc countries. Even more to the point, the much proclaimed *Reformpolitik* whose essentials were the *Kombinat* system, high technology development, and export promotion was premised on a significant advantage other command economies were in no position to avail themselves of, namely, the GDR's unique relationship with its wealthy Western neighbor who provided credits, much-needed supplies of material, even know-how and management expertise when the latter were requested. In two key areas, CAD/CAM and robotics, the GDR was largely if not wholly dependent upon Western technology and know-how. The directors of the *Kombinate* could gear their production to nearby open markets and reliable supply sources in a manner other East Bloc economic bosses could only dream of. SED claims to offer a model for socialist development thus had to be preceded with a few important caveats. In light of the uniqueness of the GDR's economic position, the country's utility for Moscow as a sort of laboratory for socialist reform was limited, even though some in the Soviet Union would continue to entertain the notion.

Given the conceptual disagreements about reform, the SED would encounter increasing difficulties maintaining the cloak of socialist solidarity with the fraternal states. In fact, the GDR had undergone a rather marked transition from being the East Bloc's conscientious team player and leading proponent of alliance cohesion in the 1970s to becoming the spokesman of bloc differences in the 1980s, even to assuming the loner's role. The autonomy theme found vent in official writings, as for example in a 1984 article by the director of one of the Central Committee's research institutes, and appearing in the foreign policy journal *Horizont*.[4] It argued that each communist party should trust in its own achievement, and base policies upon its own experiences. It went on to say that different experiences and assessments could result in diverging views, a "natural occurrence" in the international communist movement which was, after all, a voluntary community of "equal and independent" parties.

In the foreground of this transition, which began as early as 1980, stood two issues. The first was Honecker's effort to preserve inter-German detente in the face of the superpower mini cold war whose origins dated back to the Soviet invasion of Afghanistan. Although some differences of opinion surfaced at the time (the row over Honecker's visit to Bonn, for example), the SED general-secretary cautiously avoided any statements or actions that might have been construed as constituting a challenge to Soviet bloc leadership. The second issue, that of economic and political reform following Gorbachev's ascension to power in the Soviet Union, was more disturbing to East Berlin, and proved to be far more divisive. SED rhetoric and conduct after the summer of 1988 disclosed a growing rift with Moscow that showed signs of evolving into a challenge to Moscow's authority unprecedented during Honecker's eighteen years in office. The absence of suave SED statements after 1988 to the effect that the airing of tactical differences in bloc members' views was "completely natural" in the voluntary community of "equal" parties suggested that the disagreement was more fundamental. What is more, it seemed that bloc cohesion ceased being of paramount importance to Kremlin reformers. Gorbachev, in a complete reshuffling of the deck, finally expressed his lack of confidence in Honecker's leadership and effectively left the SED twisting in the wind.

THE OUTLOOK IN 1989

Clouds were conspicuously forming on the GDR's economic horizon in the late 1980s. There were signs that the GDR's economy was suffering from declining investment at a time when demand for capital remained high and investment was desperately needed for infrastructure improvement and the increase in labor productivity crucial to the retention of international competitiveness.[5] Exacerbating the decline in investment activity was the lingering problem of low capital productivity in the GDR. Investment had nudged up only slightly in the years before 1989 and this uptrend followed the downturn that was reported in the period 1982-85.[6] The most critical year from the central planners' standpoint in the 1980s was undoubtedly 1982, when, largely as a result of the events in Poland, sources of Western credit almost dried up.[7]

What was widely regarded as an absence of a coherent investment strategy in the 1980s was primarily attributable to two factors. The first was, quite matter-of-factly, scarcer capital as the West became less generous with loans. The second and weightier one was the hesitancy on the regime's part to extract sacrifices from its people, much less to engage in the sort of forced savings schemes that would have significantly curtailed private consumption. The SED's chief concern, in all likelihood, was with the popular unrest a downturn in living standards would have triggered. The overall trade surpluses the GDR had been registering in the 1980s were in large part the result of fostered import reduction to improve the balance of payments. What funds did become available through these surpluses were as a rule not employed for investment, but plowed into the consumer sector, the hope being that additional spending in this area would more than compensate for the effects of import reduction upon the living standard. As a consequence of receding investment, economic growth began to sag in the GDR, which had in fact been the only East Bloc country to have produced higher growth rates in the first half-decade of the 1980s than in the 1970s.[8] National income growth in 1988 was reported to have dipped below 3 percent, by and large not unsatisfactory, but lower than prior growth rates, and short of the SED's plan targets. Even the fairly healthy growth rate of 3.5 percent in 1987 was considerably below the plan target of 4.1 percent. Repeatedly, the central planners' projected growth rates were not being met. In three sectors, agriculture, housing construction, and machinery export, growth decline was unmistakable.[9]

Poor harvests contributed significantly to slowdown in overall growth. Net product in agriculture in 1987-88 by some accounts shrank by as much as 8 percent.[10] Housing starts were continuously sluggish, and output in construction was reported to have risen at most 2.8 percent for several years running. This is to be compared with the whopping 7 to 10 annual percentage growth that was part and parcel of Honecker's main task drives. More disconcerting for the SED in all likelihood were trade figures. Foreign trade was visibly stagnating. The GDR market for West German suppliers was indicating very little increase over a several-year period prior to 1989.[11] Projections at the beginning of 1989 suggested West German sales would not exceed the levels of previous years and non-West German sales remained flat at around DM 4 billion.[12] To what degree such figures reflected import reduction schemes was difficult to assess, but the GDR's trade sector received a fair amount of bad press in the FRG and elsewhere.

Such economic trends spelled major trouble for the GDR, not least because the economic sectors showing arrested growth were among those the central planners had identified as being critical target sectors for the late 1980s and early 1990s. Between one-fourth and one-third of national income was export generated, meaning that the GDR was as dependent upon trade as many Western European countries. The prominent place assigned to the export sector in economic planning was clearly evident, since trade with the West increased 745 percent in the period 1960-80 and total foreign trade volume registered nearly 10 percent annual average increases in the same period, more than twice the yearly increase in national income.[13] An economic index of openness to foreign influences is the ratio of exports to GNP; employing this index, the GDR's economy had achieved the openness command economies typically were designed to avoid.

What was going wrong? Several explanations present themselves. First, certain broad currents in the world economy beyond the GDR's control were affecting its production. Chief among these was the shift in economic activity to East Asia. The emergence of highly competitive, relatively low-wage countries on the Pacific rim, especially but not exclusively, the "four dragons" of Asia, South Korea, Taiwan, Singapore, and Hong Kong, who had made considerable inroads into Western markets, were squeezing some of the basic manufacturing sectors of the GDR that had heretofore been price-competitive abroad.[14] Earnings from durable consumer goods manufacture constituted a not insignificant percentage of yearly East German trade turnover. Official statistics were typically sketchy, but it did seem to have been the case that this number dropped several percentage points from a high of over 20 percent in the 1970s to around 15 percent of total exports in 1980, then tapered off a few percentage points thereafter.[15] In at least one area, textiles, efforts to establish an export industry proved fruitless, no doubt due to the difficulty of competing in international markets. Hardest hit was machine tool manufacture, a flagship industry in the 1970s. According to some Western estimates, machine tool export declined by 75 percent in the years 1973-89.[16] This represented a significant loss of foreign exchange earnings. Over 40 percent of light industry production was designated for export, an amount earmarked for increase in the late 1980s.[17] The goal was not achieved.

Many East Asian producers were able to vie with the GDR in microelectronics and computer-aided manufacturing. By the end of the 1980s, Taiwan alone was selling twenty times as many machine tools to industrial countries as the GDR. In consumer electronics and vehicle production the GDR wasn't playing in the same league as South Korea, not to mention Japan. Although the direct impact upon the GDR of East Asian economic expansion did not lend itself to easy quantification, the trend portended a downturn in East German international competitiveness and suggested a general inadequacy in adapting to global structural changes.

There were growing indications in the 1980s that the GDR confronted industrial decline. Whereas 2.5 marks in investment generated on average 1 mark in foreign exchange in 1980, by the end of the decade the amount of needed investment rose to 4.5 marks and was continuing to increase. Prestige sectors soaked up huge amounts of investment funds, depriving other sectors of finances and exacerbating growth imbalances. The microelectronic industry, for example, which was intended by the central planners to put the GDR on the cutting edge of high technology manufacture was consuming 14 billion marks annually.[18]

Second, the continuing inability of the energy sector to meet basic requirements of the GDR's economy was a drag upon national income growth. The GDR had been only partially shielded from the oil price shocks of the 1970s, since even the price of imported Soviet crude oil rose more than fivefold over the course of a decade. Between 1972-75, total price increases for GDR exports were 17 percent, whereas import prices rose 34 percent, most of this attributable to rising energy costs.[19] The conjunction of high energy consumption rates and increasing reliance upon Western-produced materials whose prices were affected by rising energy costs caused the GDR to have been severely rocked by the price hikes. Consumption rates, not cost-responsive because of price distortions, continued to rise. Despite official measures to reduce imported energy, especially in years 1979-80, there was no indication that wastage of relatively expensive energy abated, nor did imports significantly decline. The GDR produced less than 70 percent of its needs through domestic production, nearly all of this through lignite burning, meaning that over 30 percent of domestic energy needs had to be met through oil and natural gas imports.[20] The Five-Year Plan 1981-85 envisaged considerable reductions in amounts of imported fuels with a concomitant expansion of lignite production.[21] Quite apart from the horrendous environmental damage caused by extensive lignite burning, dependence upon this source incurred considerable direct economic costs since open-face mining ruined areas for agriculture and forestry.

Third, full employment schemes exacerbated the intrinsic problems of inefficient human resource allocation. Put another way, the GDR's economy suffered chronic labor shortages as well as an excess of workers in many industries and offices at the same time. Factories typically held employees in reserve. Redundant labor in many enterprises thwarted the operation of labor markets, preventing rechanneling of human resources. Further difficulties were caused by a declining work force. Unfolding social and political problems, manifested in higher numbers of young, educated emigrants, were not without effect. Labor shortages and labor force decline were widely regarded as a significant growth inhibitor.[22] The GDR confronted a taut labor supply situation and a substantial, almost predetermined downturn in the new supply of manpower in the late 1980s. In light of this, prospects for economic expansion hinged exclusively on raising the productivity of labor and capital.

Finally, the continuation of marginal declines in trade with the West, a trend which started in 1985, was a symptom of underlying structural weaknesses in the GDR's economy. The late 1980s were boom times in Western Europe when the FRG was chalking up record export surpluses. Yet intra-German trade volume flattened out and the GDR seemed unable to reap the benefits offered through association with the EC which was experiencing a considerable economic upturn. Stagnating foreign trade, lagging productivity, production bottlenecks in key industries that could be overcome only by Western supplies—all were signs of serious imbalances in the industrial production structure.[23] Evidence of economic degeneration was to be found in the multiplier effects of the various shortcomings. For example, bureaucratically determined prices were causing energy wastage that in turn resulted in unnecessary foreign exchange expenditure. Faltering productivity and imbalanced growth, also attributable to price distortions, necessitated more "emergency" supplies and technology transfer from the West, both of which drained hard currency reserves. Growing dependence upon imported raw materials and capital goods subjected the GDR to price fluctuations and global inflation. Diminishing amounts of available foreign reserves, exacerbated by bills accumulating for growing quantities of imported fuels, induced import reduction, which in turn might have adversely affected living standards. But Honecker would not allow such a decline to occur and instructed the planning authorities to dip into the savings pool if necessary. Thus, commitment to the maintenance of the living standard even in lean years prevented the increases in investment needed for building infrastructure and boosting productivity.

THE TIGHT SQUEEZE

GDR leaders found themselves caught vicelike in the grip of continuing liberal influence from the West on the one side, and the pressure of *glasnost* and *perestroika* from the East on the other. Increasingly, the latter became the more immediate and less manageable challenge for the SED. Over the years East German leaders had learned to live with the siren song of decadent capitalism.

The party blinked at the prevalent viewing of West German television and the tuning in to Western radio programs. Confinement or expulsion from the country awaited those East Germans who became too enamored of Western ideas or publicly criticized the socialist order. And Honecker's administration had become fairly astute at manipulating the German "special relationship," wresting funds from Bonn for such things as construction projects, postal services, waste disposal, and liberation of political prisoners. Visa fees and amounts of required exchange were altered more or less arbitrarily either to lower the numbers of Western visitors or to raise state coffers.

But Soviet "new thinking" proved more difficult to handle. The campaign for reform put East German leaders on pins and needles, sapping the public self-confidence many had been displaying. The reasons were palpable. For years the country had been spoon-fed laudatory slogans bordering on the obsequious, for example, "Learning from the Soviet Union means learning to be victorious." The younger generation had been indoctrinated with the notion that the Soviet Union was the most advanced society on earth, one to be unfalteringly emulated. Schools required children to learn and internalize basic political concepts such as why the Soviet Union represented a vital force and was an eternal friend of the GDR, and why it possessed original "revolutionary legitimacy." A quote from an elementary school text is instructive:

> Socialist Countries (*Sozialistische Länder*)—Countries where the factories and fields belong to the people. The working people rule here. These countries want peace. We are bound in intimate friendship with them. The GDR belongs to this community. Among them, the Soviet Union is not only the largest and richest member, it is also the strongest and most powerful country in the world. Socialist countries support each other. They live in friendship together. They have good trade relations.[24]

With *glasnost* the enormous economic deficiencies of the Soviet Union were being brought to light. Soviet economists, including some of Gorbachev's advisors, began providing statistics and prognoses that made the most case-hardened Central Intelligence Agency analysts look like optimists. Radical Soviet reformers and regime critics were calling socialism the "economics of the lunatic asylum" and getting away with such insolence. The SED's old guard was simply mystified, and in the back of every East German leader's mind was the thought that the Soviet Union ultimately underwrote the regime's security. With any significant attenuation of the Soviet guarantee, the SED might have stood naked in front of its own people.

This is what happened in 1989. Years of Western influence converging with a homegrown variety of "Gorbymania" ignited the fire for reform throughout the society. I noticed the flame's first smoldering during Christmas week 1988 in the GDR. By that time the Politburo was already chiding the Soviet Union for tolerating "revisionism by bourgeois characters run wild." More than a few East Germans were talking in private about the departure of the old guard, the opening of borders, eventual pluralism in the GDR. I took pains to avoid being insensitive, but inwardly I could not imagine change of such magnitude taking place in the foreseeable future.

Some observers now suggest that political firebrands were already being thrown up around the middle of the year 1989. For example, in June during a West Berlin rock concert, whose vibrant percussions and shrill guitars cascaded into East Berlin, unifying parts of the divided city in rhythm and blues, a crowd of youths assembled and began chanting "Gorbachev, Gorbachev," followed by an accompanying chorus of "Away with the Wall!" Security forces dealt harshly with the demonstrators, hauling some off to jail and beating many, including a few West German camera crew personnel.

To think, though, that an unofficial demonstration involving a few dozen people, in a country renowned for its self-gratifying and self-glorifying mass assemblies, would have been newsworthy as late as the spring of 1989. In October hundreds of thousands took peacefully to the streets to demand sweeping reforms. One fall demonstration in East Berlin drew an estimated one million people.

Rock concerts did have a way of precipitating notable unrest in East Berlin. In 1977, on the GDR's national day (October 7), I witnessed a scuffle at the Alexanderplatz that turned into a serious incident. As the music stimulated listener pulses, a group of youths quite obviously affected by alcohol as well began shouting insults at the police on duty. Push quickly came to shove, and chants of *"Russen 'raus!"* ("Russians, get out!") could be heard echoing across the square. In the foray that followed, several people were injured and at least two killed. At the risk of reading too much into an isolated occurrence, I couldn't help thinking how fast a tussle at a public gathering acquired political overtones.

The SED did not fully appreciate the effect the blending of Western and (new) Eastern ideas was having on East German society, although official actions beginning in the fall of 1988 reflected some foreboding. The customary edginess about the West that translated into *Abschirmung*, or "screening off" procedures inverted into a queer "screening off" to the East, and so, with its deep-seated misgivings about reform, the SED alienated the principal guarantor of its security. "Alienation" was in fact the term reportedly used in a 1989 memorandum to the Soviet leadership by the Kremlin's chief advisor on German affairs, Valenin Falin, to describe relations between Moscow and East Berlin.[25] He suggested there was but a "small reservoir of common political views" remaining between the leaders of the two countries, exemplified by the "harsh rejection" of the Soviet reform course by SED leaders and the recent significant decline in Soviet influence in the GDR. Assuming the reports to have been correct, Falin was providing his government with prescient assessments of the situation in the GDR in the summer and early fall, and these assessments were instrumental, in all likelihood, to the development of the Kremlin's "new thinking" about its East German ally. In words now carrying conviction, Falin was said to have written about the need "to be concerned about the possibility that the widely distributed dissatisfaction (in the GDR) will in a relatively short time—by the spring of next year at the very latest—lead to mass demonstrations which would be difficult to control."[26] By October, with little room left for maneuver, the GDR proved incapable of adjusting to changing political circumstances. The final challenge to the SED came from the people, who had for years been using as an economic and political standard that fraternal Western society they had come vicariously to know, and who vindicated their demands for change with *glasnost* and *perestroika* in the Soviet Union.

NOTES

1. Hannes Adomeit, "Gorbachev and German Unification: Revision of Thinking, Realignment of Power," *Problems of Communism* 39, no. 4 (July-August 1990): 3.

2. Daniel Hamilton, "Dateline East Germany: The Wall Behind the Wall," *Foreign Policy* 76 (Fall 1989): 178-84.

3. *Der Stern*, April 10, 1987.

4. Quoted in Wolfgang Pfeiler, "Intra-German Relations in a Period of East-West Tensions," CISA Working Paper, No. 50 (June 1985), 30-31.

5. *Business Eastern Europe* 7, February 17, 1986, 52.

6. *Economic Bulletin* 2 (April 1989): 4.

7. *Economic Bulletin* 2 (April 1986): 4.

8. "GDR: On a New Path of Growth?" *Mitgliederinformation* (Wiener Institut für Internationale Wirtschaftsvergleiche), no. 8 (1989): 9.

9. *Economic Bulletin* 2 (April 1989): 4.

10. Ibid.

11. *Business Eastern Europe* 5, January 30, 1989, 36.

12. Ibid.

13. *DDR Handbuch*, vol. 1, 127.

14. Hamilton, "Dateline East Germany," 182-83.

15. *Statistical Pocket Book of the German Democratic Republic 1978*, 76-77; *DDR Handbuch*, vol. 1, 126-27.

16. *Der Spiegel*, November 20, 1989.

17. *DDR Handbuch*, vol. 1, 823-24.

18. *Der Spiegel*, November 20, 1989.

19. Lawrence Whetten, *Germany East and West* (New York: New York University Press, 1980), 148.

20. David Childs, *The GDR* (London: Unwin Hyman, 1988), 148-49.

21. *DDR Handbuch*, vol. 1, 354-56.

22. "GDR: On a New Path of Growth?" *Mitgliederinformation*, 9.

23. *Business Eastern Europe* 5, January 30, 1989, 36.

24. Quoted in John M. Starrels and Anita M. Mallinckrodt, *Politics in the German Democratic Republic* (New York: Praeger, 1975), 45.

25. This is discussed by Adomeit who cites information received by West German intelligence as reported in *Die Welt*, September 15, 1989. The report did not specify the exact date or context of Falin's assessment. See Adomeit, "Gorbachev and German Unification," 6.

26. Ibid.

7

The Iron Curtain Corrodes and Shakes

GLASNOST? NEIN, DANKE!

As early as 1986 indications of significant political differences between East Berlin and Moscow began to emerge. Honecker's triumphal visit to Bonn in September 1987, marking the pinnacle of his career, somewhat covered over evolving discord, and since no friction arose from what had been a contentious issue in the preceding years, there was even the temporary illusion of a warming in Soviet-GDR relations. But the tensions that unfolded over the next two years ultimately involved deeper matters than prior Soviet concern about German-German coziness.[1] The first intimation of this was to be found in the East German media's unmistakable disregard for the growing number of Soviet pronouncements about *glasnost* and *perestroika* that suggested genuine Soviet commitment to reform. Confronted with what appeared to be growing Soviet resolution, GDR leaders oscillated between nonchalance and quiet uneasiness.

It was more than reform discussion that the SED found worrisome. Within a year of taking office, Gorbachev made clear he would upbraid East Bloc leaders clinging to the "old thinking." Addressing the 1986 Eleventh SED Party Congress, Gorbachev said:

> All of us, I think, are aware that the socialist countries are entering a period in which their mutual collaboration must be raised to a higher level. It must be raised not just by a few degrees, but—to borrow a term from mathematics—by a whole order of magnitude.[2]

The general secretary's speech had significant connotations, even though a good deal of it consisted of statements that were fairly typical of the sterile platitudes of communist party gatherings. As Honecker and his Politburo were later to discover, "mutual collaboration" à la Gorbachev foreshadowed something very different from business as usual in the East Bloc. In fact, it entailed the adoption of economic and political reforms that would change the face of communist societies. The "cooperative effort" Gorbachev envisaged was to take place within a reconstituted political framework East Bloc rulers wished no part of. Though Gorbachev himself did not anticipate the immensity, and above all the swiftness of the change *glasnost* and *perestroika* would eventually bring about, his disdain for the old thinking was conspicuous, and he was visibly unsettled with the absence of *glasnost* he encountered in the GDR during his 1986 visit.[3]

In his address to the SED Congress Gorbachev took the East German leaders firmly to task for a variety of alleged iniquities including abuse of office, nepotism, party favoritism, and improper acquisition of authority.[4] To Western ears there is something gratifying about hearing one communist leader chide another for abusing power, but to an SED leadership that had successfully weathered a political squall over detente issues in 1983-84 and was coming forward as increasingly self-contented, this was a most unwelcome development. For their part, top apparatchiks preferred complacency in "actually existing socialism" where they were resolutely working for the "perfection of the system of planning, management, and cost accountancy." *Perestroika* had no place in the German Democratic Republic, as Hager's public rejection of Gorbachev's proposals for stronger trade unions and the election of factory managers made clear.[5] "The strategy for social development outlined in the SED's program," Hager stated, "has proven correct under the most difficult international circumstances of the past decade-and-a-half."[6] Highlighting Hager's remarks, Honecker heralded the great achievements of the GDR's socialist economy in the 1980s.

The other side of this coin was the underlying but increasing disdain SED officialdom harbored for the Soviet Union, an example of which is to be found in a remark made in June 1986 by Hans-Dieter Seguett, then editor of *Junge Welt*, the orthodox FDJ newspaper. "For me the Soviet Union earned great historical merit because it defeated Hitler and won the war," Seguett said. "It is not, however, a model for us in terms of technology and progress."[7] Party newspaper editors were not in the habit of speaking off-the-cuff, nor was his attitude unrepresentative. His interjection begged the question, though: If the Soviet Union was no longer a model for the GDR, what was?

Having in the main ignored *glasnost* and *perestroika* for the better part of two years, by the fall of 1988, the GDR began to regard in earnest the reform debates occurring elsewhere in the East Bloc, so much so that SED leaders felt it necessary to launch verbal assaults against Soviet publications and films reflecting purported heresies. Quite suddenly, in November, the German-language edition of *Sputnik*, a digest of the Soviet press with an average monthly circulation of 180,000, was banned from the country. The move signified increasing nervousness with the Soviet reform course. Long a notoriously dull magazine subscribed to by the party faithful as a routine duty, *Sputnik*, in a breathtaking about-face, posited itself on the cutting edge of reform. Such transformations put East Berlin decidedly ill at ease. That *Sputnik* "no longer strengthens GDR-Soviet friendship," but instead "distorts history" was the succinct official explanation of the prohibition.[8]

The GDR had banned publications from other communist states on prior occasions. During the Prague Spring, for example, the German-language weekly *Volkszeitung* disappeared from public view. In early 1988 several issues of *Novoye vremya* containing extracts from Michael Shatrov's *Onwards, Onwards, Onwards*, a play critical of Stalinism, found their way onto the SED's hit lists and off the newsstands. Never before had the SED imposed an outright ban on a Soviet publication, though. Honecker, it seemed, had set out upon a new course of ideological screening off, this time directed toward the East.

An article suggesting that the pre-war KPD was partly responsible for the rise of Hitler made the October 1988 edition of *Sputnik* singularly contemptible in SED eyes. According to the piece:

> The German Communists did not risk joining the Social Democrats in the struggle against the Nazis. Had they done this, Hitler would not have succeeded in winning national parliamentary elections, and European history would have probably taken an entirely different course.[9]

Toeing Stalin's line on the German Social Democrats, by denouncing them as "social fascists," the pre-war KPD chose strange bedfellows in the 1930s. Concluding tacit accords with the extremist right on occasion, the KPD fought bitterly against moderate democratic forces in the Weimar Republic. In collusion with the Nazis, the KPD organized strike actions to undermine elected governments. It voted with rightist groups in 1931 in favor of a Nazi-sponsored referendum on the dissolution of the Prussian *Landtag*, where the moderate Social Democrats held a majority. Given the composition of Weimar Germany, the state of Prussia was a mainstay of democracy and an important bulwark against radicalism. The list of extremist actions was long, and the KPD by its own admission was determined to do away with Weimar democracy.

To SED leaders the *Sputnik* accusations had all the earmarks of sacrilege. Not only did they cast a long shadow upon the KPD leader, Ernst Thälmann, the greatest hero of the GDR, but they were considered something on the nature of a personal affront by those SED dignitaries, especially Honecker, Axen, and Sindermann, who had been persecuted by the Nazis and took considerable pride in their impeccable antifascist credentials. Since antifascism was a critical component of the GDR's self-identity, much was on the line for the SED. By challenging the KPD's antifascist tradition, a Soviet publication was sapping the foundations of a pillar of SED legitimacy. Few issues of *Neues Deutschland* were devoid of some mention of the antifascist struggle. Factories, schools, collective farms, and streets throughout the GDR bore the name of Thälmann and other prominent figures in the fight against fascism. The party youth organization for children aged six to fourteen that was affiliated with the FDJ was appropriately called the Thälmann Pioneers. Speaking in September 1988, only weeks prior to *Sputnik*'s astonishing revelations, Honecker offered a visiting Bulgarian youth group the following laudation:

> True to the revolutionary legacy of Ernst Thälmann and Giorgi Dimitrov, the greatest sons of our peoples, the resolutions of the Eleventh Congress of the SED contribute to the realization of the provisions of the 1977 Treaty of Friendship, Cooperation and Mutual Assistance between the two fraternal socialist states.[10]

The SED had hitherto lashed out furiously against any inference in Western analyses that the KPD had not willfully resisted the Nazis. In his writings Honecker rebuked Western authors for perpetrating the "historic lie" that German communists underestimated the extent of the right-wing threat.[11] To substantiate his argument that the KPD never discounted the Nazi menace, he offered Thälmann's description of the Nazi party even before its ascension to power as the "deadly enemy of the workers' movement and of the Soviet Union."[12] He singled out for castigation those "social democratic and bourgeois historians" hypothesizing that leftist and rightist terror destroyed the Weimar Republic.[13]

By disclosing how the German Communists were responsible in no small way for the Nazi seizure of power, *Sputnik* breached a time-honored taboo and precipitantly touched raw nerves. From the *Sputnik* article emerged the specter of deplorable allegations about the KPD being made by a Soviet observer. The charge leveled was poignantly thought-provoking in the part of Germany where the effects of war had lasted longer than in the West and the scars of defeat were more palpable. Reputations tarnish easily in an era of reform. Adding insult to injury, *Sputnik* reprinted a previously unpublished letter to the Soviet writer Illya Ehrenburg that presented hard evidence of the numerous warnings Stalin received about the impending German attack on the Soviet Union in 1941. In it Stalin was termed "blind as a mole" for brushing aside the ominous and plainly evident signals.[14] SED functionaries must have rubbed their eyes in disbelief. The Soviet reform press was transgressing the cardinal principle of GDR media policy that required the depiction of socialist development as altogether positive and inherently progressive.[15] From the SED's perspective, reappraisals of the Stalinist period were agonizing and dismaying enough. Any association between the Nazis and the antifascist, progressive forces that laid the foundations for socialism on German soil was utterly alarming. In a rebuttal of *Sputnik*, *Neues Deutschland* wrote:

> This publication has defamed German Communists and their allies who fought for a new Germany and whose struggle brought about the establishment of the

German Democratic Republic. . . . It argued that Stalin was basically Hitler's puppet. . . . Until now such things were to be heard only from the unscrupulous Western apologists of fascism. Distortions of this kind are simply unfathomable for those who lived through this period or who have been raised in the spirit of anti-fascism and thus know the historical truth about fascism.[16]

Along with the banning of *Sputnik*, the GDR Ministry of Culture ordered the immediate withdrawal of five Soviet films from movie theaters countrywide, while the FDJ received instructions to cancel indefinitely all discussions of the Soviet reform course. Underscoring the official position, the secretary of Regional Councils in the GDR proclaimed: "Whoever wants *perestroika* here will be excluded."[17]

The scale of SED reaction was striking and, as might have been expected, the measures backfired. Nothing whetted popular appetites for information more than official instructions about what one was not supposed to read. *Sputnik*, the forbidden fruit, all the more tempting because of the *Verbot*, gained considerable notoriety, and cynical new jokes about SED narrow-mindedness made the rounds. Fresh winds from the East were bringing waves of criticism against the aging leadership of a country already awash with Western ideas. Over and above the piquing of interest in the occurrences and issues themselves was a more telling effect. Popular intuition increasingly sensed that Soviet admonitions held out possibilities for genuine reform in the GDR, and the presentiment subsequently began to spread among East Germans that SED rule was in fact more tenuous than generally assumed. Many correctly perceived that official nervousness about the *Sputnik* revelations was a sign of regime weakness, a point widely overlooked in the West. By mid-1988 *glasnost* and *perestroika* had become household words, and in private conversations these subjects were inevitably broached. Above all, the *Sputnik* incident testified to the extent East German public opinion was being swayed by Soviet "new thinking."

THE PARTY RIGS AN ELECTION

Efforts to seal off the GDR reflected not only apprehension on the leadership's part, but indicated an enduring aloofness alongside an abiding sense of unreality. The staging of communal elections on May 7, 1989, furnished additional testimony of this. With popular dissatisfaction clearly on the rise, and despite signs of possible unrest, SED leaders resolved to engage in election machinations, crude even by GDR standards. In a Politburo meeting five days prior to the communal polling, several members were alleged to have remarked that some "trouble" in the form of dissidents encouraging people to vote against the SED lists had to be reckoned with. Suggesting the possibility of embarrassing consequences, Mielke reported that small opposition groups were attempting to organize protest votes and to check for election rigging. To think that people might have the audacity to interfere in their own internal affairs!

Chairing the election commission and serving as chief overseer of the polling was Egon Krenz. On the evening of election day, he announced a triumph for the SED. Of the 12,182,050 valid votes, there were 142,301 against, giving the party a margin of 98.85 percent.[18] That the SED would have been turned out of office anywhere was, of course, inconceivable but the enormity of the success caused skepticism even among loyal party functionaries. Lest the liberalization bacillus infect any part of the population, Hager and Mielke kept close tabs on the public mood thereafter. Identifying in his security reports the "inner enemies" who were coming forward with proof of election manipulation, Mielke issued an executive order to the effect that "all responsible organs are to reply to any complaints about election procedure by denying the existence of any evidence of irregularities."[19] He instructed post offices not to deliver letters that the Ministry for State Security indicated to contain citizen protests about the elections. Mail contents were, of course, no secret to the ministry.

According to classified ministry estimates, as much as 10 percent of the populace had voted against the SED lists, the source of this information being not election officials but various sources, including one the Ministry of State Security described in reports as "treasonous circles," presumably independent citizen groups, with which it maintained contact.[20] From his own sources Hager claimed to have obtained more disquieting indications of potential citizen discontent. At a number of universities, he pointed out in a Politburo meeting following the elections, large percentages of students had struck out the party lists. In the Berlin Academy of Fine Arts a reported 51 percent of the students voted against the SED; the corresponding numbers were 43 percent at the Dresden Art Academy and 35 percent at the Dresden Academy of Music. Although a discussion item on the Politburo's agenda, such voting results remained unpublicized at the time.

Neither the actual results of the election, nor information about the extent of manipulation are available, and thus the observer is left to conduct analysis piecemeal with fragmentary evidence. As polling in the small town of Quedlinburg in the eastern Harz region in all likelihood typified countrywide election returns, this municipality might be employed by way of example as something of a political microcosm. As elsewhere, the party candidates duly received 99.5 percent of the vote. Some candidates were supposedly elected unanimously. "Naturally there was election rigging," the mayor unhesitantly admitted in late November 1989.[21] To make a point, he indicated that in the fall of that year over 20,000 people marched week for week in the local demonstration against the regime. In light of the fact that virtually every adult in a town of less than 30,000 was a participant, there was sufficient reason to question the amount of genuine citizen support reflected in the SED election victory just six months previously.

In the spring of 1989 the Politburo chose impulsively to present the people with fraudulent election results, while unreservedly disregarding visibly growing citizen annoyance. Krenz spoke of the returns as "an expression of the voters' will to participate in the shaping of the developed socialist society."[22] Honecker saw in them "an impressive popular acknowledgment of the SED's policies of peace and socialism."[23] Subsequent to a large FDJ parade organized less than two weeks after the communal elections and featuring the slogan "Western Freedom: Nein Danke!" Honecker called the events of the month "overwhelming indications of the political-moral unity of our people."[24] Angelika Unterlauf of the official television news, who, by her own admission had repeatedly lied on the regime's behalf, would later provide a more sobering assessment. In an interview late that autumn she commented that even she had encountered difficulty keeping a straight face when announcing the *Sputnik* banning in the autumn of 1988 or the communal election results of the spring of 1989.

LIBERALIZATION IN HUNGARY

Catching the SED off balance, the first acid test of citizen loyalty came sooner than anyone expected. In May 1989 Hungary began dismantling frontier fortifications with Austria, and announced that the border would be completely open within a year. With this expanding "green border" between Austria and Hungary, a largish breach was being rent in the iron curtain.

Meanwhile, the uppity Hungarians tendered an ideological challenge that struck the SED with consternation. Budapest began thinking out loud about neutrality. In April the *Budapester Rundschau* opined: "The status of neutrality has many advantages. Inter alia the military budget can be reduced as seen fit and foreign troops have no business being on national territory."[25] Such talk came on top of countrywide discussions about reform measures, including the eventual introduction of a market economy and a multi-party system. Hungary, renowned (or chided depending on the perspective) for its "gulash communism," had begun eliminating obligatory economic production plans and compulsory production targets for agriculture and foreign trade enterprises some time before. Trade relations with the West had broadened considerably, mirroring a reduction of Hungarian trade in the period 1979-89 with the CMEA countries as a percentage of overall trade from 70 to 45 percent.[26]

By the middle of 1989 expressions of SED anxiety about the situation in Hungary could be heard. During the June congress of the Central Committee, the Politburo announced: "Under the banner of 'renewal of socialism' there are forces at work striving for the removal of socialism. In this context developments in Hungary fill us with great concern."[27] Honecker weighed in with the following prodigious remark, the gist of which was plain enough. "Only in the GDR are socialist values solidly anchored in the people," he said, because the party leadership "always works for the good of the people."[28] For its part, Budapest was posing a twofold threat to SED orthodoxy. It was breaching the extended wall providing the GDR's first line of protection, while bidding defiance to the SED's neo-Stalinist underpinning. In Honecker's way of thinking, other East Bloc states including the Soviet Union, by deviating from the true socialist path, were pursuing policies inimical to popular well-being. The stage was set for Stalinism-in-one-country.

In a speech to the West German *Bundestag* on June 17, 1989, the West German holiday commemorating the 1953 East German uprising, SPD politician Erhard Eppler identified what was becoming increasingly accepted as the SED's central dilemma in a changing Europe. The old men of the Politburo, he said, harbored fears that reforms at home or elsewhere in the East Bloc threatened their lifework.[29] They were quite simply unequal to the challenges facing them, were reactionary, detached, and self-important, he added, and they unremittingly conducted the affairs of state according to the dictum "stay the course." A prominent example of the leadership's shortsightedness, he averred, was the May 1989 election fraud in which the party issued its standard single-candidate lists, received 85 percent of the vote, then proceeded to inflate this to 98 percent. The SED had affronted its own people yet again.

With the gradual emergence of liberalized states around the GDR, it would be inconceivable for the SED to maintain its Stalinist island, complete with monopolies on power and truth, Eppler argued, and thus the GDR would eventually be forced by the pressure of events to assume an entirely new democratic socialist "function" in Central Europe, or, alternatively, the state would simply not survive. The new GDR, Eppler suggested, could have an extensive public sector but, in contrast to the existing state, would have guarantees of basic liberties and civil rights; the regime's legitimacy would be based upon free elections; and market forces would be allowed to work in the economy.

Here was the rub, though. Eppler stressed that the Politburo, at least in its configuration at the time, was singularly unsuited to initiating such change. Who then was to have effected it? Renunciation of the party's power monopoly and the creation of a pluralist society corresponded, in the view of the Honeckers and Stophs, to a dismantling of their life's work. The puzzle's pieces simply did not fit. What was to be the SED's role in a multi-party state? Would a basically Stalinist party be willing to release its iron grip on the economy?

To this latter question the SED had ready, and none too encouraging, responses. In a *Neues Deutschland* commentary appearing in the summer of 1989, Karl Morgenstern, a leading East German professor of economics said "the retreat from economic intervention would mean a retreat into capitalism," adding that "an abandonment of central economic guidance and planning was out of the question."[30] In response to questions about economic reform, Otto Reinhold insisted that the system of central planning in the GDR was inviolable. There was little in the SED's history that suggested a willingness to share power or to carry out the kind of economic reform necessary to shape a wholly new society. To be sure, economic reconstruction would have had highly disquieting effects in the SED's view. Freeing of markets would have meant keener competition, belt-tightening, and the potential bankruptcy of state-owned firms. For rank-and-file citizens it would have meant harder work and more discipline. The short-run success of reform might have been measured by the lengths of queues before shops or by visible inflation. The SED would not have been able to generate sufficient popular support to carry through such a program.

THE BREACH

By the summer Hungary had become an escape route for East Germans. Between May and August thousands crossed into Austria. In the span of just a few days in early August, over 2,000 turned their backs on the GDR for good. At any given time that summer nearly 1,000 East Germans lived in tents in Budapest while seeking permission to go to the FRG. Hundreds walked across the partially open border into Austria. The estimated 200,000 East German "vacationers" in Hungary portended ill for the regime and the Politburo waited anxiously to see how many would return when school commenced again in the autumn. According to estimates at the time, a minimum of 10,000 weren't planning on a return.

Although Budapest at first assured East Berlin that border crossings would be controlled as tightly as ever in accordance with the Warsaw Pact treaties, the Hungarians showed only a halfhearted disposition to stop people from fleeing across the green border. For a period of weeks border patrols were actually strengthened, and Hungarian authorities did on occasion discourage East Germans from bolting. During an August 19 "pan-European picnic" in a Austrian frontier area, though, thousands of East Germans decided to enjoy their picnic baskets in the West and Hungarian security forces did nothing. Organization of the picnic by Imre Pozsgay, Hungary's leading communist reformer, and Otto von Habsburg, a member of the European Parliament, suggested to an increasingly edgy East Berlin that the Hungarians were conspiring with the West against it.

Growing numbers of East Germans not willing to risk a border crossing that presented some difficulties and which was still officially illegal, attempted another route: storming the West German Embassy in Budapest, requesting a West German passport, and demanding the right to leave. Exit from an East Bloc country at the time was possible only if one had a valid visa and entry stamp in one's passport. By August 1 over one hundred East Germans had sought refuge inside the embassy compound and were attempting to force exit to the West. The West German Embassy in Prague and the Permanent Mission in East Berlin became destinations for would-be refugees as well.

In the past, the GDR had to come to terms with a certain percentage of its citizens who wished to take leave of the country, but with close to 80,000 departures from the GDR in the first eight months of 1989, nearly one-third of these illegal, the SED was confronted with an exodus crisis as severe as that of 1961 which precipitated the building of the Berlin Wall to stem the tide. By voting with their feet, the GDR's citizens were once again silently refuting the viability of their country. In the middle of the year 1989, Bonn expected close to 100,000 legal emigrants; this estimate was, of course, later overtaken by events.

Krenz, chairing the Politburo that July and August in place of the ailing Honecker, advocated a hard line vis-à-vis the embassy refugees. He asserted that West German diplomatic missions would become "endless escape routes" if the way out were not barred. Consequently, security forces kept the permanent mission in East Berlin under control by preventing East Germans from entering the premises, but there was little the GDR could do in Budapest and Prague if the authorities there were unwilling to cooperate. The Hungarians in particular resisted, not wishing to anger the FRG or to display outward signs of repression. Shrill GDR media attacks reflected the Politburo's stand on the unfolding events. Bonn was assigned primary blame for the problem, and accusations of "provocations" and *Menschenhandel* ("slave trade") abounded. According to the Bonn correspondent of the East German television: "Warning voices have been pointing out that Bonn's campaign of interference in the GDR's internal affairs is intended to provoke a tougher posture from East Berlin."[31] Not to be missed either was the customary tactic, when the GDR confronted difficult circumstances, of saddling Bonn with the perpetration of alleged atrocities. On August 12 *Neues Deutschland* published photographs of "brutally murdered" East German border troops, offering these as yet additional examples of Bonn's "heinous instigations."[32] Throughout the fall months, as the difficulties mounted, the SED resorted to pointing an accusing finger at the West Germans for a plethora of alleged misdeeds as a distraction from the real situation.

But in any event reports filtering in about the appreciable effects of the exodus were alarming. The flight of doctors, nurses, and medical staff were leaving large gaps in the GDR's health services. Over 500 doctors and nurses had left the East Berlin region alone, and health services in many parts of the country were increasingly taxed. Many areas including East Berlin were drawing up emergency plans to maintain basic services. In some rural areas medical facilities were facing the possibility of closure, and ambulance services were more and more difficult to maintain. With personnel leaving regularly and hundreds of applications for emigration on file, the situation clearly would worsen. Some areas were reporting that trainee nurses were being sent to polyclinics for regular service, and in several cities nurses were even performing minor operations. Dresden, one of the hardest hit urban areas, lost dozens of doctors and hundreds of nurses.

Although the official media characteristically never made mention of it, one source of the problems which came to a head in the late summer and fall of 1989 went back many years. In point of fact, health services were in many respects not held in very high repute in the GDR. Central planners classified health service personnel as nonproductive workers, and the health service in general as a nonproductive sector. Many in the profession considered their salaries inadequate, and remuneration by Western standards was astonishingly low. A pediatrician, for example, with twenty-five years of experience earned on average 300 marks more than a shipyard worker.[33] The shortages and bottlenecks that plagued the economy as a whole were prevalent in rural medical facilities, with the result that frustration in the profession was great. Adding to the frustration was the general perception of the existence of class medicine in an allegedly classless society. Central planning organs tended to fund large and prestigious city hospitals, while neglecting small-town and rural facilities. Imbalanced growth appeared to have been as great a problem, if not a greater one in medical services as it was in other sectors. The operation of special government clinics caused considerable resentment on the part of medical personnel as well as ordinary citizens. In short, the state of the profession furnished powerful incentive to many to turn their backs on the GDR.

Events in late August took a dramatic turn for the worse from East Berlin's perspective. Some one hundred East Germans, holed up in the embassy in Budapest and insisting upon the right to emigrate to the FRG, were permitted safe conduct to Vienna under Red Cross protection. Although described as a "unique and not-to-be-repeated" measure by the Hungarian government, for the first time an East Bloc country had sanctioned the departure of East Germans to the West. Given the Hungarian track record, assurances meant little to an indignant East Berlin, which lambasted Hungary for violating its solemn obligations to the GDR, while charging the FRG with "nefarious slave trade" and "egregious" interference in others' internal affairs. But through its rhetoric the Politburo was awkwardly painting itself into a corner. Any dealings with Bonn on the matter would have been tantamount to negotiation on interference in the GDR's internal affairs, and by itself East Berlin was effectively powerless. To this the Politburo could not have been oblivious, yet it seemed to be going out of its way to alienate all parties.

By late August the GDR teemed with rumors that East Berlin was about to take the unprecedented step of placing Hungary administratively into the category of a Western country, segregating it from the fraternal socialist countries. A few leading West German newspapers surmised that East German officials planned to restrict travel to Hungary drastically, if not completely, by September 1. The East German media also made noises about such an eventuality, a sure indication of Politburo contemplations since East German journalists were not accustomed to speculate idly. East German commentators spoke of the Hungarian "betrayal of the socialist camp" and "growing Western provocations." Visitors to the GDR felt the force of the party's fury, as delays on the borders became more frequent and controls tightened. In the first week of August I experienced the greatest amount of border chicanery I ever had in years of travel to and from the GDR. Upon exiting the GDR we were delayed for over three hours as border guards rummaged through cars and luggage. The GDR appeared poised to seal itself off.

In the last days of August East Berlin sent a special envoy to Budapest in a desperate effort to enlist Hungarian support for a tougher line on the refugee problem. Upon his return, he was reported to have resignedly told the leadership that Budapest had no inclination to shore up the GDR, and had, moreover, lost control of matters. He expressed his belief that Bonn's influence with the Hungarians was far greater than East Berlin's. Another attempt by the SED shortly thereafter to lean on the Hungarians was equally unavailing. On September 5 Budapest discreetly notified East Berlin that six days later, beginning on September 11, East Germans would be authorized to cross the border into Austria legally and without special formalities. Speaking for an outraged Politburo, Sindermann called the move "a frontal assault against socialism."

In a later statement Schabowski recalled that several Politburo members realized at the time that the challenge East Berlin faced was fundamental; at stake was the system itself. "The weightiness of the situation had suddenly rolled onto the Politburo's table," he remarked.[34] And yet, an odd sense of unreality still prevailed. Honecker, returned from vacation and a hospitalization thereafter, seemed incapable of grasping what was happening around him. He blithely brushed aside official reports candidly warning that the large number of people wishing to emigrate was symptomatic of a more general mood in the country, that outright resignation was assuming massive proportions. A few in the Politburo pressed for clear official statements, even for some new accents. Loosening travel restrictions was one obvious way of attempting to get a handle on the matter, but such a bold move was fraught with risk and was not to be undertaken with Honecker in charge. In fact, no actions were taken, nor significant decisions made, and the Politburo appeared more or less content to assume a wait-and-see posture.

STIRRINGS AT HOME

In August came the first stirrings of genuine and open dissent in the GDR. These began as citizens' initiatives affiliated with the churches. The first to come forth publicly was organized by four pastors from Greifswald and Halle and an East Berlin member of a hitherto unknown group called Initiatives for Peace and Human Rights. The group's declared goal was the eventual establishment of an opposition social-democratic party. An August paper specified the principal demands:

1. rule of law and the strict separation of government powers;
2. parliamentary democracy and a multiplicity of parties;
3. a "social" state with ecological orientation;
4. regional political institutions and a "social" market economy;
5. independent unions with guaranteed right to strike;
6. freedom of information and assembly.[35]

Faint murmurings of opposition also began to surface in the media which the party had always undertaken to keep on the tightest leash. A commentary in the newspaper *Sonntag* criticized both emigration policies and travel restrictions, calling the former "a kind of poison . . . nurturing dissatisfaction and aggression."[36] The commentary recalled that the GDR had ratified the CSCE "Final Act" warranting freedom of travel and the right of all citizens to emigrate, a fairly bold memorandum of the sort circulated by dissidents, and quite remarkable appearing in a newspaper.

The soon-to-be-famous Leipzig Monday demonstration made its debut the third week of August, beginning quite modestly in the Nikolai Church in central Leipzig with the peace prayers that would precede each subsequent demonstration. Only a few hundred attended the initial prayer meetings and demonstrations, but the number of participants grew rapidly in September. On the fourth consecutive Monday over a thousand people turned out to demonstrate, a dramatic event in the GDR. Taking part in a public demonstration was risky business at the time and participants exposed themselves to brutality and arrest. But within six weeks of the first meeting the Nikolai Church was filled to overflowing, peace prayers were being held in many places of worship in the city, and afterward people were marching by the thousands.

Pastors in Leipzig and elsewhere began openly to advocate that the authorities commence public discussions about the acute problems facing the GDR. That so many citizens, the young in particular, were turning their backs on the country was distressing church officials, and the fashioning of a society where people truly wished to live had become an urgent task in the view of the religious communities. Pastor Friedrich Schorlemmer of the Leipzig Reformed Church called for a "democratic, social and ecological society." Describing the emigration and refugee waves as "indicative of the entire unhappy situation in the GDR," and denouncing the GDR's rulers for being rigidly bound by "yesterday's thinking and behavior," he insisted the GDR's problems could be solved only through openness and pluralism.[37] Expressing a fairly common opinion, a lay leader of the Nikolai Church said to a Western news agency at the time: "Political dissatisfaction is very strong. The feeling of people is that nothing is going on, that we have reached a state of stagnation. People have no trust that the government is even trying to solve the problems."[38]

Not by coincidence the demonstrations quickly acquired political overtones, spread beyond small groups of dissidents, and began drawing from a significant cross-section of society.[39] At the September 4 demonstration people were carrying placards demanding freedom of assembly, an open country for free people, and freedom of travel. Occasional chants of "Stasi out!" and "We shall overcome!" could be heard, and many protesters sported Gorbachev lapel pins as testimony of their desire for *glasnost* in the GDR. "Gorbachev is our hope. He allows people to speak out, to say what they think. If he succeeds, things here could change," commented a student taking part in the demonstration.[40] Security forces and police took most of the signs away from the demonstrators, arrested a few, but did not attack people or attempt to break up the assembly.

In the first week of September one also found the first mention of the occurrence of demonstrations in the GDR media. Prior to this time, protests were simply non-events. Then the press began to wield the propaganda mace. The party youth newspaper, *Junge Welt*, on September 6 called the Leipzig demonstrators "enemies of the state." In one of the first press articles concerned with protest and civil disturbance, *Junge Welt* disclosed the official frame of reference.

> How else, other than as enemies of the state, is one to describe those exclaiming "Away with the Wall" or "Away with the Communists"? Those are words which are against the laws of the GDR and against the Constitution. Involved is the defamation of millions of people who have built and are building the GDR, who work diligently, and in contrast to no-goods and drop-outs, appreciate our republic and wish to make it more attractive and friendlier, undisturbed by egoists and political rowdies. From this provocation we could ascertain how West German television in its continuous search for anti-socialist elements made a point of inviting itself once again. We were also able to see on West German television screens what was most decisive: that those who disturb the peace don't have a chance here. The comrades of the "People's Police" and the security apparatus acted decisively and prevented any public incitement to violation of GDR laws, as the Western media does often enough.[41]

Several days later in *Neues Deutschland* Axen provided a commentary. Though not necessarily a response to the demonstrations of that week (the page layout for the party organ is often done weeks in advance, an indication of the timeliness and accuracy of news reporting), the piece bespoke party delusions.

> With the socialist revolution . . . the gate of freedom has been swung open in our fatherland. With the socialist achievements in this socialist democracy human rights in their entirety, individual and collective, the right to a life in peace, the right to work and education, the equality of women and the basic rights of the younger generation have become reality.[42]

NOTES

1. *This Week in Germany,* October 13, 1989.
2. Quoted in Mike Dennis, *German Democratic Republic* (London: Pinter, 1988), 189.
3. David Childs, *The GDR* (London: Unwin Hyman, 1988), 326.
4. Dennis, *German Democratic Republic,* 100.
5. *Neues Deutschland,* April 10, 1987.
6. *Neues Deutschland,* November 25, 1988.
7. Quoted in Childs, *The GDR,* 326.
8. *Neues Deutschland,* November 25, 1988.
9. Julian Semyanov, "Stalin und der Krieg," *Sputnik* 10 (October 1988): 127-29; see also *Der Spiegel,* November 28, 1988.
10. *Neues Deutschland,* September 26, 1988.
11. Dennis, *German Democratic Republic,* 8.
12. Ibid.
13. Erich Honecker, *From My Life* (New York: Pergamon, 1981), 58-59.
14. The full text appeared in *Der Speigel,* December 5, 1988.
15. Childs, *The GDR,* 230-31.
16. *Neues Deutschland,* November 25, 1988.
17. *Der Spiegel,* November 28, 1988.
18. *Der Spiegel,* April 16, 1990.
19. Ibid.
20. Ibid.
21. *Der Spiegel,* November 27, 1989.
22. *Der Spiegel,* April 16, 1990.
23. Ibid.
24. Ibid.
25. Quoted in *The German Tribune,* April 16, 1989.
26. *Stuttgarter Zeitung,* November 27, 1989.
27. *Frankfurter Allgemeiner Zeitung,* June 16, 1989.
28. *Der Spiegel,* April 16, 1990.
29. *Die Zeit,* November 24, 1989.
30. Quoted in *Der Spiegel,* November 20, 1989.
31. *Der Spiegel,* April 16, 1990.
32. *Neues Deutschland,* August 12, 1989.
33. *Die Welt,* November 21, 1989.
34. *Der Spiegel,* April 16, 1990.
35. *Archiv der Gegenwart,* no. 22, October 2-18, 1989.
36. *Sonntag,* September 3, 1989.
37. *Archiv der Gegenwart,* no. 22, October 2-18, 1989.
38. *The Washington Post,* September 6, 1989.
39. *The Economist,* September 30, 1989.
40. *The Washington Post,* September 6, 1989.
41. *Junge Welt,* September 6, 1989.
42. *Neues Deutschland,* September 11, 1989.

8
Marx and God

CHURCHES IN THE GDR

The GDR was the only predominantly Protestant communist state of the East Bloc. In 1946 in what was to become the GDR, 81.6 percent of the population or 14,132,174 people at least nominally belonged to the Evangelical churches, while 12.2 percent of the population or 2,110,507 were Catholic.[1] Although devoid of party domination, the churches of the GDR were officially nonpolitical and operated in the main within certain accepted parameters. It is largely a matter of judgment whether the churches in the SED state, or under any other regime for that matter, adequately endeavored to uphold the central canons of Christianity, for example, worth of the individual, the dignity of the person, and the transcendent nature of earthly existence, or whether they were in fact over-accommodating. One must not, however, underestimate the essential nature and the intensity of the conflict between Marxism and Christianity. The categorical opposition of Christianity to communist designs nurtured permanent disapproval of the SED on the part of numerous believers, and accordingly, the churches in the GDR never had a completely harmonious relationship with the party. That said, since the late 1950s the state plainly attempted to muster church support in its quest for legitimacy. A 1958 meeting between the all-German Evangelical Church organization (EKD) and SED officials ended with the following communiqué: "In accordance with their beliefs, Christians will fulfill their responsibilities as citizens on the basis of law. They will respect the development of socialism and will participate in the peaceful building of the community."[2] Concurrently, the SED insisted upon the founding of the so-called Organization of Evangelical Pastors, which committed itself to the internal and external strengthening of the socialist society of the GDR in a program announced at the time. This group, for unspecified reasons, voluntarily dissolved itself in 1974, possibly for lack of interest.

In October 1960, Ulbricht, citing the communiqué of 1958, stated in a *Volkskammer* speech promulgating the end of what had in fact been a decade of fostered atheism and anticlericalism in the GDR that Christianity and the "humanistic goals of socialism" had a great deal in common.[3] Thereafter, in several well-publicized meetings with religious leaders, the SED chief stressed the "very deep humanistic goals" of the socialist society as well as the "commonalities between Marxist and Christian principles." In the Wartburg Talk of August 1964, Ulbricht and the Bishop of Thuringia, Moritz Mitzenheim, the Protestant Church leader willing to go furthest in cooperating with the SED, released a statement to the effect that Marxists and Christians were bound by their "common humanistic responsibility."[4] Hoping to increase church support for his regime, Ulbricht endeavored to gain explicit EKD endorsement of the building of socialism, as opposed to a mere tolerance of it. Not content with a modus vivendi, he went so far as to encourage church leaders to condemn the (West German) "NATO churches," which would have been a startling position for a nonpolitical religious community but was a potential propaganda coup the SED would never bring off.[5]

In 1969 the SED achieved a significant breakthrough in its church policy when the eight regional organizations of the Evangelical Church withdrew from the all-German EKD. The move seemed to accord church recognition to Germany's division, while obviating the need on the SED's part to deal with large church organizations straddling the inner-German border. It had the added feature from the SED's perspective of rendering the Evangelical Church more amenable to state control.[6] The SED had removed the "all-German" attributes of the organized Protestant churches it had found so objectionable. The State Secretaries for Church Affairs rather unabashedly attempted thereafter to play one church off against another, while the bloc parties, including the East CDU, to the chagrin of many Christians, lent the SED support in the ongoing campaigns against remaining all-German church associations.[7] Mitzenheim's not uncontroversial statement at the time that "The borders of the GDR correspond to the limits of the churches' organizational possibilities"[8] displayed an aura of resignation. The Catholic Church, while not following suit, did nonetheless recognize the reality of the situation, and accordingly furnished its dioceses in the GDR with more independent authority.[9] Catholicism, however, maintained a more circumspect distance from the SED, resisting any schemes to redraw ecclesiastical boundaries to coincide with national boundaries, and stipulating in some cases that the Politburo deal not with local bishops but with the Vatican.[10]

Honecker, who it may be presumed felt rather more comfortable with the faithful than Ulbricht, took additional steps to improve relations between church and state, conceding in 1973 to allow greater contacts between East and West German religious communities, secure in the knowledge most of these would remain organizationally separate.[11] He approved of more extensive ties between East German churches and co-religionists in other East Bloc states, and, in addition, promised to reduce discrimination against those practicing their religion. Setting the tone for what it doubtless hoped would be an improved rapport with the state, the East German Organization of Evangelical Churches announced in 1971: "We do not strive to be a Church against socialism or alongside socialism, but a Church within socialism."[12]

Nonetheless, the churches did not limit their activities to the religious sphere in a way that would have been to the liking of Honecker, and as a consequence some frictions ensued. The church position that "The individual Christian and the Christian Community as a whole can understand the divine service only as divine service of life in its entirety" was widely and correctly taken as an expression of abiding church interest in social development.[13] The religious communities insisted upon maintaining at most "critical solidarity" with the GDR, the very principle of which disturbed Honecker, since criticism of any sort was not something the SED countenanced. On those occasions when the churches were perceived to be addressing political issues, as for example, when the East German Protestant bishops publicly opposed the 1975 UN General Assembly resolution condemning Zionism as racism that the GDR was strongly endorsing, the SED warned the religious communities about interference.

TENSIONS GROW

Following the ratification of the Helsinki Final Act, the SED demonstrated a somewhat greater willingness to advise church officials of the purposes and goals of its policies, without requesting any direct church input into these. For all that, considerable ambiguities in church-state relations marked the years 1976-1978. On the positive side the Politburo consented to allow additional construction of churches and community centers in the new socialist settlements ringing major cities, which had for the most part been without religious facilities or spiritual guidance and were thus subjects of considerable preoccupation for church officials. But discrimination against believers persisted in education and on the job, and irrefutable evidence of this continuously surfaced. The matter gained wide currency in a grisly fashion, when on August 18, 1976, Pastor Oskar Brüsewitz publicly lit himself ablaze in an act of self-immolation to protest regime policies.[14] The suicide shocked not only religious leaders but some state officials as well, for it was rather evident the man was neither insane nor a crank. Such a desperate act, suggesting all was not well in the workers' and farmers' state, was hardly the sort of publicity the SED wanted at any time, let alone just after the GDR had emerged proud and triumphant from the CSCE negotiation. Individual spiritual leaders and to some extent the church organizations were inclined thereafter to take firmer moral and political stands.

Subsequently, the churches began to voice concerns about the quite evident contradiction between the official view of the overtly materialistic socialist personality and Christian principles. On several counts these were plainly incompatible and it was hard to escape the conclusion that the faithful were subjected to regular chicanery in the GDR. Yet another bone of contention involved the constitutional guarantee of freedom of religion and conscience.[15] Promulgation of the new party program in 1977 would disclose that all the basic rights anchored in the 1974 Constitution with the exception of guarantees of freedom of religion and conscience were included. All churches expressed bewilderment. According to Article 39 of the Constitution:

(1)   Every citizen of the GDR has the right to profess religious faith and to practice religion.
(2)   Churches and other religious communities conduct their affairs and carry out their activities in conformity with the Constitution and legal provisions of the GDR. Specifics can be settled in follow-on agreements.[16]

It is against this background that the March 1978 meeting between Honecker and the governing committee of the Evangelical Church must be seen. To this day no one has provided a satisfactory answer to the question why exactly the constitutional provision on religious freedom was deleted from the 1977 party program, especially in light of the fact that the GDR had ratified a set of ground rules for international conduct in the Helsinki Accords which included such a provision in the Basket Three section.

Following the 1978 meeting the churches received some modest concessions from the state. More time was allocated for religious broadcasting on radio and television. Permission for more church construction in urban areas was provided.[17] In an official Council of State proclamation Honecker praised the "positive and humanitarian role" of the religious communities in socialism, while highlighting the complete equality of opportunity in the GDR, notwithstanding certain differences in *Weltanschauung*.[18] Honecker assured church leaders that Christians would always find "purpose and perspective" in the workers' and farmers' state. In reply the Protestant bishops somewhat austerely stipulated the criterion they would in the future apply in judging the actual situation of the faithful in society, namely, that church-state relations would be measured according to the specific circumstances of each individual Christian. In other words, discrimination against one would be regarded as discrimination against all. Although Honecker did not formally reject this notion, the likelihood of East German society ever having been able to meet such a criterion was a remote one.

Any relaxation of tensions, though, received a significant check from the church-state controversy surrounding the militarization of the society that developed the same year. January 1978 had brought the introduction of compulsory paramilitary training (*Wehrerziehung*) in the schools which virtually all religious communities resolutely decried.[19] In addition to finding fault with the policy generally, the churches insisted upon the accordance of conscientious objector status to individuals, a right never recognized in the GDR and a delicate issue. Both moral and political arguments against *Wehrerziehung* were advanced, with not a few religious leaders cautioning the state about the tarnishing of the country's international image that greater bellicism in an already highly militarized society would effect. Rather brusquely rejecting the criticisms, the SED pursued its new educational policy undeterred, a course of action ensuring the continuation of church-state disaccord. Making little effort to conceal its dismay, the Evangelical Church issued the following statement later in the year

> As we understand it, church officials and laypersons are called upon in deed and in witness to strengthen the German Democratic Republic, to preserve peace and to administer to mankind and each individual . . . the chief issue being a new orientation toward salient societal questions with a more definitive Church position in our socialist society.[20]

The Evangelical Church then proceeded to proclaim its own program entitled Education for Peace.[21] SED leaders were not pleased.

Following the emergence of the free trade union Solidarity in Poland, the SED became acutely nervous about the possibility of church appeals for peace and individual professions of pacifism in the religious communities evolving into grass-roots peace movements that might eventually have formed the nucleus of a veritable political opposition. The GDR responded with repressive measures which further exacerbated church-state relations. Foreign correspondents were routinely denied permission to cover church conventions and other meetings. Church newspapers printing anything considered political, for example, articles about Poland or the Soviet invasion of Afghanistan, were not permitted to be delivered through the mail and were sometimes seized. On several occasions the Evangelical News Agency (ENA), along with all five weekly Evangelical newspapers, alluded to an increase in official pressure upon them. Religious leaders called attention to what they perceived to be the notable rise in discrimination against young Christians, especially ones not displaying enthusiasm for military training and service.[22] The official press openly criticized the joint consultations on the "responsibility for peace" and other issues between East and West German churches. Church reminders of the nondiscrimination criterion were for the most part unavailing.

Then the SED unhesitantly offered to join hands with the Evangelical Church to celebrate the five hundredth anniversary of Martin Luther's birth in 1983. The Luther Committee established for this purpose was divided into secular and religious components, headed by Honecker and Bishop Werner Leich of Eisenach, respectively. The importance the state attached to the celebration underscored the anniversary's role in the GDR's quest for legitimacy. Sizeable secular and religious celebrations took place, although these remained for the most part separate. Bishop Leich, who was to find himself thrust into an influential position during the upheaval in the fall of 1989, spoke of Luther in a not altogether uncritical manner at the inaugural meeting of the committee in 1980. His words, reprinted verbatim in the official press, today seem almost prophetic.

> (Luther) respected the social order and the administrative prerogative of government as ordained by God for the preservation of life and human society on earth. Grasping the problem of tension-laden freedom, Luther boldly contradicted princes and disassociated himself from social developments if they did not in his judgment live up to their God-given task of guaranteeing life, justice and peace. . . . We want to be serious about the fact that Martin Luther was never regarded as a guiltless or infallible man and that he exposed himself to the judgment of others. . . . We find ourselves in inner agreement with the Reformer when we say openly what in our view is to be considered as a wrong decision.[23]

THE CHURCHES NURTURE DISSENT

In a word, equivocacy was always a keynote of church-state relations in the GDR, and superficial partnership was punctuated by phases of tension, along with scattered rounds of repression. The Luther anniversary celebrations and period thereafter represented no exception to this rule. During the anniversary year, party representatives referred to the desirability of "mutual respect" between Marxists and Christians. In an April 1984 speech in Brandenburg, Klaus Gysi, State Secretary for Church Affairs, spoke of the "splendid chances" for Christians in East German society and appealed for more "reciprocal understanding."[24] All the same, on at least two separate occasions in 1987, security forces raided church publishers in East Berlin on trumped-up charges, and in the following year, police employed brutal force against an outdoor prayer meeting, arresting dozens of people, and putting several in the hospital, including members of a West German camera crew filming the unusual event.

But the relative independence of the churches in the GDR usually enabled them to serve as sanctuaries for the exercise of rights that would have been unthinkable outside their walls. As the only places people could assemble legally, in the 1980s churches became forums for the free expression of political ideas. Only in the churches did one hear objections to the militarization of East German society, to the stationing of more nuclear weapons on German soil, to the arms race. As the SED had feared several years earlier, embryonic peace movements centered around the churches did indeed catalyze opposition in the GDR. Churches in 1989 became tribunals of protest and havens of opposition. There, people young and old, political and apolitical, from all walks of life, could express dissatisfaction and exchange ideas relatively freely. Within church walls, people could air views the party branded "unsocialist" at best, and more likely "counterrevolutionary." But police and security forces didn't dare as a rule enter church property to crack down on dissent the way they did unflinchingly anywhere else. The forerunner of the ubiquitous Gorbachev pins of the late 1980s that were among the first visible signs of outright defiance, was the "swords into plowshares" badge of the East German peace movements emerging around 1981. That this phrase from the Old Testament was embraced by the Soviet Union when advancing its disarmament proposals, and was, in fact, rendered tangible for the United Nations by Soviet sculptor Evgeny Vuchetich, is one of the paradoxes of the GDR's revolution. Wasn't it the SED that coined the phrase, "Learning from the Soviet Union means learning to be victorious?"

Not by coincidence did the fall demonstrations begin with church assemblies and divine services. At the outset of the now famous Monday demonstration in Leipzig were the obligatory prayer meetings in the city's major churches. Just the same, the blending of the spiritual and the political was seldom as complete as it was in Poland. Religious fervor did not reach the intensity it had there. But this arguably was in keeping with the somewhat staid nature of Prussian Protestantism and the Lutheran gospel of obedience to secular authority. One must also be cautious about criticizing the churches for complacency in the GDR. It would have been illusory to believe that Lutheranism by itself could have solved any of the longer-term social or political problems of the GDR had only the churches become more involved in politics. The churches repeatedly, and correctly, asserted that they could not assume the role of the political opposition. To do so, it was argued, would have meant a transgression of the churches' pious and unworldly mission. There was at least one other quite apparent reason: the Church spoke for a far smaller percentage of the population than did the Catholic Church in Poland.

With certainty many people with no particular religious leanings used the churches as a refuge from repression. At the same time, churches were pulled by events to help bring about reform. The churches assumed an important mediating role in the fall of 1989, when, on several occasions, church leaders discouraged the police from using force against demonstrators and assisted in persuading party leaders not to order the police to crush demonstrations.

The first major church initiative in response to the crisis in the GDR came in the form of a letter dated September 2 from the Conference of Evangelical Churches to the Politburo, appealing for a reduction of tensions and calling for across-the-board political rethinking. Expressing particular disquiet about the mass exodus from the GDR (it should be remembered here that the Hungarian border wasn't yet officially open), church representatives stated categorically that, as Christians have a moral duty to change themselves, so too do they bear social responsibilities, especially in times of trouble. Thus, the Evangelical churches considered themselves obliged to work for a better society which people would no longer wish to leave.

> The Conference does not pretend to be able to offer any short-term solution to the present difficulties. It regards official rejection of long overdue reforms in the society as the salient cause of the large-scale exodus. It regards a process facilitating majority participation in social life and a fruitful public discussion of current problems, one enhancing popular trust of state organs as imperative. We therefore urgently and once again request the following:
> - an open and realistic discussion of the causes of dissatisfaction and of the serious flaws in our society but above all the avoidance of stereotyped public information or threats;
> - consideration of citizen criticisms with an aim to effecting the change that will benefit all;
> - the furnishing of accurate information in all areas of politics and economics as well as honest media reporting, putting an end to the daily contradictions between everyday life and official portrayals;
> - an acknowledgment that state officials have to respect all as fellow citizens and to treat no one as a subject;
> - that all citizens be free to travel to other countries;
> - that former citizens who left the GDR be allowed to return without prejudice.[25]

The Politburo failed even to respond to the missive. Less than two weeks later on September 14, the East German Catholic Bishops' Conference announced its growing apprehensions about the situation in the GDR. That "too many people desire to leave the GDR, while others withdraw to the private sphere in resignation" worried the bishops most, as was the case with their Protestant counterparts.[26] Underscoring the urgent need for sweeping reform, the bishops proclaimed their intention "to raise these problems and their causes in discussions with state authorities." The latter, however, showed no inclination to listen. The Catholic Church could not even, as O. Henry put it, "inject a few raisins of conversation into the tasteless dough of existence."

Marx described his concept of "otherworldliness" in the following way:

> Religion is both the expression of real distress and the protest against real distress. Religion is the sign of the oppressed creature, the heart of the heartless world and the spirit of a spiritless situation. It is the opium of the people.[27]

Marx's words seem almost uncanny. Wraithlike, they would come back to haunt the GDR's rulers, for the churches had an instrumental, albeit indirect, role in their toppling.

NOTES

1. Kurt Hutten, *Christen hinter dem eisernen Vorhang* (Stuttgart: Quell-Verlag, 1963), 26-27.

2. *DDR Handbuch*, vol. 1, 721.

3. Roland Smith, "The Church in the German Democratic Republic," in *Honecker's Germany*, ed. David Childs (London: Allen and Unwin, 1985), 66-68.

4. *DDR Handbuch*, vol. 1, 722.

5. *Die Zeit*, August 29, 1967.

6. Arthur Hanhardt, Jr., *The German Democratic Republic* (Baltimore: Johns Hopkins University Press, 1968), 83.

7. *DDR Handbuch*, vol. 2, 1299.

8. *DDR Handbuch*, vol. 1, 720.

9. Childs, *The GDR*, 93.

10. *DDR Handbuch*, vol. 2, 1300.

11. A. James McAdams, *East Germany and Detente* (Cambridge: Cambridge University Press, 1985), 138.

12. *DDR Handbuch*, vol. 1, 723.

13. Ibid.

14. Ibid., 724.

15. Childs, *The GDR*, 93.

16. *The Constitution of the German Democratic Republic*, 28.

17. *Frankfurter Allgemeiner Zeitung*, March 7, 1978.

18. *Neues Deutschland*, March 7, 1978.

19. *DDR Handbuch*, vol. 2, 1,467-70.

20. *EPD Dokumentation*, no. 15 (1978).

21. *DDR Handbuch*, vol. 1, 725.

22. Ibid.

23. This appeared in the official publication *Panorama DDR 1980*, quoted in Childs, *The GDR*, 94.

24. *DDR Handbuch*, vol. 1, 726.

25. *Archiv der Gegenwart*, no. 22, October 2-18, 1989.

26. *Frankfurter Allgemeiner Zeitung*, September 16, 1989.

27. Smith, "The Church in the German Democratic Republic," 66.

9
The SED Alone

THE MEANING OF THE EXODUS

Observers subsequently began to grasp the deeper problems confronting the GDR. There had in fact been indications of fundamental difficulties more than a year before, when, for example, requests for exit visas surged and the SED started to face a veritable departure wave.[1] The greater leniency the regime had been showing when processing applications to visit the West did not result in a reduction in the number of citizen requests to emigrate, as had been hoped. On the contrary, the number continued to climb. A tougher line on travel and the arrest of some filing for exit visas brought despair and disgruntlement which, in turn, drove the numbers higher. The SED found itself caught in a impasse that was to be a preview for the following year.

Why had the magnitude of the GDR's political and social problems been so widely underestimated? Relative openness to the West notwithstanding, the GDR, it must be recalled, was a tightly controlled society, devoid of a free press, where unbiased opinion polls were rare and findings kept secret anyway, where expressions of citizen concern remained unvoiced, where opposition was swiftly suppressed. In short, the GDR remained a largely closed, somewhat enigmatic society. Because of the difficulty of seeing into that society and uncovering concealed features of it, few in the West foresaw the events of the fall of 1989 until the floodwaters poured out. Not surprisingly perhaps, some in the Soviet leadership had a better perspective of SED problems than did many in the West. A spokesman of the CPSU Central Committee, Nikolay Shishlin, commenting on the situation in the East Bloc, said in January 1989, "I hope everything will be changed. You are seeing these events in East Germany. We do understand the meaning of these events." Shishlin did not elaborate upon the "meaning" of events he was discussing, but his words now seem almost premonitory.

What the mass exodus beginning that August demonstrated above all was that nearly thirty years of supposed societal consolidation replete with "socialist intensification" had achieved little in the way of rallying people to the goals and purposes of the SED. The drastic measures of 1961 gained the SED an extended reprieve, but the regime failed in the longer term to inculcate its values in the population, and to develop popular allegiance to the cultural values representative of the system. Largely absent were the cultural and social resources which were indispensable to the party's championing of citizen attitudes that the regime was proper and deserving of support. True, the SED seemed increasingly comfortable invoking national identity and fostering a sense of history, but in spite of marked efforts to attune the East German present with the all-German past, the party's socialist purposes and goals failed to supplant a popular feeling of Germanness, or to convince the citizenry that the regime safeguarded German values. Nor did the regime succeed in establishing the structures that would have made possible a generalized respect for the correctness of decision-making and adjudicative procedures. The SED was closely identified with a foreign power, and the final guarantee of regime security was the Soviet army, a disaffecting combination in the minds of most East Germans. Furthermore, the SED's articulated set of ideals remained empty, devoid as these were of any notions of popular participation. For, despite party acclamations of socialist progress and achievement, in the forced stabilization period after 1961 people in the GDR failed to gain the least amount of self-determination.

SOCIALIST NATION-BUILDING

Some Western observers were given to arguing that what had emerged twenty-five years after the building of the Wall was a fundamentally stronger and more self-confident East German state.[2] The outward self-confidence and smooth manner of Honecker and his cohorts were often interpreted in the West, not wholly without basis, as evidence of growing regime strength as well as emerging national identity. The GDR was, by most accounts, an industrialized, relatively modern, highly militarized police welfare state, and many considered it reasonable to suppose that East Germans prized the modest security of this welfarism, notwithstanding the GDR's obvious political drawbacks.[3]

It was not only Westerners who thought this way. Bahro, who did time in Honecker's jails for airing his views, and thus had learned his anti-Stalinism the hard way, can scarcely be imputed to have been a regime apologist. His comments to the *New Left Review* are noteworthy:

> You find that workers will grouse and swear about conditions when they are in their factory, but when some well-heeled uncle arrives on a visit from West Germany, they stand up for the GDR and point out all the good things about it,

all the disadvantages they had to overcome after 1945, and so on. Although the state's demands for loyalty are widely resented, I would say that in normal, crisis-free times there is a sufficiently high degree of loyalty to assure the country's stability. . . . The increase in international recognition has certainly boosted the sense of loyalty to the state.[4]

Outward appearances can deceive, however, and the East German state's track record on nation-building was, as so many things in human affairs, fraught with discrepancies. For the SED the 1980s was the best of times and the worst of times. Whatever position Western analysts might have taken with respect to the nation-building process in the GDR, the SED itself viewed this process as incomplete. The walling-in of people and the operation of a meddling security apparatus were signs of regime insecurity, tacit admission of the short measure of a veritable civic culture. The regime's basic mistrust of its citizens induced it to handle them callously, even with condescension. The people, for their part, felt put upon by a regime so wary and suspicious that it prevented them from traveling abroad, and maintained a brutal secret police to harass them.

Yet, prior to 1989, the true standing of the regime with its people was not easy to assess, and gauging the progression of nation-building in the GDR remained for the most part a matter of conjecture. Inherently related to nation-building issues was the SED rapport with Moscow. Beyond the ideological affinity, the SED judged the relationship with the Soviet state as the country's most vital self-interest, assuming the SED thought in such terms at all. This self-interest was constitutionally enshrined by Honecker's government in Article 6 of the 1974 Constitution, which stated: "The German Democratic Republic is forever and irrevocably allied with the Union of Soviet Socialist Republics. The close and fraternal alliance with it guarantees the people of the German Democratic Republic continued progress along the road of socialism and peace." This was also unmistakably expressed in the 1975 Treaty of Friendship, Cooperation and Mutual Assistance between the GDR and the USSR which spoke of "relations of eternal and inviolable friendship and fraternal mutual assistance in all fields."[5]

A typical bit of national self-praise, as in Honecker's statement, "the citizens of our republic need not fear social insecurity, unemployment, inflation, or any of the other faults of capitalism; they have no fears of tomorrow," was invariably followed by a provision of credit to the Soviet Union. East Germans tended to regard such glorification with distaste, not only on a more rational level because few acknowledged, rightly or wrongly, that the Soviet Union deserved any credit for the GDR's accomplishments, but viscerally as well since the close identification conjured up in many minds something distinctly foreign about the regime. In this way the paramount vital self-interest of the SED state in fact militated against popular acceptance of it, and consequently represented a stumbling block to nation-building. And it was ironic that in the end Honecker would have the tables turned on him, whereby a people hitherto ungratified by accolades to Moscow began lauding the Soviet Union for policies SED leaders found anathema: *glasnost* and *perestroika*.

Strains in relations that were the innate product of the GDR's will to self-assertion and Moscow's alliance policies surfaced as early as the 1960s. The unpitying grindstone of daily policy making had taught Honecker that he would have to accept certain contradictions and quandaries. Chief among these was the incongruity between his country's national interests, chiefly the GDR's relations with the West, and fraternal alliance interests. "National interest" is not a term that passed communist lips easily, and the West German position on the special relationship between the German states that was grounded in common nationality, was vigorously rebuked by East Berlin. In regime propaganda the FRG remained the "class enemy."

In the 1970s, though, inter-German relations started rapidly evolving into that knotty and complex community of interests it became in the 1980s. However ideologically unpalatable a special relationship with the enemy might have been for the SED, the latter acquired a certain vested interest in rapprochement between the Germanys. One example of the importance Honecker attached to inter-German detente was the one already examined—his appeal for a coalition of reason during the mini cold war in the 1980s. Honecker apparently feared, as did many Germans on both sides of the border, that a chill in the *Grosswetterlage* ("the overall climate") would adversely affect the Germanys who, it must be said, had the most at stake in the detente process. Honecker's subsequent damage limitation policies, widely perceived as being designed to maintain a business-as-usual relationship with the FRG, were on occasion roundly condemned by Moscow as crude efforts to pursue pan-German interests at the expense of neighboring states.[6] The Kremlin went so far as to suggest that the national interests of some of its socialist allies—the GDR and Hungary were singled out—were incompatible with its own. Later, in a stunning reversal of roles, East Berlin would launch verbal attacks against the Soviet Union, the point of contention being the latter's reform policies that raised much broader issues. In one view, the debacle of the GDR stemmed principally from its inability to reconcile national interests with international ones. Foreign policy has been described as the management of contradictions: in its short history the GDR confronted more than its share of these.

Such a line of reasoning rests upon a number of assumptions, chief among these being that SED leaders harbored national sensibilities, and thought in terms of national interests. There are, of course, differing interpretations. Some observers suggested that the SED, being a Communist party, never regarded the GDR as a country with national interests, and that to employ such terms was to project Western concepts and values onto a party elite not sharing these.[7] Using such terms in analyzing a communist society, went the argument, was to run the risk of saying things that were essentially meaningless. According to Seiffert, the party leadership was not disposed to think in terms of national interest, but instead considered the GDR first and foremost the "instrument of Soviet power in Germany."[8]

The use of dubiously applicable terms in communist settings wasn't the only problem one encountered in analyzing German national issues, as we have already seen. In addressing such issues, one entered what Schweigler described as "the thicket of confusion created by the various German distinctions between *Staat, Nationalstaat*, and *Nation*."[9] SED policies had to be viewed in the context of a divided nation with an uncertain identity. The diverse SED interpretations of German identity and nationhood over the years—the efforts to create state-supporting myths through historical reinterpretation, the seemingly contradictory positions taken by party officials with regard to the nation and identity—indicate that the SED was prone to considerable cross-currents. The GDR leadership endeavored to maintain a certain level of national consciousness, while working to consolidate a socialist state whose ultimate goal was the development of the "new man." Claiming to be the inheritor of positive German traditions and the best strands of progressive German history, a posture that became much more distinct in the 1980s, the GDR undertook to combine the new with the old in awkward ways. The goose-stepping soldiers of the NVA (National People's Army) who wore uniforms remarkably like those of the *Wehrmacht* evinced a German (or Prussian) national consciousness to a far greater extent than they did a socialist state consciousness. Nationhood questions necessarily entered into SED thinking, but certainly SED leaders did not believe that *Nationalbewusstsein* coincided with socialist state consciousness on all points. Even if most SED leaders agreed in principle that the party's chief task was to further Soviet interests, Soviet leaders themselves were not always of one mind about those interests. Determination of national interests is an involved and subjective process even in mature polities unhampered by the ideological shackles of Marxism-Leninism. And sufficient ambiguity in Soviet policy existed on such fundamental matters as the U.S. presence in Europe, relations with Western Europe, and the plethora of German issues, to unsettle SED leaders from time to time. The Gorbachev era not only increased differences of opinion in the Soviet Union, but openly encouraged the venting of these.

In 1989 the Soviet Union began to force the pace of political reform, an enterprise that, in the course of things, led to Soviet sanctioning of an end to the power monopoly in the GDR, at which point the SED confronted the horrible paradox of being implicitly charged with its own radical restructuring, if not its eventual dissolution. The dilemma for the SED in the wake of the Soviet decision to apply the principle of freedom of choice to the East Bloc was acutely agonizing. The principle brought with it the obvious risk of the ultimate elimination of the GDR. If Germans chose some form of federation, the Kremlin was prepared to drop its instrument of power in Germany. SED leaders had cause in fact to fear such an eventuality before, in March 1952, say, when Stalin offered German unification in exchange for neutrality.[10] Whether Stalin meant the proposal seriously is largely beside the point. As Samuel Johnson once commented: "Depend on it, when a man knows he is about to be hanged in a fortnight, it concentrates his mind wonderfully." Similarly, a regime does not negotiate about its existence. If the great paradox of 1989 was that the SED was being ordered to obliterate itself, fears that the party's dissolution would be sanctioned in one way or another by the Soviet Union were not new ones.

Anxieties about civil turmoil in the GDR or a political arrangement leading to dissolution weighed heavily on SED minds before 1955. With the specter of social unrest resurfacing in the late 1960s, Ulbricht recoiled in horror at the prospect of multi-party pluralism in Czechoslovakia, and thereafter adamantly resisted detente with the West. Ulbricht actually went so far as to challenge Soviet leadership when he felt that the latter, principally through the pursuit of detente, was not acting in the best interests of the bloc. In the abstract, therefore, GDR and Soviet interests diverged at a particular point, and in 1989 such divergence ceased being theoretical. Even if Honecker and Ulbricht, as devout communists, had no German national sensibilities, both were in all likelihood cognizant of the potential deviation of Soviet interests from those of their state. The contention that SED leaders harbored few strong feelings about the nation furthermore begs the question whether they were clear in their own minds with respect to differences between feelings about the GDR and feelings about the German nation, that is, whether there was an unconfused distinction between GDR *Staatsbewusstsein* and German *Nationalbewusstsein*.

One can presume that the widening gulf between East Berlin and Moscow in the late 1980s triggered a Soviet decision to let the GDR go. Gorbachev's verbal assaults on ideological stereotypes beginning in 1986 put him at odds with Honecker and his Politburo, since Gorbachev unquestionably had Honecker in mind when launching them. If the principal mission of SED policies was to further Soviet power interests in Central Europe as the SED defined these, this constituted the sort of ideological "old thinking" Gorbachev wanted to change. It was this expanding rift between East Berlin and Moscow that prompted Falin to speak in the summer of 1989 of the "alienation" between the SED and the CPSU, and the "small reservoir of common political views" between the two parties. The Falin memorandum suggests the Soviet leadership determined that differences of interest between the USSR and the GDR were becoming irreconcilable. Had Honecker and his Politburo wanted to persuade the Kremlin that the GDR was an expensive (and expendable) outpost, their statements and actions after 1987 could hardly have been more persuasive.

NATIONAL QUESTIONS REVISITED

However harsh the rhetoric of inter-German relations might have been at times, Honecker frequently insinuated he took pride in the forging of a tacit German community of interests, and both at home and abroad he was closely identified with this achievement. Through it he presumably garnered personal support within the party, in spite of the friction the German rapport might occasionally have caused with the eastern neighbors. Whatever his true motives, it is altogether possible that Honecker had a certain emotional attachment to inter-German detente. Gaus and other observers submitted that he pursued such a course in part because of national sensibilities. Paradoxically, in the face of Soviet criticism for pursuing pan-German interests and ignoring internationalist obligations in the early 1980s, Honecker received unaccustomed commendation from his countrymen for "standing up to Moscow." As a politician Honecker could not have been completely oblivious to such public acceptance of his actions, however grudging this acceptance might have been. Did public acclaim affect his actions?

To this question no easy answer comes. But the GDR's national problem stemmed in large part from the widespread popular rejection of Soviet politics and culture, which in turn promoted dissatisfaction with the local political structures these were accredited with having established. The use of Soviet troops first to install, then to prop up communist regimes had intensified popular resentment. Citizen antipathy toward foreign military forces was as great if not greater than it was in any other European country, East or West. Sheer numbers added to the vexation. Since World War II, the GDR served as the Soviet front line against NATO. The Virginia-sized country teemed with Soviet weaponry and troops. It was virtually impossible not to encounter Soviet military units when visiting an East German city, and traffic tie-ups due to the movement of armored columns were not infrequent. Common citizen displeasure did not focus on single issues only, though, but instead were directed against the system, and East Germans saw no distinction between theirs and the Soviet version. What was at times lost in the myriad of debates about identity and national consciousness was the basic fact that the average East German regarded the GDR far less as a homeland with its own interests than as a Soviet vassal state. Until 1989 East Germans were unable to express their opinions on such matters, but it was their views which ultimately counted. As an everyday example of citizen resentment vis-à-vis the system, the Russian language had been a compulsory subject in schools since the 1940s, and yet many East Germans were defiantly proud not to be able to speak it.

The example is prosaic, the implications profound. For a proper perspective, one need only think of the English that crept into the West German vocabulary, the American slang that was part of every West German schoolboy's speech, and the zest of many young West Germans for rock-and-roll. There can be little doubt that the Americanization of West Germany, and of Europe for that matter, was much more extensive than the Sovietization of the former GDR.[11] Even fleeting observation of the GDR revealed the intense Germanness one did not find in the FRG. People are predisposed to associate most closely with a system when they view it as representing themselves, or in some fundamental way being extensions of themselves. They become most attached to it when they deem it a vehicle for realizing their own ends. The lack of popular identification with system roles in the GDR undoubtedly elevated German national consciousness among the populace, giving added emphasis to the *Bewusstseinsnation.*

It follows then that the GDR citizen's notion of freedom had acquired a dual connotation: freedom *to* and freedom *from.* "Freedom to" referred to directing one's own life and to personal liberties generally. "Freedom from," on the other hand, meant at one and the same time freedom from domestic fear and from external domination. Fear and external domination were different sides of the same coin. Though too little attention was paid to this crucial juxtaposition in the West, and it presided, in all likelihood, mostly within the subconscious of East German minds, its identification explains the totality of the break with the system once the old guard departed the political scene. In a bit of star-gazing at the end of 1988, Michael Howard suggested the GDR would become a very different place once the aged SED leaders had been removed either through political or biological attrition. He could not have been more correct, though no one could have foreseen the immensity and, above all, the suddenness of change.

If one can accept this premise about the duality of the East German notion of freedom, the next step in the argument seems clear. As the regime tottered, "freedom from" to many East Germans, certainly to a majority of them, rapidly became synonymous with the dissolution of the GDR, since this would have brought about the freedom from fear as well as the freedom from foreign domination nearly all wished. Notwithstanding occasional rows, the SED state always strove to make itself indispensable to Moscow. But an inescapable dilemma for the SED, a seemingly irreconcilable regime predicament, was that affinity with the Soviet Union remained a domestic liability. Citizens of the GDR had not internalized its values, and complicating matters immensely was the pull of a common German nationality. National identity in the GDR was one of the unknowns of the German question, but in the final analysis the civic orientation of GDR citizens was toward a German *Nationalstaat.*

The rapport between the Germanys that developed from the detente process compelled the SED to be continuously mindful of the potential domestic instability exposure to the West might have generated. Apprehension on the SED's part about forces considered threatening to the GDR's social order dated back to the founding of the GDR. Fearing in the 1960s that their internal efforts to strengthen regime legitimacy would be undermined by exposure to the West,

SED leaders resisted the detente process altogether, only later, in yet another paradox, to become earnest advocates of the process. What caused such a volte-face?

The explanation lies in the character of the relationship that emerged. The limited opening of the country in the 1970s did not immediately endanger the GDR's social order, and many political as well as economic benefits began to accrue to the GDR from the detente process. The "one nation, two country" formula of the 1972 Basic Treaty, though not wholly satisfactory to the SED, nonetheless motivated it to accept detente, especially after the process seemed to be one working to the GDR's advantage. That detente offered a means of getting a grip on systemic legitimacy was very likely a notion entering into SED thoughts.[12] Universal recognition of the GDR, it was reasoned, would enhance the country's stature, and thereby enable it to overcome lingering legitimacy problems. Such was the modern East German version of the *Primat der Aussenpolitik* ("the primacy of foreign policy"). Hence, the SED position on the detente process had come full circle: from believing it would undermine efforts to bolster legitimacy to employing it for that very purpose. For most of the 1970s and 1980s detente seemed to be serving the country's interests at a minimum cost, that is, with only sporadic dissent and domestic unrest. For a number of years the GDR's bargaining position vis-à-vis the FRG had doubtless improved, and the former did seem to be obtaining numerous concessions, especially from the West German SPD after 1983. In the longer term, regime suppositions about surmounting legitimacy problems through the detente process proved illusory, though, and largely unanticipated forces were unleashed that the SED was increasingly incapable of controlling. The lessening of tensions that had begun in the 1970s was only a preliminary audition for the true tests that would present themselves in the form of rapid liberalization in neighboring countries.

In a slightly different interpretation, other observers argued that Honecker was far less interested in developing a relationship with the FRG, and later limiting damage to it, than he was in obtaining concessions from the West.[13] The detente process, according to this viewpoint, extended to Honecker an opportunity for political extortion. The fact that the GDR was so successful diplomatically for the better part of a decade lends some credence to this argument. Assuming the role of the innocent and injured GDR leader advocating peace and detente, Honecker plainly equipped himself to induce the FRG to accept many of his policies. And by suggesting that Bonn had to make concessions to help him, Honecker often prevailed.

A GREAT LEAP FORWARD

By the late summer of 1989, from within and from without, pressure mounted on the SED. To the East, the Polish liberalization process coming in the wake of semi-free elections held earlier in the summer was moving ahead more quickly than most thought possible. In the second week of September the first noncommunist prime minister since World War II presented a liberal-to-the-core cabinet to the parliament (*Sejm*), complete with a finance minister unabashed in his determination to put in place a "normal market economy of the Western kind," and a minister of industry whose ideas were shaped by no less than those of Milton Friedman. The *Sejm* voted 402-0 for the new government whose twofold aim was a final break with over forty years of communism and the eventual establishment of liberal democracy.

The new government's economic program read like a list of SED bugbears. Poland's huge budget deficits were to be cut, and subsidies were to be phased out. Prices would be freed and the money supply tightly controlled. Once these initial steps had been taken, the operation of the private sector would foster genuine market competition, a system of commercial banks would be created, and a stock market established.

As was the case in the GDR, Stalinist economics loomed large in Poland, and that legacy was the starting point for Poland's transition to a market economy. Over 90 percent of industrial plant was in state hands, and the usual substantial bias toward heavy industry was manifest. State planning organizations whose be-all and end-all were centralization of economic control and maximization of overall output, not product quality or consumer satisfaction, maintained their grip on the production process. Policies of blanket industrial growth were sustained in large part by deliberate distortion of the price structure which was designed to hold input prices, especially energy costs, artificially low. The proposed changes had to be enormous.

The Polish reformers stressed that bureaucratic price and cost determination prevented rational pricing of any sort. International trade, explicitly accepted by the new government as the most efficacious way to instill competition into the economy, required the unfettering of markets. Foreigners would need to invest in Poland freely, the reformers believed, primarily to encourage the economic efficiency crucial for exporting to the West. Even before the emergence of a Solidarity-led government in September 1989, many leading figures in the trade union movement such as the labor minister Jacek Kuron had been urging Solidarity to employ its wide public backing to implement sweeping reforms.[14] Poland's leap forward in the fall of 1989 had the following key components:

- Subsidies were to be phased out and prices decontrolled. The problem of "soft budgets" was to be dealt with by introducing financial discipline based on an unforgiving credit regime.
- Hindrances to international trade were to be eliminated. The basis for free trade with the West was to be the establishment of a convertible currency.
- Restrictions on the private sector were to end as soon as was feasible.[15]

Always ones to follow events elsewhere, East Germans took a keen interest in Poland's spirit-stirring course. As if there could have been any lingering doubts, Polish developments attested to the fact that economic and political reforms in communist regimes went hand-in-hand. Even the proverbial man on the street in the GDR, a country with a relatively high level of political sophistication, had some grasp of this. In the GDR *glasnost* and *perestroika* had long since begun catalyzing popular expectations heightened by years of partial opening to the West, and passions there sharpened as a society lost all confidence in its leadership. But through the clouds of dissatisfaction there shone a ray of hope. Change considered unthinkable even short months before had come in Poland. If possible there, then why not in the GDR? Few East Germans believed Honecker's Politburo capable of carrying through any sort of reform, or even comprehending the need for it. But what if the ruling clique were replaced, as in Poland? What if . . . ?

NOTES

1. *The German Tribune*, April 17, 1988.

2. A. James McAdams, "Inter-German Detente: A New Balance," *Foreign Affairs* 65, no. 1 (Fall, 1986): 148.

3. Timothy Garton Ash, "Which Way will Germany Go?" *The New York Review of Books*, January 31, 1985, 34.

4. Quoted in Ash, "Which Way Will Germany Go?" 34.

5. Hartmut Zimmermann, "The GDR in the 1970s," *Problems of Communism* 27, no. 2 (March-April 1978): 34.

6. A. James McAdams, "The New Logic in Soviet-GDR Relations," *Problems of Communism* 37, no. 6 (September-October 1988): 54.

7. For a discussion of this problem, see Wolfgang Seiffert, "Die Natur des Konflikts zwischen der SED-Führung und Moskau," *Deutschland Archiv* 17, no. 10 (October 1984): 1,043-59.

8. Wolfgang Seiffert, "Moderner, sozialer Nationalstaat als Ziel," *Die Welt*, January 24, 1986.

9. Gebhard Schweigler, *National Consciousness in Divided Germany* (London: Sage, 1975), 156.

10. See the analysis by Rolf Steiniger, *Eine vertane Chance Die Stalin-Note vom 10 März 1952 und die Wiedervereinigung* (Bonn: J. H. W. Dietz, 1986).

11. Ash, "Which Way Will Germany Go?" 35.

12. McAdams, *East Germany and Detente*, 6.

13. David Gress, "The Politics of German Unification," *Proceedings of the Academy of Political Science* 38, no. 1 (1991): 148-52.

14. Jeffrey Sachs and David Lipton, "Poland's Economic Reform," *Foreign Affairs* 69, no. 3 (Summer 1990): 54-55.

15. Ibid.

10
The Dam Bursts

HUNGARY OPENS THE BORDER

In late August a senior Western diplomat is reported to have said, "I really don't have the impression that the situation [in the GDR] is out of control. The system is going through some creaks and strains." He could not have been more wrong, of course. The second week of September 1989 marked a watershed for the GDR and for Europe. On September 10, the Hungarian government, as it had stated in private six days before, dispensed with all border formalities, effectively allowing all East Germans still "on vacation" in Hungary to leave. Within seventy-two hours over 12,000 transited into Austria. Before the month was out, 22,000 trekked through Hungary on the way west. Some were on foot; many chugged along in their two-cycle engine cars which would later become one of the symbols of German unity; the vast majority were young. It was far and away the largest exodus since the construction of the Wall. Prior worst case scenarios regarding numbers were proving overly optimistic.

Outraged, East Berlin delivered bitter protests, charging the Hungarians with violation of a twenty-year-old agreement requiring that East Germans be returned for committing certain offenses, including attempted emigration. Mielke told a shocked Politburo on September 11 that on the previous day 2,250 families had asked for permission to travel to Hungary, an increase of over 250 percent in twenty-four hours, and that he was duly instructing GDR officials not to grant such permission. For Mittag the only issue seemed to be the plugging of the hole. Stoph demanded immediate investigations into the question why people were fleeing. SED leaders were caught up in events and simply reacting to them. They had done nothing, despite notification in advance from the Hungarians, and now it was simply too late for investigations into the causes of social friction in the GDR.

Honecker, incapacitated for most of the month of August by a gall bladder operation, had disappeared from public view for some little time, and consequently did not attend the Politburo meeting the day after the Hungarians opened the border. According to hearsay, he was gravely sick and would not be able to resume his duties, and to the chagrin of the Politburo, the West German rumor mill was having a field day. With the SED leaders' world slowly collapsing around them, it was said, the general secretary did not so much as make an appearance. Some West German newspapers were talking of terminal cancer and heavy sedation. Schabowski and several others expressed concern about the absence of any official clarification of Honecker's state. The impression of confusion at precisely the wrong moment was damaging to the party, he pointed out. And indeed, whose hand was on the rudder remained an open question for over a month.

The GDR media, for its part, engaged in caustic invective, accusing the West Germans of kidnapping citizens of the GDR, and implicating the Hungarians for having become bribed "tools of imperialist intrigue."[1] *Neues Deutschland* railed against the Hungarian decision as a sort of cloak-and-dagger operation involving direct interference in the internal affairs of a fraternal socialist state, a serious charge since such indictments had been hitherto reserved for capitalist states. "Under the pretext of humanitarian considerations," the party organ asserted, "organized slave trade is being conducted."[2] Certain circles in the FRG were denounced for violating provisions of the CSCE Final Act. "Their goal is to degrade the successes the GDR has made in building a socialist society, to call into question the GDR's place in the community of European states, and to interfere in the GDR's internal affairs."[3]

Desperately, the Politburo looked for backing from its erstwhile allies, in particular, from the Soviet Union. Finding little, the GDR then began slamming shut its borders, announcing an immediate visa requirement for its citizens to exit the country bound anywhere, except neo-Stalinist Czechoslovakia. Meanwhile, on September 9 Gorbachev gave a televised speech which was, oddly enough, reprinted in *Neues Deutschland* on September 11. Gorbachev described the situation in the Soviet Bloc as "complicated" and "fluid." "Political life is currently characterized by tense and emotion-laden discussion," he said. Nothing resembling the East German leadership's vitriol was present in the speech. The tone was, in fact, distinctly plaintive. Perhaps the SED party organ's editorial staff printed the speech in the hope that some party officials would peruse it and serendipitously discover support, however hesitant, for the GDR's position. Somewhat ominously for the SED, though, Gorbachev spoke of the "restructuring" that would be necessary to overcome the "alienation" of people from "the power."[4]

Notable also was the more general shift in the rhetorical tone of Soviet media coverage of events transpiring in Hungary and the GDR in the late summer of 1989. In August the Soviet news agency TASS was still vociferously condemning the FRG's "tendential" media campaign against the GDR. With apparent satisfaction the GDR media reported Soviet criticism at the time of the FRG's "blatant interference" in the internal affairs of the GDR and other socialist states as violations of the CSCE process and the spirit of detente.[5] Commensurate with Gorbachev's efforts to distance himself from hard-line East Bloc regimes, such rhetoric was scaled down and after August even the official GDR media were hard pressed to conceal the dearth of support from Moscow. Grasping at straws, the SED searched for support where there was little.

Soon the estrangement cut both ways. A review of the GDR press at the time increasingly disclosed a rebuffing of a Soviet Union too liberal for GDR tastes, and an alignment with the more orthodox communist regimes of Romania and the People's Republic of China (PRC). Scant official praise for "mankind's great historic alternative" was to be found any longer. On September 15 the party organ proclaimed almost joyfully the condemnation of the "tendential campaign against the GDR" by Yegor Ligachev, Soviet hard-liner and Gorbachev detractor. Later in September it ridiculed Soviet radical reformer Boris Yeltsin for treading the wrong path.[6] Throughout September and October *Neues Deutschland* was spangled with headlines about warm GDR-PRC relations, manifestations of which ran the gamut from official Chinese visits to East German kindergartens to unswerving GDR support for the actions in Beijing against the "counterrevolution."[7] And with quite obvious satisfaction *Neues Deutschland* reported that the Romanian media were denouncing in the strongest terms the illegal exit of East Germans through Hungary, as well as the gross human rights violations such slave trade constituted.[8] Bukarest's expressions of abhorrence with the interference in the internal affairs of socialist states by revanchist, revisionist, and chauvinist elements in the FRG could not have been better presented by the SED itself, which received these enthusiastically. North Korean strongman, Kim Il Sung, was also reported by *Neues Deutschland* to have had "high praise" for the GDR's policies, while North Korean party officials, it seemed, were very worried about Bonn's "defamation campaign."[9]

As if somehow to correct the faltering of socialist neighbors, *Neues Deutschland* launched an offensive replete with banner headlines about provocations against the GDR and ruthless trade with GDR citizens. Vexatious questions of West German journalists and the vicious night and fog actions of the Western media were damaging relations between the German states, it was said.[10] The front page of *Neues Deutschland* carried reports of the cruelties being inflicted upon East Germans by cold-blooded provocateurs and professional slave traders. Two eyewitnesses allegedly described to *Neues Deutschland* the West German preparations for outrages in Hungary and how they saw East German young people being molested by the slave traders.[11]

A most poignant story involved the case of the railway employee Hartmut Ferworn who claimed to have been drugged by a menthol cigarette given him by a West German who proceeded to kidnap him to Vienna. "Clear proof," according to the party organ, of the horrendous campaign being waged against the GDR.[12] More basic issues, for example, the flight of some 15,000 East Germans to the FRG the previous week or the continuation of streams of people seeking refuge in diplomatic missions, were not addressed. Who exactly was the intended target of such propaganda and, moreover, who was supposed to be fooled by it were enigmas of SED headwork and bafflements to human under-standing. Few East Germans lent any credence to it, and many recalled with the standard cynical amusement the equally incredulous "doping stories" appearing previously in the GDR's press.

The reference was not to professional athletes. The most notorious of the tales pertained to one Herbert Meissner, an economics professor and SED member who was picked up in a West Berlin department store for shoplifting in 1986. As the SED media told it, he was drugged by the West German intelligence service, then framed for purposes of blackmail. But notwithstanding such provocations and aggression, the socialist German state, the media assured its audience, would follow the path of peace and progress.[13]

For their part, the Hungarians riposted that their move was fully in accordance with the United Nations Convention on Refugees they had recently signed, though the invoking of this treaty in connection with the situation in Hungary was extraordinary, since Budapest classified the "vacationing" East Germans as refugees. Refugees from what? From communism? There were at least three discernible reasons for Budapest's decision. First, the Hungarians doubtless wanted the problem solved, not wishing to have their country become a refugee camp. Second, with their own reform course about to go into high gear, the Hungarians were not apt to set the clock back by supporting socialism with a Stalinist face. Third, Budapest, desperately needing Western assistance for its reform program, was disinclined to undertake any action that would needlessly anger the West. What better way to demonstrate their seriousness about liberalization than to open borders?

THE OPPOSITION DECLARES ITSELF

The SED seemed equally unprepared for what was to occur closer to home in the days after Budapest threw open the border: genuine political opposition to the power monopoly began. Although the GDR never produced an opposition leader with the popular appeal of a Lech Walesa, the social diversity of the East German opposition, as well as the ability of opposition groups to draw people from many walks of life partially compensated for the absence of such a center of attraction. Even before the open opposition spread out beyond the churches, those challenging the regime included many average, working people alongside the doctors, clergymen, and scholars. The pressing desire for change transcended age, station in life, and even profession. Although many observers saw the lack of central organization as a significant weakness in the face of raw state power, all agreed that the steadily growing opposition was in fact quite heterogeneous. The mass character of the opposition would later enable it to apply considerable pressure upon the regime in spite of the lack of charismatic figures. In rising against the regime, a downtrodden people suddenly found hope and a sense of purpose.

On September 11, the so-called "List Two for the Democratic Renewal of GDR Society" published an appeal in Hamburg to organize a countrywide opposition to SED rule: "We encourage everyone to assemble into citizens' groups and personal circles on October 7, the anniversary of the founding of the GDR, in order to discuss concepts and organizational forms for an opposition that will represent the critical potential in our land."[14] "List Two" furthermore demanded that Bonn cease its financial support of the GDR.

On September 19 the opposition group, New Forum, led by the crusading dissident, Bärbel Bohley, who had been expelled from the GDR earlier in the year, and then to the SED's great dismay, managed to return, petitioned for official recognition. New Forum notified the interior minister, Friederich Dickel, that it was establishing a "political platform for the whole GDR enabling people from all circles of life, of all professions and of all parties to participate in public discussion and in the solution of social problems facing the country."[15] Citing a need for the largest number of people to take part in the reform process, the co-founders substantiated their actions by Article 29 of the Constitution which stated: "All citizens of the GDR have the right of association, in order to implement their interests in agreement with the principles and aims of this Constitution by joint action in political parties, social organizations, associations and collectives." Dickel wasted no time in explaining in a televised interview that the establishment of New Forum was "illegal and treasonous," and, moreover, that because "no social need" for such an organization existed, there was "no social interest" in it. Bohley, undeterred by the brusque rejection, voiced her disgust, stayed the course, and encouraged others to organize into political groupings also. The SED had shot the ball into its own goal, she quipped, asserting that the official treatment of the opposition would exacerbate the mass exodus problem. At the time of its outlawing, the New Forum membership list contained over 3,000 names and was growing rapidly, a phenomenon in a country virtually without any opposition just short weeks before, and Bohley claimed over one hundred people were signing on every day. "People have no fear to come forward publicly any longer," she said in an interview. In response to the SED position, the group stated: "The desire for justice, democracy and protection of the environment lies in all efforts 'New Forum' has given expression to."[16]

Another co-founder of New Forum demonstrated equal courage. He was Rolf Henrich, a leading dissident, former SED member, and author of the acclaimed critical study of the SED, *Der Vormundschaftliche Staat*.[17] Until he broke with the regime, Henrich had been an attorney, and his disillusionment with the GDR ran very deep. He characterized state power in the GDR as simply reactionary and portrayed the legal process as an outright sham.[18] In September he began unhesitatingly to voice in public the very criticisms he made in his book, which had been published in the West and was banned in the GDR. "The status of the individual in the socialism that has developed between the Oder and the Elbe is precisely that of a ward," he thundered. Drawing upon his own experience in the courts, he described how the outcome of political trials were always foregone conclusions in the East German legal system. In "political cases," those pertaining to attempted illegal emigration, the guilty verdict had been decided in advance and invariably entailed a jail sentence, he said. In September he led the first of several open debates on the problems of the GDR, emboldening people with his civic valor, and setting in motion the public discussions in which huge numbers would later participate. Despite the warnings he had received in the past for giving any expression to his views, the state did not move against him.

By the third week in September new grass-roots opposition groups seemed to be springing out of the ground like mushrooms. Democratic Awakening announced its intention to organize a countrywide meeting in East Berlin in early October. The group Citizens' Initiative Democracy Now, led by a dozen well-known pastors, civil rights activists, and scholars, issued a proclamation whose purpose was manifest in its title, "Appeal to Interference in One's Internal Affairs."[19] It demanded sweeping political reform, condemned the brutality employed against demonstrators and openly accused the SED of rigging the May 7 elections. The already active Initiative for Peace and Human Rights, declared that recent police actions, particularly in Leipzig, showed that "the state apparatus is reacting to the crisis only with silence and responding to people's criticisms only with violence."

Musicians and writers then began to leap onto the political bandwagon. The leading figures of the GDR's rock and pop scene including Frank Schöbel, Tamara Danz, Gerhard Schöne and the group Silly all joined New Forum. To boot, fifty-four musicians issued the following resolution:

> We want to live in this country and it sickens us to have to watch idly as efforts at democratization are criminalized and social analyses are ignored. . . . We, the undersigned, are concerned about the present situation of our country, about the mass exodus of many in our age group, about the identity crisis of this societal alternative and about the insufferable ignorance of the state and party leadership who downplay evident difficulties and continue on a rigid course. At issue here are not reforms to eliminate socialism, but instead reforms to make possible the further existence of socialism. Current party attitudes endanger socialism.[20]

Other artists began to follow suit. The board of the Berlin Association of Writers, including Christa Wolf and Stephan Hermlin, sent a scathing letter to the Council of State and to the minister of culture, Hans-Joachim Hoffmann, stating:

> In light of the present mass exodus of citizens we find official declarations that "nothing, absolutely nothing" would necessitate a course correction simply unacceptable. The manner in which responsibility for the situation is fobbed off, even though the causes lie in the unsettled contradictions in this country, we find unbearable.[21]

CRACKS IN THE BLOC

From the bloc parties, known neither for spontaneity nor independent spirit, critical voices could be heard as well. Mustering self-confidence at long last, party members began demanding an earnest investigation into the reasons behind the alarming mass exodus, and called upon the Politburo to face up to the seriousness of the situation. A few CDU and LDPD party officials even started talking of reform. Following several highly critical statements from religious leaders, four CDU politicians recommended in an open letter to their party that it break with the SED and assume a politically independent role. Insisting that "change within a stable framework" was necessary, the critics said the churches must not be forced to undertake an opposition function that is the business of political organizations. "The problems of the country must be realistically and straightforwardly faced, openly discussed, and proposals put forward for their solution," they asserted. They demanded openness and democracy, within their own party, within the other bloc parties, and throughout the society. The immediate tasks, they said, were the formation of public opinion forums, respect for the expression of citizen views, publication of major economic problems, the clarification of travel issues, and a change in media policies. "Media policies based upon omission, reticence and extenuation render coverage preposterous, anger people and simply open the GDR to the influence of the Western media," they said.[22] The CDU press had also to portray more accurately the actual conditions in the GDR, it was suggested, and editorial boards had to become independent.

Such criticism from the rank-and-file of the East CDU found no echo in the highest echelons of the party, however, which ardently defended close cooperation with the SED. Accordingly, the party leadership made noises about some misguided members joining in "foreign instigated" destabilization campaigns of the GDR. A commentary in the party organ, *Neue Zeit*, attacked the dissidents, saying that the CDU "in its joint responsibility" for the entire republic would help protect East Germans from "foreign interference."[23]

In contrast, the LDPD leadership itself initiated the fissure. On September 19 Manfred Gerlach, the Liberal Democratic chairman, came out in favor of sweeping reforms. Access to reliable information is a citizen's right, Gerlach asserted. "We must not prevent change, but foster and channel it."[24] As others had already done, he voiced his grave concerns about the exodus waves, and expressed a desire to know the reasons for "mass resignation." He concluded his remarks by announcing that at the next party conference the LDPD and its program would be completely restructured.

The SED failed to respond to Gerlach's startling pronouncements. *Neues Deutschland* carefully deleted all critical passages from its reprints of Gerlach's speeches, and replaced its coverage of the LDPD meetings with a scathing attack on a Protestant church assembly in Eisenach for taking positions "inconsistent with socialism." According to the newspaper, "What was reported in the West from the synod's declaration is in the main a catalogue of measures to prepare the GDR for capitalism and reunification."[25]

Gerlach, however, was only warming up. Some days later on September 30 he suggested in another public speech that political trust in the GDR would increase through "public dialogue and critical expression." The LDPD was alarmed, he said, that "political vigilance" was beginning to be turned against cooperative and law-abiding citizens. Making reference to the yawning gap between the GDR's self-portrayal and the realities of everyday life, he contended that responsible criticism would not weaken the country. Finally, he raised a taboo subject no GDR official had hitherto dared broach. Leaving no doubt where the finger was pointing, he laid responsibility for the pre-war split in the working-class movement that facilitated Hitler's ascension to power squarely on the KPD's doorstep.[26] Therewith, decades of servitude to the SED abruptly ended.

THE REGIME TOTTERS

As the SED began preparations for its self-glorifying yearly anniversary rituals, the official media reflected the continuing sense of unreality. The print media provided its usual diatribe about increasing neo-Nazism in the FRG, widespread police atrocities there, as well as ongoing capitalist slave trade. By September the media had picked up on a new theme: the West German housing shortage, which was described as "dire." That the principal reason for the shortage were the droves of refugees from the GDR was naturally not mentioned; *Neues Deutschland* blithely assumed no one would consider the cause of the sudden growth of the West German population.

On September 22 a headline in *Neues Deutschland* read, "On the Way to the XII Party Congress of the SED: Determined and Unified We Stay the Sure and Clear Course for the Good of the People," and in a caption thereunder, "Our principle remains . . . the party is there for the people and the only privilege of a party comrade is to serve the people." One week later on September 29 the paper spoke of the secure future in the GDR, especially in rural areas where village life was retained and farm communities preserved.

During that week the number of East Germans seeking refuge in the FRG's embassy compound in Prague rose to over 1,500, and in Warsaw to over 400. GDR efforts to arrive at a solution failed. An East Berlin lawyer representing the Politburo traveled to Prague and offered safe conduct and guaranteed legal emigration within six months to those willing to return to the GDR. Not a single person consented. Within a week there would be thousands in the Warsaw Embassy, and when the GDR finally closed the border with Czechoslovakia on October 4, the number in the Prague compound had risen to over 10,000. Following an arrangement between the respective countries and the FRG to evacuate the refugees, special trains began transporting the East Germans to the West. In the first days of October when these trains passed through the GDR, East Germans attempted to board them. In Dresden on October 4 police fought a pitched battle with some 5,000 people in front of the train station before brutally clearing the area. There was every reason to believe all 5,000 were heading for the station late at night to storm the trains scheduled to pass through. The episode involved the most street violence seen in the GDR since the 1953 uprising, and similar incidents were reported in Karl-Marx-Stadt (Chemnitz) and other cities.

On September 24 the first countrywide assembly of East German opposition groups took place in Leipzig. Organized by the Leipzig Initiative Group Life, over eighty groups attended to discuss the possibilities for close cooperation. All political groups known at the time sent representatives, but new and hitherto unheard-of organizations such as Awakening Now and Free Democratic Union made appearances also. Pastor Edelbert Richter, spokesman of Awakening Now, announced that the common goal of all would be "breaking the power monopoly of the SED."

On the same day in twelve cities solidarity demonstrations with those arrested at demonstrations in the prior two weeks were held. Over 5,000 gathered in Leipzig at the usual assembly point, the prayer meeting at the Nikolai Church. The crowd then marched through the middle of the city. Security forces and police, present in large numbers, did not move against the demonstrators.

For whatever reason, September 29 appeared to be a day designated for high-level testimony as leading SED figures issued statements dismissing any possibility of dialogue with the opposition. Referring to the demands of the opposition groups, Stoph declared in *Neues Deutschland* that "there will never be such so-called reforms in the GDR and no cleverly disguised advice will move the GDR to touch socialism."[27] Sindermann, saying the "revanchist" FRG was out to overturn the post-war order of Europe, demanded reforms in the FRG that would "take the wind out of neo-Nazi sails and halt current pan-German noises."[28] Herrmann also condemned the FRG for "striving to liquidate the first workers' and farmers' state on German territory."[29] Such attempts would be in vain, he argued, in spite of the malicious propaganda campaign the West was waging. In the same vein Mielke claimed FRG "agitators" to have thrown down the gauntlet, and that the "foe in cooperation with certain domestic circles was engaged in an effort to establish an opposition aiming to undermine the economic and political foundation of our socialist state and societal order."[30] The "anti-socialist forces" were, however, receiving a clear response, he said. Finally, Dohlus provided public assurances that the SED "in a close trusting relationship" with all working people would decisively stay the course. He went on to say:

> The ruling circles of the FRG with their media and assorted lackeys who are loudly recommending reforms of socialism, who are unabashedly demanding an alteration of borders, who are illegally interfering in the internal affairs of other states, and under the motto "Heim ins Reich" are engaging in slave trade, have one chief goal—to eliminate the first German workers' and farmers' state and socialism as well.[31]

NOTES

1. *Neues Deutschland*, September 12, 1989.
2. *Neues Deutschland*, September 11, 1989.
3. *Neues Deutschland*, September 13, 1989.
4. *Neues Deutschland*, September 11, 1989.
5. *Neues Deutschland*, August 12, 1989.
6. *Neues Deutschland*, September 19, 1989.
7. For example, *Neues Deutschland*, September 26, 1989.
8. *Neues Deutschland*, September 20, 1989.
9. *Neues Deutschland*, September 20, 1989.
10. For example, *Neues Deutschland*, September 21, 1989.
11. *Der Spiegel*, September 25, 1989.
12. Ibid.
13. *Neues Deutschland*, September 13, 1989.
14. *Archiv der Gegenwart*, no. 22, October 2-18, 1989.
15. *Der Spiegel*, September 25, 1989.
16. *Archiv der Gegenwart*, no. 22, October 2-18, 1989.
17. Rolf Henrich, *Der vormundschaftliche Staat Vom Versagen des real existierenden Sozialismus* (Reinbek: Rowohlt, 1989).
18. *Der Spiegel*, March 27, 1989.
19. *Archiv der Gegenwart*, no. 22, October 2-18, 1989.
20. *Der Spiegel*, September 25, 1989.
21. Ibid.
22. *Archiv der Gegenwart*, no. 22, October 2-18, 1989.
23. *Neue Zeit*, September 19, 1989.
24. *Der Spiegel*, September 25, 1989.
25. Quoted in *Der Spiegel*, September 25, 1989.

26. *Der Morgen*, September 30, 1989.

27. *Neues Deutschland*, September 29, 1989.

28. *Archiv der Gegenwart*, no. 22, October 2-18, 1989.

29. Ibid.

30. Ibid.

31. *Neues Deutschland*, September 29, 1989.

11

People Without Fear

THE DEMONSTRATIONS SPREAD

By the first week of October the city of Leipzig had established itself as the bellwether of the public demonstrations that started to attract regularly many thousands of people in some dozen East German cities. Along with the mass exodus that was partially catalyzing them, the marches provided vivid testimony to the magnitude of citizen displeasure. On October 2 the protest demonstration for democratic reforms in Leipzig drew between 15,000 and 25,000. At least 2,500 had taken part in the initial prayer meeting in the Nikolai Church, and people appeared to be joining the demonstration spontaneously. Some with loudspeakers called "Gorby, Gorby" and demanded that Honecker finally initiate *perestroika*. Cries of "Gorby help us!" signified in an ironic way how the upheavals taking place in the East Bloc had come full circle. Past risings were intended in one form or another to loosen Soviet control of satellite nations. Now, East Germans were calling upon the Soviet leader to assist them against their own leadership. Also to be heard were calls of "liberty, equality, fraternity," as well as "no Chinas here," an unmistakable reference to speculation that the SED would employ tanks against the demonstrators. During most of the demonstration, the security forces exercised restraint, but the police formed long lines in the middle of the city, and behind these stood the paramilitary units of the *Kampfgruppen*, police vans, and water-spraying vehicles. As the demonstration began to dissipate, police attacked small groups with clubs and electric prods. Numerous people were hospitalized and more than a dozen arrested. On the same night, scattered outbreaks of violence were reported at several train stations and along rail right-of-ways, as East Germans once again attempted to board the special trains loaded with refugees from Bonn's embassies.

At the "Monday demonstration" on October 9 over 50,000 took to the streets and in the following week this number tripled. Shouts at demonstrations of "We're staying here" and "We are the people," the latter to become the rallying cry of the revolution, instead of "We want to leave" marked the new turn of the opposition spiral. Exit visas were no longer what people were clamoring for, but reform. The vast majority of those protesting, engaging in public discussion, or establishing nascent political groups were determined to remain in the GDR and change things.

Still, the party leadership refused to consider a dialogue with the people. *Neues Deutschland* referred to the unrest, when at all, as "hooliganism," "rowdyism," or "isolated provocative acts," preferring to dish out the usual fare of overfilled production quotas. In numerous East German cities including Leipzig, East Berlin, Plauen, Arnstadt, Karl-Marx-Stadt, Dresden, and Magdeburg, the guardians of actually existing socialism attacked demonstrators who had dared to take to the streets for *glasnost* and *perestroika*, for democracy, for freedom, for human rights.

Faint grumblings about the Politburo's inattention to the grave situation were becoming audible from various corners of a party supposedly united behind Honecker. Hans Modrow, the party chief in Dresden and one of the few Gorbachev adherents in the *nomenklatura*'s upper echelon, began insisting upon an investigation into the causes of the widespread dissent. Rebuffed by the party leadership and ignored by the official media, Modrow turned to the Western media to air his views about the need for change. West German television was only too pleased to provide coverage, which was broadcast in the GDR and watched by millions of viewers with considerable interest.

Modrow also backed the efforts of another reform-minded SED politician, Wolfgang Berghofer, the mayor of Dresden, who acquired the distinction of being the first party leader to open channels of communication with the opposition when he initiated discussions in the wake of the violent demonstrations in early October. Along with Modrow, Berghofer was one of the few in an influential position to see the writing on the wall at the time. With the party still balking at any notion of contact with the opposition, Berghofer advocated extensive political reform, to include free elections.[1]

PARTIES COME, PARTIES GO

On October 2 in East Berlin came a major breakthrough in efforts to establish a nation-wide political organization. Security force chicaneries induced the sixty founding members of Democratic Awakening to meet at two different locations, a private apartment and a community house, and prevented the drafting of a specific party program; nonetheless, Democratic Awakening took pride in being the first national opposition party in the GDR worthy of the name. The party's immediate objective was twofold: to achieve legalization of the organization, and to consolidate various smaller groupings in order to assemble lists of suitable candidates for local elections. The broader, longer-term goal was that of a renewed, truly democratic republic, featuring freedom of speech and information, pluralism, social control of the state apparatus, and a mixed economy.

Two days later, representatives of several opposition groups including New Forum, Initiative for Social Democracy, Democracy Now, Democratic Awakening, The Group of Democratic Socialists, and Initiative for Peace and Human Rights met to discuss possibilities for common political action, and issued a joint declaration designed to be the point of departure for party programs.

> Binding us is the will to refashion this state and society into a democracy. The present core issue is to bring about conditions in which citizens are able to exercise their political rights, as specified in the Human Rights Convention of the United Nations and the CSCE documents. We declare our solidarity with all those who are persecuted for their endeavors toward the achievement of this goal. We strive for the release of political prisoners, for the overturning of past convictions and for the termination of ongoing political trials. We consider the top priority of our country to be an open discussion of the basic conditions for a free election. Such an election must allow for different political decisions. It must be secret, i.e., that voters are required to use a booth. It must be free, i.e., no one is to be forced to vote in a particular way.[2]

Soon thereafter, 300 East Berlin artists issued a public resolution demanding open discussions of problems in light of the present crisis situation in the society. It criticized the GDR's rulers for being oblivious to the reality of looming societal collapse. Conditions had already reached the point that "the existence of the socialist society is seriously endangered."[3] The artists called for an end to repression and the elimination of undemocratic institutions in the country.

Coinciding with the day of the GDR's founding came the pronouncement by a group of forty-three reformers who had assembled just outside Berlin that they were establishing forthwith a Social Democratic party (SDP) in the GDR. Independent Social Democratic organizations had disappeared in the SBZ/GDR after the forced fusion in 1946, and had not reemerged, but there could have been little doubt about the threat such a moderate leftist party posed to the SED. Not only would its potential drawing power be considerable, but its very existence hurled defiance at the four-decade sham of working-class unity under the aegis of the hammer and compass. The SDP was to be steeped in the traditions of the democratic socialism of the European Socialists and Social Democrats, and its primary goals were to be the creation of a genuinely democratic state with a mixed economy and clearly defined rights of private property. To this end the GDR was to have party pluralism, parliamentary democracy, independent unions, the guaranteed right to strike, basic civil rights, and a genuine federal system with the attendant reestablishment of state governments. What is more, the GDR was to maintain special relations with the FRG, to include certain confederative structures. Elected to the chairmanship of the new party was the Berlin historian Ibrahim Böhme, a member of the group Initiative for Peace and Human Rights.

The proclamation caught not only the SED by surprise. Steps leading to the party's establishment had been taken so swiftly that the West German Social Democrats had received no prior notification of the founding of this kindred political organization. Meanwhile, the West German SPD had been rapidly distancing itself from the SED with whom it had developed a routine businesslike relationship, one critics described as inordinately familiar. Reported discussion in a Politburo meeting a month before indicated that the hardening SPD line vis-à-vis the SED was of some concern to the latter.[4] Having realized that the SED was in severe trouble, SPD spokesmen by mid-October were urging the GDR's leaders to share power.[5] The abrupt SPD switch from what some saw as appeasement of the SED to hostile criticism of it was characterized by political wits as the change from *Wandel durch Annäherung* to *Wandel durch Abstand*.

From Budapest came yet another hammer-blow to SED rule, and an inspiring assist to the GDR's budding opposition: communism in Hungary disappeared. On the verge of a split, the Communist party chose to dissolve itself. The Hungarians appeared to have no more room for Lenin, and many Hungarian communists ceased desiring to be that any longer, above all, because they had recognized that not even reform communists win free elections. A second East Bloc state had discarded monolithic unity and begun moving toward pluralism. True to his word, Gorbachev did not interfere; there was in fact not so much as an expression of concern from the Kremlin.

THE SED CELEBRATES ITS DECLINE

On October 5 the GDR's anniversary festivities commenced. A beaming Honecker, returned to the public limelight, and commenting how well he was feeling, opened the celebration on October 5 with the laying of wreaths at a Soviet war memorial and the Memorial for Antifascist Resistance. Meantime, eighteen East Germans took refuge in the United States Embassy in East Berlin and demanded the right to emigrate. Others were driven away from the building by police. Elsewhere, in Dresden and Magdeburg, there was sporadic violence, with over 250 arrests taking place in the latter city.

In banner headlines the next day *Neues Deutschland* greeted all citizens of the GDR on the occasion of the fortieth anniversary of its founding. At the same time it printed a warning from defense minister Heinz Kessler:

In order to distract from the peace-endangering activities of NATO, as well as to miscredit the workers' and farmers' state and its peace policies, a crude campaign of agitation and defamation has been initiated against socialism in the GDR. What the enemies of the socialist German state, despite great efforts, have not succeeded in achieving in four decades, namely, the counterrevolutionary elimination of socialism, which is the power of the workers and farmers on German soil, they will also fail to do in the future.[6]

As the goose-stepping elite units of the NVA were marching past the review platforms in East Berlin and the bands were playing, civil disturbances and scattered outbreaks of violence swept across the GDR as a regime assaulted its own people. Concurrently, thousands of refugees boarded trains in Prague for the journey to the FRG. More attempts were made in Dresden to storm a refugee train that was passing through. Police, using water cannon and truncheons broke up another demonstration in the city. In Arnstadt near Erfurt, Stasi units assailed 800 peaceful demonstrators with truncheons and dogs, badly injuring several.

Police cordoned off the train stations in Zwickau and Plauen to thwart any efforts to board trains to the West. The GDR media made casual mention of "misguided" and "misled" people wishing to leave the country, but on the whole the media treated the unofficial events occurring during the anniversary celebrations in a breathtakingly simple manner: they were merely ignored. But antiregime demonstrations in East Berlin and other cities during the October festivities cast a long shadow upon the anniversary jamboree. In East Berlin police dealt brutally with demonstrators who numbered over 7,000. Some Western journalists were roughed up in the foray, and a few were expelled from the GDR on October 8 simply for covering the events of the previous days. Several West German news photographers had film torn out of their cameras for photographing the protests.

A church protocol of the East Berlin demonstrations recorded the security force and police savagery.[7] It told of teenage girls being struck with truncheons. One woman recalled how her fourteen-year-old daughter was beaten for holding a candle at a protest vigil. The protocol recorded that many people had vivid memories of the terrible dull thud of clubs hitting heads. The police appeared not to discriminate between demonstrators and bystanders, and a number of older people not participating in the protests felt the full force of the state's wrath. It was not the GDR's finest moment.

In other cities, Leipzig, Plauen, Potsdam, protest assemblies drew tens of thousands. Any festive mood soured as police attacked demonstrators, hauling some off to jail and injuring quite a number. SED politicians showed no sign of particular concern, and in his anniversary statement Krenz displayed what might be described as the characteristic lack of Politburo perspective. He said proudly that with the founding of the GDR "a state enjoying great world-wide admiration as well as respect for its peace policies and the high living standard of its people" had been established. GDR policies "preserve antifascist traditions," he went on to say, and the country was renowned for "its constructive contributions to international cooperation and security."[8] In an article reprinted in *Pravda* on the occasion of the anniversary, Honecker confidently spoke of the GDR's "positive influence on the situation in Europe and the world over," and of the superb performance of the socialist economy "that serves the people's interest and is based upon societal ownership of the means of production." He made only one vague reference to the turmoil in his country, with a swipe at the "FRG's provocative campaign" to annex the GDR. With respect to reform he had the following to offer: "We regard any suggestions to look for socialism's salvation in a retrogression to capitalism to be as absurd as to claim the rain comes not from above, but out of the ground."[9]

In a speech in the Palace of the Republic, the GDR's parliament building, before over seventy delegations, Honecker spoke once again of the great achievements and superior economic performance of the GDR.[10] Referring to the founding of the GDR as an "historical necessity," he described the country as a "keystone of stability and security in Europe." He claimed the GDR to have been the work of millions of people over several generations. It was, he said, a country with modern industrial and agricultural sectors, with a socialist educational system, flourishing culture, and superb athletic achievements. He spoke of the need to continue with socialist development which he depicted as an "historical, long-term process of wide-reaching change and reforms in all areas." He then furnished a few words of warning to those "striving to alter the status quo in Europe": the GDR would remain a breakwater against neo-Nazism and chauvinism. "If the foe is engaged in a defamation campaign of hitherto unknown proportions, then this is hardly coincidental. . . . Forty years of the GDR's existence equate with the 40-year defeat of German imperialism and militarism."[11] Those in the West anticipating the collapse of socialism, he said, should simply be more realistic in their assessments. He referred to an "unbridled and internationally coordinated defamation campaign" designed to confuse people and cause doubts about the creative power of socialism. After attacking the "revanchist demands" of West German politicians that caused worldwide concerns and protests, he emphatically rejected all notions of an open German question. "Our position," he said, "springs from the imaginative application of Marxism-Leninism, from the interests of the working class and all working people. In a word, our position is one of a policy whose first principle is to do everything for the good of the people and their peaceful future." Honecker closed, saying that "socialism and peace" would go hand-in-hand as before and would remain the fundamentals of future achievement. "We are carrying on with determination and confidence," he said. "In its fifth decade as well," he sanguinely predicted, the socialist German state of workers and farmers would continue to demonstrate "that the founding in October 1949 was a watershed in the history of the German people and of Europe." But the state that was celebrating its fortieth anniversary that October had no future, and Honecker stayed in office less than two weeks after making the speech. His socialist state of workers and farmers did not survive the year.

The guest of honor at the anniversary celebration was paradoxically also the person bearing the greatest responsibility for the turmoil sweeping the GDR, and the message Gorbachev delivered in his speech in East Berlin on October 7 was hardly welcomed by the SED. The Soviet leader had traveled to the GDR with reform on his mind. "New thinking," he pointed out in a short speech at the wreath-laying ceremony at the Treptow Soviet War Memorial earlier that day, had already gained wide currency in the Soviet Union, and the Soviet people strongly favored democratic reforms.[12] His response to a reporter's question whether *perestroika* should be applied in the GDR was bodeful for the SED. The matter, he said, was for the people of the GDR to decide. The Soviet Union knew its German friends well and had a high regard for their ability to reconsider issues and to effect corrections when necessary. Whoever duly regards impulses issuing from the society, and formulates policies accordingly, he suggested, need have no fear. "Dangers await only those not reacting to life."[13]

In his address in the Palace of the Republic, Gorbachev expressed his conviction that the GDR would eventually initiate what he considered necessary changes. He said that every country had its own development problems; all were affected by integration processes; all were influenced by international political and economic conditions. He praised the high quality of cooperation between the GDR and the USSR, but affixed an admonition: attempts at standardization in questions of social development—imitation on the one hand and coercion based upon rigid models on the other—belonged to the past. Choice with respect to forms of development should be the sovereign decision of every people. But the greater the numbers of such forms, the greater was the need of an open exchange of experiences, as well as a discussion of theoretical and practical problems.[14]

Gorbachev minced no words about what he knew were sensitive topics for SED leaders. "*Perestroika* is a most difficult task . . . it is nonetheless vitally necessary for us," he said. Pursuit of realistic policies have had "very positive results" for the general improvement of the European climate, for the betterment of relations between the two German states, and the widening of interpersonal contacts. "Realistic Soviet policies," for their part, have encouraged the development of a mutually advantageous relationship with the FRG, he added.[15]

One cannot help speculating what was going through Honecker's mind at that point. He and his Politburo were of the orthodox school, dogmatic and inflexible, men of a past era, isolated, nonplused, for the most part unable to fathom what was going on around them. Hadn't the GDR achieved much in forty years? Didn't the people have a lot to be proud of? Why did Moscow wish to destabilize the GDR? Why were the people leaving in droves? Gorbachev's barely concealed warnings, such as "one who is late with reform will be punished," might have astounded Honecker. Sounding the anniversary keynote,

Neues Deutschland acclaimed the great accomplishments of the GDR and extolled the virtues of "staying the course." And as a sort of final mocking gesture to his people, Honecker warmly received Nicolae Ceausescu, the Rumanian party boss. In the past, meetings with Ceausescu corresponded in the GDR, not by accident, with displays of unhappiness toward Moscow, a new round of domestic repression, and usually both.

THE SED BACKS DOWN

The Politburo's outward unity ended with the anniversary celebrations, and divisions within the party became conspicuous the following week. The first unmistakable sign came on the October 11 East German evening television news. The standard vitriol about West German imperialist intrigues was noticeably tempered by appeals of solidarity to all those believing in the socialist cause. Although words like "opposition" or "reform" were not yet part of the Politburo's vocabulary, and as if to underscore this a commentary stated the GDR had no need of organizations like New Forum, the news program added that "all opinions and suggestions concerning a more attractive socialism are important."[16]

Leaks to the West German media indicated that the combined effects of Gorbachev's admonitions, the weekend violence, and the huge Monday demonstration in Leipzig had provoked open strife in subsequent Politburo meetings. Honecker was coming under increasing pressure, and there was even talk in the Politburo of his resignation, according to the reports.[17] Krenz and Mielke, it seemed, were advocating a modicum of flexibility, a few cosmetic changes in the Politburo's complexion, and were entertaining the possibility of limited dialogue. They planned to set things right by issuing a few promises and rolling a few heads at the top, the likely candidates being Honecker, Hager, Mittag, Sindermann and Mückenberger, the health problems of the latter three already a matter of public record and thus convenient for the purpose. Adding to the convenience, on his recent visit Gorbachev had rather impertinently conveyed uneasiness about the advanced age of Politburo members: average age at the time approached sixty-five. Propaganda chief Herrmann came under pressure also, ostensibly because of the increasing unevenness of media coverage.

The dissenting opinion was voiced in the main by Herrmann and Mittag, both of whom advocated a tough line, even a crackdown. Available sources, including the party press, suggest Herrmann to have been operating on the assumption that yielding an inch to opponents would have been tantamount to a breach of the political front, hence his consideration of a "Tiananmen Square solution."[18] Honecker's exact position is difficult to determine. Whether for reasons of illness or despondency, or some combination, he had already begun his slide into political oblivion. He clearly ceased being a major player in the drama after

October 7, but in all likelihood, this had been the case as early as August. If Honecker had still been in control at that time, why would the man, self-satisfied to the point of vanity, not have appeared in public to refute the rumors circulating in the Western press about the state of his health? Shyness was certainly not the reason. There was even some idle speculation in the Western press, for what it was worth, about on-coming senility. Honecker, it seemed, was given to reciting nursery rhymes in public, and included one in his jubilee address on October 6.[19] Gorbachev did not appear to have regarded the recital as a highlight of a visit he did not find especially entertaining anyway.

During the week following the anniversary celebrations Politburo members blew hot and cold as they endeavored to adapt to a rapidly changing situation, and hedged to save their own positions. The employment of police truncheons, attack dogs, and water cannon, broadcast in living color on the Western television news, had considerably heightened the dissent potential of an already restive population. East Germans, no doubt surprising even themselves at times, were exerting pressure with increasing confidence. What is more, the number of people emigrating to the FRG reached record levels in the middle of October.

Now the political weather vanes began to adjust to the prevailing winds. The first to come forward was Kurt Hager who denied on West German television any differences of opinion in the "unified leadership," then proceeded to criticize the "outmoded thinking" of certain unnamed individuals. He indicated how the Central Committee was "working out precise conceptions for the realization of necessary renewals in certain areas."[20] Thus did the very same Hager who had scoffed at the reform course in the Soviet Union begin to burnish his image with fresh wallpaper. Hager, the chief censor in the GDR, who had for thirty-four years foisted the party's views on artists while persecuting the nay-sayers, who had prevented much of the GDR's best literature from being published there, became an advocate of renewal and change. He announced the convening of a special party congress complete with a "large open discussion" of social problems. "There will be every possibility," he declared, "for comradely parties, societal organizations unified in the national front, and all citizens to express their views on SED proposals."[21]

The next to join the pragmatic group was Götting, the chairman of the East CDU, who had long been the loyalest of SED allies, and was one of Honecker's deputies in the Council of State. This was the same Götting who short weeks ago had so bitterly attacked his fellow party members for criticizing the SED. In the same vehicle he used for such attacks, the party organ, *Neue Zeit*, he stated that "the media must be more realistic in its portrayal of life."[22] In proposing "fresh rethinking" of Honecker's social and economic policies, he was publicly distancing himself from the man he had so long served.

It was then the turn of Politburo veteran and chairman of the East German Federation of Unions (FDGB), Harry Tisch, to become a born-again reformer. "Now it is time," he said, "through trusting, thoughtful and reasoned dialogue to discuss current problems with the workers. Criticism must be exercised where criticism is necessary. . . . We are being asked and we are prepared to make bold decisions. Dissemination of rapid and complete information at all levels, especially in the media, is essential."[23]

This was the same Harry Tisch who had been a member of the Politburo since 1975. The FDGB, by its own admission, followed the SED's leading role and served as a transmission belt of the party. This was the same Harry Tisch who had hitherto been inattentive to the departure of union members in droves from the organization. He was now anxious to talk with his fellow members about problems he did not concede the existence of the prior week.

Adding his name to the list was the almost notoriously hard-line president of the Writers' Organization, Hermann Kant, who in the FDJ paper, *Neue Welt* started to complain about the censorship in the GDR media which any person with a memory of more than a few weeks would recall he was in large part responsible for.[24] This was the same newspaper that short weeks ago had lashed out so fiercely at regime critics and protesters. This was the same Kant who had expelled dozens from the Writer's Organization over the years for being politically unreliable, who had ruined careers at the slightest provocation, who had instigated the expulsion of Wolf Biermann from the GDR.

Rounding out the field among the prominent that week was the East Berlin lawyer and Honecker confidant, Wolfgang Vogel, who began publicly demanding "constitutional practices" and the release of all political prisoners and detainees. This was the same Wolfgang Vogel who was the chief agent in the dissident export schemes that yielded the GDR hundreds of thousands of marks, the man who showed so little concern for the refugees in West German diplomatic missions, while making promises to them about safe conduct home and the guaranteed right to emigrate.

Mirroring these changes, factions within the party then cautiously attempted to buy time, and evidence of sidestepping and about-faces began to surface in *Junge Welt* and *Neues Deutschland*. At last acknowledging the existence of open criticism of the SED, the former put to press a dissenting opinion for the first time ever. Under considerable pressure from several artists, it published a resolution of 3,000 musicians calling for political reforms.[25] *Neues Deutschland*, for its part, printed in full a declaration of the directors of the Academy of Fine Arts, which censured both the SED and its media organs. An excerpt provided the flavor: "In our country daily experiences of people very often differ from the official view. This contradiction leads to painful disturbances of the moral and intellectual climate in our society."[26]

On October 13 Honecker made his first and last statement about the upheaval. Alluding to the "not minor challenges" associated with the situation in a meeting with representatives of the bloc parties, the general secretary, flanked by Mittag and Herrmann, said the party would begin investigating the causes of the current difficulties.[27] The great economic potential of the country would enable it to overcome these, he said, but in any case the party was considering certain measures to improve the general welfare, to include improvement in the supply of consumer goods, a more realistic media policy, and more travel possibilities. The latter in particular hardly represented a significant concession in light of the fact that the GDR's borders at the time were effectively closed for its citizens. Any foreign travel amounted to greater liberalization at that point.

HONECKER STEPS DOWN

Following the GDR's inauspicious birthday party, as pressure for change mounted from within, the Western media frequently conjectured about SED intentions. Not surprisingly, much of the commentary doubted the leadership's sincerity about reform or its willingness to engage in genuine dialogue with the people. And there was no shortage of rumors about Honecker's resignation. On October 12 without explanation, the general secretary canceled his trip to Denmark scheduled for the twenty-fifth and twenty-sixth of the month. A few West German newspapers speculated (incorrectly, as it turned out) that Hager would replace him the following day. Then the boulevard paper, *Bild*, obtained the news scoop. On its front page it said Honecker's last working day would be October 18. That afternoon, in a special Central Committee meeting, Honecker, citing health reasons, resigned all his official posts and was replaced by Krenz, the groomed heir apparent. In his resignation speech before the Central Committee Honecker stated:

> My entire life I have devoted with unflinching zeal to the revolutionary cause of the working class and to our Marxist-Leninist goal of the establishment of socialism on German territory. The founding and the successful development of the socialist German Democratic Republic, whose achievements we celebrated together on the fortieth anniversary, I consider to be the crowning triumph of the struggle of our party and my activity as a communist . . .[28]

In addition, Herrmann was dismissed from the Politburo and the Central Committee, and Mittag lost all his official positions as well. Krenz assumed office promising a *Wende*, or "turnaround." In a lengthy televised speech Krenz spoke of "new beginnings" and an "historic hour." He said that cooperation and "constructive criticism" were more necessary than ever, but he was vague on many matters of popular concern and danced around contentious issues. "It is certain," he began with lurid understatement, "that in the last months we have not realistically assessed social development in its essence and did not draw the proper conclusions early enough."[29] He assured his audience that the SED had the necessary strength for solving the current spate of problems as well as for the tasks that lay beyond. "Always at the forefront of revolutionary change," he argued, the SED was uniquely qualified to usher in a "new epoch."

Conceding that much renewal of the economy was necessary, he voiced understanding of the need for the extensive popular discussions of efficiency, wage policies, and the ecology that had been taking place in the GDR of late. Particularly in the economic sphere, he said, "glossing over" must cease. All should accept, indeed encourage, "criticism and self-criticism," he said. He went on to acknowledge that in the mass exodus over 100,000 had fled the GDR. This flight from the country he described as a "symptom of a complicated situation," although he did not specify what sort of situation he meant. The emigration waves he characterized as a "great human and economic loss" and a "social wound" for the GDR, and he entreated East Germans entertaining the possibility of emigration to remain. "Our homeland, your friends, your colleagues, we all need you. Each who leaves is one too many."[30]

On the matter of dialogue he stated that "the socialist society must have debate precisely because it is an enlightened society." This society, he said, must have critical and confident citizens. But in the next breath he lashed out at the West German media for "hindering" proper dialogue and interfering in the GDR's internal affairs: "NATO concepts and counsels aiming to reform away socialism will have no chance here." Wavering yet again, he held out the expectation of closer relations with the FRG "in accordance with the Basic Treaty."

With regard to actual political reform, Krenz offered thin gruel. While underlining his commitment to equality before the law and "socialist constitutional rights" on the one hand, he spoke of "practicing democratic centralism in the sense of Lenin" on the other. Finally, he announced new government openness and laws permitting more extensive travel.[31] The government was preparing a bill on travel abroad, he said, that would lift all travel restrictions to socialist countries. Travel possibilities to the West, though, were "seriously hindered," he claimed, by the refusal of the FRG to recognize a separate GDR citizenship.

"KRENZ MACHT KEINEN LENZ"

The selection of Krenz as Honecker's successor met with considerable skepticism, and a fair amount of cynicism, in both Germanys, and few found his "new course" very credible. Representatives of New Forum pointed out that nothing in Krenz's background suggested a commitment to liberalization, that indeed, he had been one of Honecker's closest cohorts. Bohley publicly deplored his record on civil rights, bringing to recollection that he had been responsible for the suppression of certain religious groups, and had rigged the local elections the previous May. She correctly predicted he would be hard pressed to overcome the people's great mistrust of him. Many East Germans recalled with dismay that

Krenz had brazenly supported the harsh crackdown in the PRC the previous summer. East Berlin bishop Gottfried Forck commented that open dialogue would be a completely new and challenging field for Krenz.

FRG Chancellor Kohl welcomed the public's success in forcing Honecker out of office, but added somewhat ruefully that a mere change of personalities at the top was no guarantee of reform. The decisive issue for Kohl was that "fellow countrymen" should no longer be denied freedom, human rights, and self-determination.[32] Krenz, he said, would be judged by his willingness to carry out necessary reforms. Hans-Jochen Vogel, chairman of the West German SPD, referred to Honecker's removal as an important first step, but added that fundamentally new policies were essential. People in the GDR and throughout Europe, he remarked, were expecting expeditious democratization, recognition of opposition groups, freedom to travel, and basic reforms of the state and society.[33] The Hamburg weekly, *Die Zeit*, commented: "If [Krenz] himself does not refurbish the system from the ground up and make the GDR liveable, then another will do so, and he will remain merely a transitional figure . . . his 'transformation' will be credible only if it involves genuine change."[34] A considerable rolling of heads, the commentary went on to say, would have to be the first step in the process.

Krenz quickly received the popular view of his "turnaround." Mass demonstrations, the party's chief instrument of pretentious self-gratification in the past, had boomeranged. On the Monday after Honecker's resignation, some 250,000 participated in the Leipzig protest march with a palpable enthusiasm the SED could never have dreamed of generating. In Plauen that week 50,000 demonstrated, and tens of thousands took to the streets in virtually every city. After the official celebrations on October 7, the SED tried once or twice to organize demonstrations for the regime. The efforts were to no avail, however. One party demonstration scheduled to be held in Halle and to be entitled, Red Flags Against White Candles, was unceremoniously canceled for lack of popular interest. The regime was no longer able to mobilize people, nor recruit them to attend its rallies.

Neues Deutschland and other party-affiliated papers now spoke daily of the "dialogue throughout the country," but the popular notion of this differed greatly from what the SED leadership had in mind. Krenz's election as chairman of the Council of State occasioned a spontaneous demonstration of over 12,000 in the streets of East Berlin, with protesters clamoring for a separation of party and state. By assuming Honecker's posts of SED chief and Council of State Chairman, Krenz was the embodiment of the fusion of high office. Just prior to Krenz's scheduled election, a joint declaration of the SDP, Democratic Awakening, and Democracy Now appealed to the *Volkskammer* representatives to relinquish their "undignified role" as a rubber stamp, and to refuse Krenz their votes.

Twenty-six *Volkskammer* members voted against Krenz and an equal number abstained, an occurrence without precedent in a parliament where unanimity had been the practiced rule. Most of the negative votes came from the bloc party ranks, a sure sign the unraveling of the coalition was far advanced. And there was sufficient dissent among SED members to show that the leadership was coming under pressure from its own rank-and-file. *Volkskammer* President Sindermann, having been spared the trouble of counting votes in the past, was visibly stunned.

But what was truly remarkable in such a repressive state, and was of far greater import, was the swift dissipation of people's fear. In all major East German cities the young, the not-so-young, and the old began simply to defy their rulers. Families marching in protest with small children called to on-looking police to join in the demonstrations. Ordinary persons, for years browbeaten into docility by officialdom, suddenly became tenacious, intrepidly taking to the streets to demand control of their own lives, and addressing that officialdom with an audacity that would have been inconceivable six weeks before. Some would later remark they were putting their own internal affairs to rights for the first time. They would suffer the lie no longer. Thrice and four times blessed were those who witnessed people lifting their heads in dignity and prodigiously relishing the cup of freedom.

By early October there could no longer be any doubt that the demonstrations were of a resolute character, and had an overtly political flavor. Where there had been much uneasy reticence the month before—the legacy of grisly authoritarianism—there were shouts for Krenz and his cohorts to resign, for lying demagogues to be gone, even for the SED to depart altogether. Protest signs and banners called for free elections, the release of political prisoners, and open borders. Nor was humor wanting in the mass movement of a society renowned for its acid, but largely fruitless, political wit. Now that wit would be enlisted in freedom's cause. Large protest signs in Leipzig calling for Schnitzler to be sent to the "Muppet Show" were received with much amusement. Other placards read: *Krenz macht keinen Lenz.* The pleasantry translates loosely to "One swallow does not make a spring" but it cleverly (and flippantly) employed the new general secretary's name. All this was transpiring in a country where a mere two months before, public criticism of the regime was virtually unknown and those voicing modest political demands risked jail sentences. Almost in a twinkling, to stand up and be counted became intrinsic to a new sense of self-worth. The people were on the move, the party on the run.

The sense of purpose East Germans had discovered almost overnight seemed to surge forth in spontaneous outpourings. A society where for four decades no independent structures were permitted to exist was organizing itself and revamping a totalitarian state from below. Toward the middle of October in the county of Dresden political discussions were regularly being held in some 400 auditoriums and clubs, these often packed full.[35] Over 100,000 people attended an open-air meeting in Dresden on October 26 with Modrow and Berghofer, who both pledged a truly new era. In the city of Leipzig there were over thirty such assembly points where people talked of political reform, and not infrequently boldly shouted down party officials not saying what they wished to hear. In the official press there were merely subtle regrets that dialogue with the people was so late in coming.[36]

Instead of gaining any time, the supposed dialogue between a leadership and its people only whetted appetites for change. Concessions incurred no popular contentment, but had the opposite effect of bringing on a fresh round of demands as pressure from below increased. When thousands of Berliners formed human chains one October weekend, Schabowski went amidst the demonstrators to engage them in conversation. With East German television cameras running, people on the street in a vivid display of newly discovered courage cleared the air with Schabowski, standing no nonsense on political issues, and inquiring to boot when the privileges of the party elite would be eliminated. It was not necessarily the sort of dialogue Schabowski had planned for, but he did go on record saying party privileges would be discarded. Several days later Politburo members met for a frank discussion with two founding members of New Forum, Jens Reich and Sebastian Pflugbeil. Afterward, Reich said he was cautiously optimistic.

There was reason to be. On October 27 the Council of State announced an immediately effective amnesty for refugees and for all demonstrators taken into custody. Those convicted of illegal border crossing would be released, and prosecutions of those caught fleeing were halted. Bohley termed the move "the first signal that we have waited for so long."[37] On the same day *Neues Deutschland* intimated in a commentary that the *Volkskammer* would soon be reformed.[38]

As the people exerted pressure on the regime with greater confidence, the press could no longer conceal the enormity of the political and economic crises facing the SED. The faltering uncertainty of the press reflected the bewilderment and vacillation of the party it depended upon for guidance. While continuing to show some obligatory animosity toward the FRG, a vestige of the party's defensive posture, the press trumpeted the "serious discussions" and dialogue that were taking place within the GDR. As was visibly the case with the party, the press oscillated between the inclination to assail socialism's foes and the requirements of reconciliation. A major problem seemed to be that the party, having relied heavily upon verbal assaults as standard operating procedure in the past, found itself at a loss without the barrage. Nonetheless, a considerable transformation of the official press occurred in a very short time. On October 26 *Neues Deutschland* wrote that the "police do not wish to criminalize the demonstrators." The overwhelming majority, it went on to say, meant well and were acting out of conviction to achieve a new beginning in the society. Two weeks before, these same demonstrators were mere "rowdies" and "bandits." The next day, October 27, the party organ acknowledged the existence of opposition groups and even had a few words of praise for the contacts taking place between the SED and New Forum.[39] On the following day it contained an article about the plight of the refugees in the diplomatic missions, heretofore a non-issue altogether. Other formerly taboo subjects such as the pressing need for inner-city renovation, the regrettable suppression of artistic creation in the past, the allegations about recent police brutalities, all saw the light of print. On the last day of October a theater of the cold war closed its shutters for good after twenty-nine years, when the termination of *Der Schwarze Kanal*, along with the retirement of Schnitzler, was announced.

KRENZ IN MOSCOW

On October 31 Krenz traveled to Moscow for consultations with Gorbachev on developments in the GDR. In a press conference he stated that "full agreement" on principal issues had been reached in the "openhearted discussions."[40] The GDR, he said, was committed to using Soviet experiences with reform and restructuring "as these pertain to the concrete conditions of the GDR." The change he was initiating in the GDR, Krenz claimed to have assured Gorbachev, would strengthen socialism on German soil. Turning to other issues, Krenz emphasized that German reunification was "not on the agenda," and was in fact out of the question. European stability, he insisted, was far more important than "unrealistic ideas" about unification of the Germanys. For its part, the Berlin Wall, he said, broaching a most delicate topic, was not designed to hinder contacts between persons, but stood as a "certain wall of protection between two social systems and military blocs." Moreover, he asserted, there were numerous "economic reasons" for the Wall's existence.

To a question concerning the party's leading role, Krenz responded that such a function was anchored in the Constitution to which he had sworn an oath. This would not change, he stated categorically. On the matter of his predecessor, he remarked: "Under the leadership of Erich Honecker many accomplishments were made and much good was done, so that during this time I have nothing to be ashamed of."[41] This was hardly what East Germans wished to hear. With such pronouncements Krenz stood to lose whatever credibility he had with his people.

NOTES

1. *Der Spiegel*, October 16, 1989.
2. *Archiv der Gegenwart*, no. 22, October 2-18, 1989.
3. *Der Tagesspiegel*, October 5, 1989.
4. *Der Spiegel*, April 16, 1990.
5. Interview with Egon Bahr, *Der Spiegel*, October 16, 1989.

6. *Neues Deutschland*, October 6, 1989.

7. *Der Spiegel*, October 16, 1989.

8. *Archiv der Gegenwart*, no. 22, October 2-18, 1989.

9. Ibid.

10. *Neues Deutschland*, October 7, 1989.

11. Ibid.

12. *Archiv der Gegenwart*, no. 22, October 2-18, 1989.

13. *Der Tagesspiegel*, October 7, 1989.

14. *Archiv der Gegenwart*, no. 22, October 2-18, 1989.

15. *Süddeutsche Zeitung*, October 9, 1989.

16. *Der Spiegel*, October 16, 1989.

17. *Die Zeit*, October 13, 1989.

18. *Der Spiegel*, October 16, 1989.

19. See *Die Zeit*, October 13, 1989. Honecker was fond of these two: "Den Sozialismus halt in seinem Lauf/weder Ochs noch Esel auf" and "Vorwarts immer, ruckwarts nimmer."

20. *Der Spiegel*, October 16, 1989.

21. *Die Welt*, October 12, 1989.

22. *Der Spiegel*, October 13, 1989.

23. *Süddeutsche Zeitung*, October 10, 1989.

24. *Der Spiegel*, October 16, 1989.

25. Ibid.

26. *Neues Deutschland*, October 14, 1989.

27. *Süddeutsche Zeitung*, October 12, 1989.

28. *Archiv der Gegenwart*, no. 22, October 2-18, 1989.

29. *Frankfurter Allgemeine Zeitung*, October 19, 1989.

30. *Neues Deutschland*, October 19, 1989.

31. *Archiv der Gegenwart*, no. 22, October 2-18, 1989.

32. *Frankfurter Allgemeine Zeitung*, October 19, 1989.

33. *Archiv der Gegenwart*, no. 22, October 2-18, 1989.

34. *Die Zeit*, October 20, 1989.

35. *Der Spiegel*, November 27, 1989.

36. See, for example, *Neues Deutschland*, October 21, 1989.

37. *Der Spiegel*, October 30, 1989.

38. *Neues Deutschland*, October 27, 1989.

39. Ibid.

40. *Archiv der Gegenwart*, no. 22, October 2-18, 1989.

41. *Neues Deutschland*, November 2, 1989.

12

The Wall Opens

THE HEADS BEGIN TO ROLL

The GDR was in turmoil and events were following one another with stirring celerity. The economy, already troubled by labor shortages, was feeling the tight pinch of a rapidly shrinking work force. Medical care had become in large part dependent upon the military for supplying ambulance drivers, paramedics, even doctors. Other service sectors, public transportation, automotive repair facilities, and public works were in some cases only slightly better off. The official news admitted that transport services in East Berlin were functioning only with the help of overtime workers and students. The city was short of over 30 percent of its tram operators and nearly half of its bus drivers. Leipzig, the GDR's second largest city, had lost over 30 percent of its bus drivers and an equal percentage of its nurses to emigration.[1]

On November 2, FDGB boss Harry Tisch resigned. Long associated with Honecker, he had been more an executor of SED policy than a union leader. As a Politburo member, he was well-known for his aloofness from working people, and had come under increasing attack from the unions and the press for his authoritarian manner and for neglecting worker interests. In his resignation statement he acknowledged in yet another bit of SED understatement that "political and organizational mistakes" on his part had brought on a "certain loss of confidence" in him.[2] His successor was Annelis Kimmel, a member of the FDGB board of directors and chairperson in East Berlin. The chairman of the GDR's metalworkers' union, Gerhard Nennstiel, concurrently resigned in the wake of public accusations of improprieties, as did the chairman of the artists' union, Herbert Bischoff.

Later that day, the chairmen of the CDU and the NPDP, Götting and Heinrich

Homann, respectively, threw in the towel. Götting had been under considerable pressure from his own party and finally decided to "accede to the wishes and demands of party members and leaders."[3] Both men had been closely affiliated with Honecker. The next to go was Margot Honecker, Minister of Education, unabashed Politburo hard-liner, and spouse of the former party chief. She had been widely accused of operating a school system that raised children with untruths, one that innately "damaged, propagandized, disheartened and browbeat," according to allegations.[4] No great surprise, this: As minister she had demonstrated a remarkable gift for generating lies. Relinquishing their positions also were two SED regional chairmen, Herbert Ziegenhahn of Gera and Hans Albrecht of Suhl. Both had been sharply criticized by the media.

In a television appearance on November 3 Krenz announced more housecleaning at the top. Politburo members, Hager, Mielke, Axen, Neumann, and Mückenberger all stepped down. These "long-serving comrades," Krenz said, "had requested to be relieved of their duties to make room for fresh blood."[5] He appealed to the people for patience, again underscoring the willingness of the SED to reform. In the "new socialist society" there would be an end to censorship, complete freedom of expression, and toleration of all opinions, he claimed. To this end, Krenz said he was proposing the establishment of a court that would oversee adherence to the Constitution. Sweeping administrative reform was indispensable, he added, expressing empathy for widespread citizen dissatisfaction, especially with regard to excessive bureaucracy. Finally he promised a general "renewal" of the party.

Gusts of popular impatience issued forth the following day, when nearly a million people demonstrated in East Berlin for free elections, freedom of expression, the resignation of the government, the end of the party's monopoly of political power, and official recognition of opposition parties. Official television broadcast the demonstration live, as well as several taking place in other cities. Preceding the huge Berlin rally was a smaller march in the city center organized by various artistic organizations, and authorized by officialdom, a first in the history of the GDR. Some placards demanded deeds rather than mere words on the matter of political reform, others that the government step down. The demonstration ended with a rally at the Alexanderplatz where dissident artists, members of the opposition groups, and even a few party functionaries addressed the crowd. Gerlach once again publicly demanded the government's resignation. Former deputy chief of the security service, Markus Wolf, now turned Gorbachev-style reformer, demanded social reforms and nonpartisan investigations of security service activity. Amidst the cheering of thousands, self-critical intellectuals called for the regime's end. In a memorable speech, dissident writer Stefan Heym told the "exalted ones" that their hour had struck. Chief among the organizers' demands were the elimination of Article 1 of the Constitution, specifying the leading role of the party in society, and an overhaul of the criminal code, particularly Paragraph 99 (dissemination of treasonous information), Paragraph 106 (treasonous assembly), and Paragraph 217 (conspiracy).[6]

On November 6 *Neues Deutschland* provided front-page coverage of the huge Berlin rally, and acknowledged that large demonstrations had occurred in every region of the GDR. Notably, the paper also carried an article entitled, "State Security—the Basic Condition for Renewal and for Guarding Achievements," in which it partially vindicated the operation of the state security apparatus. The deputy minister for state security who was interviewed for the article insisted that "total state control" had always been a myth in the GDR, one perpetuated by the Western media. "The Ministry of State Security," he claimed, "does not attempt to control the people, but works together with citizens in the interest of those holding socialism and humanity's peaceful existence close to their hearts."[7] The article had to be viewed within the context of the party's disarray and consequent vacillations. A sizeable number of party members were hedging their bets and soft-pedaling the totalitarianism the SED had long aspired to.

Krenz and the Politburo were by then coming under intense pressure from the SED rank-and-file, and the anxiety even of the senior comrades was unmistakable. On November 7, the Constitution and Legal Committee of the *Volkskammer* rejected by a large margin the draft of a law easing travel restrictions promulgated just the day before, and the subject of strong popular criticism. The proposed law would have permitted East Germans to travel abroad and would have facilitated the reuniting of families separated by Europe's division.[8] Nevertheless, both a passport and visa would have been required to leave the country, time spent abroad limited to thirty days, and the application to travel made three months in advance. In the event officialdom did not authorize travel, an administrative appeal process would have been possible, but the very wording of the bill that, "rejection of authorization . . . will be made under unusual circumstances," aroused considerable suspicion. This was, after all, a bill drawn up by a government that had long denied its people travel rights and, less than two months prior, had closed its borders with fraternal socialist states. The committee substantiated its rejection of the bill on the grounds that it was clearly not in accordance with popular expectations about freedom of movement, and thus would not contribute to the restoration of regime credibility. At a minimum, the committee report said, the visa requirement for private and business travel would have to be eliminated. It furthermore recommended that the thirty-day limitation on the length of a sojourn be reconsidered. Following the criticism, the government admitted to certain deficiencies in the bill, and subsequently retracted it.

In point of fact, the SED was fast losing its authority. On November 8 the professors of Potsdam's Political and Legal Science Academy, party comrades without exception, sent an open letter to the 163 members of the Central Committee charging them with responsibility for the turmoil in the GDR.[9] "The party leadership's ignorant and arrogant behavior over the years towards reserved and moderate criticism provoked the crisis," said the letter, the entire text of which was published by the official news agency. If major problems were not immediately addressed, the letter went on to say, "the mass of party members will challenge party authority."

Junge Welt, now on the side of radical reform, demanded that the leadership resign to make way for the reform-minded, "those free from hatred, selfishness and reproaches." Accordingly, "we need a new Politburo and a new Government with an unencumbered ability to act."[10] *Tribüne*, the union paper, asserted that the Politburo had a major credibility problem and should step down. The lack of credibility, it suggested, was the chief reason people were exiting in large numbers.[11]

Since the Czechoslovak announcement on November 3 that East Germans would be permitted to cross the frontier to the FRG with only GDR identification cards, in technical violation of border agreements, the exodus of people unwilling to wait for reform shifted largely to that exit route. In one week, over 50,000 fled through Czechoslovakia, and up to 100 automobiles containing on average 350 persons were crossing the border every hour. Queues of fuming East German cars miles long tarried at the main crossing point at Schirnding, while West German authorities desperately strove to find accommodation in already overflowing refugee camps. The outflow reached new record highs, and the GDR was hemorrhaging perilously. The SED had lost its last effective authoritarian ally, and only the frontier with West Germany remained safely sealed.

THE GOVERNMENT AND POLITBURO RESIGN

On the day of the Legal Committee's challenge, November 7, came the startling announcement that Stoph's entire forty-one-member government had resigned in "the interest of society and of the people." The new government spokesman, Wolfgang Meyer, read the declaration of the parting officials appealing to the people, "in this politically and economically critical situation to make every effort to maintain vital social and economic functions."[12] It closed by imploring East Germans not to turn their backs on the country.

Reporting the resignations to gathering crowds, hoping to mollify testy citizens, Meyer and other functionaries were jeered by thousands demanding free elections. The resignation move, orchestrated chiefly by Krenz, represented an effort to move dissent from the streets to a more controlled and manageable form into the *Volkskammer*. It was another exercise in locking the stable door after the horse was gone. By merely reacting to events for so long, the party continuously responded with too little too late. With his back to the wall, the general secretary had now to placate a turbulent population. Internecine struggles within the party suggested that the SED was for the most part groping aimlessly.

On the following day, in an occurrence without precedent in a communist country, all the more extraordinary in the orthodox GDR, the entire Politburo resigned. Later in the day the Central Committee elected a new executive body of only eleven members. Krenz was retained as general secretary, but several new faces appeared in the leadership forum, in particular that of the outspoken reformer, Hans Modrow, whom the Central Committee proposed as the new premier.

Krenz, in a speech before the Central Committee, thanked the departing Politburo members for their work over the years. Several, he pointed out with some veneration, had participated in the antifascist struggle against the Nazis, and had been incarcerated as a consequence. As "activists of the first hour," they had contributed to the building of socialism in the GDR and could not be blamed for the current state of affairs, he said. Indeed, he contended, it was not the workers, not the intelligentsia, not the artists, teachers or students, not the millions of honest communists who bore responsibility for the "extremely difficult and tense situation," but rather the comrades who practiced "subjectivism" in decision making, and who proffered such subjectivism as "the general opinion of party members."[13] The subjectivism theme was intended to facilitate attacks on Honecker's leadership style, setting the stage for Krenz's personal turnaround on his way to Damascus. In an article in *Neues Deutschland* on November 9, Krenz began with the question: "What has led to the present situation in our society?" In his answer he acknowledged the existence of "individual errors" as well as "basic deficiencies in the present system." With these pronouncements Krenz was inviting accusations of being a wryneck. Was this not the same Krenz who, upon assuming the highest SED office, extolled Honecker's great accomplishments, and insisted that no one affiliated with his administration had anything to be ashamed of? The marred public image he was trying to mend was tarnished all the more by the gibing retort on West German television of Wolf Biermann, expelled from the GDR by the very Politburo in which Krenz had made his career, who said he found Krenz "a walking encouragement to flee the GDR."[14]

Krenz was attempting a clean break with the past that was virtually impossible for someone in his position. In a speech to the Central Committee following his re-selection as party leader, Krenz rebuked Honecker and Mittag, holding them accountable for the crisis. He stated, "From the understanding we have acquired from current analyses, it is clear that the basis of past economic policies has not been reality, but subjective wishful thinking."[15] The general secretary did not specify which path-breaking analyses he was referring to, but with his fresh assessment of the Soviet reform course, he conceded that the GDR had repeatedly missed crucial opportunities. "The proper conclusions" about developments in the Soviet Union and other socialist countries were not always drawn, and as a result "many negative symptoms" presented themselves in the economic sphere, in the media, in cultural and intellectual life, in education, in the functioning of state institutions, and within the party itself, Krenz argued. "Instead of discussing solutions to problems," he said, the party under Honecker made a business of claiming to have put things in order that were simply not in order. The ever-widening gulf between "everyday experience and the official portrayal of the GDR," by then SED Newspeak for egregious lying, undermined the trust of the citizenry, he added.

For the record, Krenz provided full particulars about the fall of Honecker, some of which are worthy of our attention. That the ailing Honecker had chosen Mittag to represent him as general secretary beginning in August was common knowledge. This choice, according to Krenz, resulted in dithering and lack of leadership at precisely the moment decisiveness was needed. The void at the top contributed powerfully to the destabilization that was exacerbated by the visible symptoms of crisis in the country as well as by Western media theatrics. Later in August, he said, certain members of the Politburo tried in vain to address the increasingly acute problems of the country, the mass exodus in particular. Mittag for his part adamantly refused to initiate partywide discussions or to convene a conference of local party secretaries. Propaganda chief Herrmann and others rejected out-of-hand suggestions for revised media policies and for the dissemination of more information to the public, Krenz stated. Upon Honecker's return, he (Krenz) and several others demanded that the Politburo begin a rethinking, and confront directly the challenges the country faced. "Honecker would hear nothing of this," Krenz insisted, and there followed a bitter two-day Politburo debate centering on the question whether any special action should be taken.

Krenz's version corresponded fairly closely with what had been reported in the Western media at the time. Herrmann and Mittag attempted to stonewall serious deliberation of the crisis, while Honecker somewhat docilely sided with them. Mittag, as usual, said Krenz, issued his "grossly manipulated facts and figures" in an effort to diminish the severity of problems. On October 12 the confidence question was raised, and on October 17, following more altercation and an ensuing motion by Stoph, the Politburo voted to discharge Honecker, Mittag, and Herrmann. Thus, only after October 12, Krenz claimed, could the Politburo begin with urgently necessary reforms.

The weekly *Der Spiegel* would afterwards flesh out Krenz's exposition. In what is to date still the most plausible analysis of Honecker's ouster, *Der Spiegel* suggested that the beginning of the episode can be traced back to a coup plot in January 1989.[16] Krenz and Schabowski, it seemed, were becoming increasingly concerned about the possibility of domestic unrest resulting from the old guard's stubborn resistance to reform. At the time the Politburo was split into several groups over an old issue that had begun smoldering like a spark dropped in a forest. On the one side there were the "hard-liners" who continuously opposed policies easing emigration and allowing greater openness, who argued that these would not relieve tension at home, and might in fact lead to turmoil.[17] On the other side were Honecker and the status quo adherents. Such divisions had been faintly perceptible in the nuanced public positions taken by the respective SED leaders vis-à-vis reform discussions in other East Bloc states.

Krenz and Schabowski formed yet a third group, having become convinced that personnel changes, and perhaps some cosmetic reform would be necessary if the party was to maintain its grip. The two planned therefore to eject Hager, Mittag, and Herrmann from the Central Committee and to bring several regional party bosses, including Eberlein, the Magdeburg regional party leader, and Modrow into the Politburo. Honecker, for his part, would either be eased out or kept on in a symbolic role. The scheme was, of course, especially attractive to Krenz since it would at one and the same time rid him of party rivals and smooth his transition to SED general secretary, the post he was being groomed for but risked losing to Hager or someone backed by him.

For several reasons the plan couldn't be carried through in the winter of 1989. Honecker, after eighteen years as SED chief, was apparently more obstinate about holding all his party and government positions than Krenz and Schabowski had anticipated. Such obstinacy later resulted in his sudden political demise. What is more, Modrow balked. He preferred remaining an outsider in Dresden than going to East Berlin on the terms Krenz was offering. He was, in fact, reported to have told Krenz he would rather play soccer with his grandchildren along the bank of the Elbe River than to be Krenz's right-hand man.[18] The situation changed when Mielke cast in his lot with Krenz and Schabowski, and sometime later in the year approached Gorbachev, telling him that stability in the GDR required Honecker's departure. Honecker's incapacitation that summer worked to the plotters' advantage. Moscow offered its assistance in toppling the party chief. What exactly the Kremlin did is not known, and probably never will be, but by the time Gorbachev visited East Berlin in October he had plainly distanced himself from the aged East German leader.

THE SED REFORM COURSE AGAIN

In the same Central Committee meeting Krenz expressed his conviction that only "fundamental reform and reorganization" of the political system held out any chance of quelling the crisis. An "unweaving" of state and party was essential, he stated, as was the establishment of a veritable coalition government and a genuinely democratic decision-making process.[19] He spoke of the need for political control mechanisms including an independent judiciary, and announced the future enactment of laws guaranteeing freedom of assembly and speech, as well as an election law "ensuring free, universal, democratic and secret elections."[20] The overriding objective, he said, had to be the "development through consensus of our country's socialism into a performance-oriented and socially just society."

Following the reform of the party and of political institutions, Krenz proclaimed, large-scale economic restructuring with the goal of creating a market-oriented socialist plan economy would take place. According to Krenz, the GDR's economic difficulties presented no proof of the failure of the plan economy, but merely how economic subjectivism, waste, and the neglect of economic equilibrium conditions could cause dislocations. Nonetheless, planning in the new GDR was to be limited and would be oriented toward common societal interests, he said. But of foremost importance in the stabilization scheme was the expansion of foreign trade. To promote Western investment the GDR was prepared to consider all forms of cooperation with the firms of capitalist countries, he emphasized. He then announced Plan 1990, his program of economic stabilization, that would expand production of consumer goods and provide a wider selection of foodstuffs. He further promised a careful reevaluation of subsidization procedures and more balanced social policies. Also, "all elements contrary to economic performance principles as well as those leading to waste and speculation," he said, would be eliminated.

Finally, he pledged the amending of the criminal code, an investigation into the working of, and the possible reorganizing of the Ministry for State Security, and a redefining of the police role in the society. In particular, laws dealing with flight from the GDR and with treasonous acts would be rewritten or thrown out altogether. Thereafter, the Central Committee decided to convene a party conference, scheduling it for December 15 to 17. According to the party statute, a party conference would deal with urgent questions of party politics and tactics and was empowered to dismiss Central Committee members and candidate members who have failed in their duties. It could increase the number of Central Committee members and elect candidate members to the committee. In the SED's history there had been only three party conferences, the last in March 1956 following the Twentieth Party Conference of the CPSU when Khrushchev denounced Stalin's crimes.

The Central Committee concluded its meeting with a communiqué stating the Politburo's new composition, and expelling Mittag and Herrmann from the committee. Mittag was accused of the "most flagrant transgressions of inner-party democracy and party discipline" in addition to seriously damaging the party's image. The Central Committee ordered the party control commission to initiate an investigation of the "mistakes" of Mittag as well as those of "other comrades who have committed infractions against the party statute."[21] A special committee was to be formed to examine causes and responsibilities for the present economic situation in the GDR.

The so-called Action Program of the SED reflected the suggestions contained in Krenz's addresses to the Central Committee. The program self-critically conceded that only after massive peaceful protests, the involvement of various Christian organizations, the formation of opposition groups, and growing pressure from the party rank-and-file, did the leadership finally realize the need to begin eliminating "encrusted political structures and to take the first steps toward change."[22] Certain reforms, according to the Action Program, were long overdue. Party and state were to be separated, and democracy was to provide socialism with a new dynamism. Opposition parties were to be accorded recognition. There would be parliamentary representation and a genuine coalition government. Complete freedom of religion was to be guaranteed and a new relationship between church and state was to be fostered. Fundamental economic changes were to result in the creation of a market-oriented economy.

Then there came more firings. Newly selected Politburo member Hans-Joachim Böhme asked to be relieved of his responsibilities in the face of protest demonstrations against his election to high office. Candidate members Johannes Chemnitzer, Werner Walde, and Ingeburg Lange resigned also. The latter, since 1973 Central Committee secretary for women's issues, had been the subject of particularly strong attacks from the party ranks.

SCHABOWSKI'S BOMBSHELL

The real historical significance of November 9 came with an almost incidental announcement by Schabowski, just reelected to the Politburo. Schabowski informed assembled journalists that, pending the passage of new travel laws, the following provisional regulations would take effect immediately:[23] (1) It would be possible for citizens to apply for permission to travel abroad without the usual preconditions, that is, special invitation and/or visiting relatives. Permission could be given on short notice by the local police departments. (2) Respective sections of police departments in the GDR have been instructed to grant travel visas without prejudice and without delay, and without considering the reasons for travel. (3) Continuous travel from the GDR would be possible at all frontier checkpoints with the FRG and West Berlin, and there would be no additional formalities or requirements.

Schabowski's message followed what had become a crisis meeting of the Central Committee, and the SED's move was widely seen as a last gamble to regain public confidence. What all Germans had been dreaming of for decades had happened suddenly and unexpectedly in a brief announcement on the evening of November 9, the date that went down in history as the day the Wall opened. Schabowski's press conference appeared live on East German television, and by 10 p.m. masses of people had assembled on the eastern side of the Berlin Wall. It was true! The barricades were being lifted and the border guards were merely glancing at identification cards, stamping them only occasionally. The surge of people quickly became so great, however, that even minimal formalities were dispensed with.

What followed in Berlin was a spontaneous multi-day celebration in a city that had been brutally divided for over twenty-eight years. Hundreds of thousands sang and danced in the streets, people cried, strangers embraced one another. Many climbed over the Wall; pictures of Berliners standing on top of that architectural monstrosity were seen worldwide. There were similar outpourings of emotion on the border with the FRG. Upon hearing the almost incredible announcement, many East Germans drove straight to the frontier. Traffic backed up for miles in many areas, and quickly reached gridlock in Berlin, where the public transportation system came to a virtual standstill.

The news of the border opening struck the FRG like a thunderbolt. Chancellor Kohl and Foreign Minister Hans-Dietrich Genscher on an official visit to Poland at the time broke off the trip and hurried to Berlin. A government spokesman described the development at the time of its occurrence as an event of "great significance." He underscored the preparedness of the FRG to assist the GDR, but quickly added:

> Cosmetic correction will not suffice. We will not attempt to stabilize untenable conditions. But we are willing to provide extensive support once fundamental reform of the political and economic situation in the GDR has been mandated. The SED must renounce its monopoly of political power, and must consent to free elections and the establishment of independent parties.[24]

He exhorted all Germans to show solidarity in the great historical process taking place in the GDR.

SPD chairman Vogel agreed that the most crucial step in the reform process in the GDR, would be free elections. He immediately called upon the West German parties to put aside their differences and to work to improve the situation in the GDR so that people would no longer have cause to flee.[25] FDP parliamentary leader Wolfgang Mischnick praised the East Germans for their courage and decisiveness. He expressed his great satisfaction that East and West Germans never lost their belief in a common nation.[26] East Germans, he said, "had regained a belief in themselves as well." The "historic hour" would present Germans with a true test, he said.

On November 10, the West German parliamentary upper house (*Bundesrat*) held a memorial session for those who died in escape attempts from the GDR. On the same day a large assembly was held before the town hall in West Berlin. Among the speakers were Brandt, who was mayor of West Berlin when the Wall was built, and the current mayor, Walter Momper. In his speech, Brandt uttered the now famous words: "In the situation now, what belongs together is growing together again. It has been a long way and we are not yet at the end of the path." With his statement Brandt was revitalizing the concept of nationhood at a crucial time. Perhaps more than any other person he understood the attraction of, even the compulsion of, German unification. In the coming months, however, few in his party took heed.

Commenting on the deep popular emotions surrounding him, Momper remarked: "On this Friday the German people are the happiest in the world." He remembered all those who had died on the Wall, and recalled the suffering division had caused. He referred to the development in the GDR as a "fascinating chapter of German history," one written by the East Germans themselves.

Chancellor Kohl also spoke of a great day in German history. The most immediate issues in the GDR, he said, were free elections, freedom of expression, and independent parties and unions. He emphasized that the FRG stood at the East Germans' side. "We are and remain one nation," he asserted, "and we belong together." Genscher stated that even forty years of division had not resulted in separate German nations. "There are not capitalist and socialist German nations, but only one German nation, obligated to peace and freedom," he proclaimed. Careful to provide assurances to Germany's neighbors, he stated that "no people on earth and no people in Europe must harbor fears with this opening of the gates of freedom, once democracy in the GDR has been realized." We Germans, he said in addressing the country's neighbors, "have decided in favor of the community of Western democracies."

FRG president Richard von Weizsäcker, eloquent as usual, characterized the developments as a "significant historical turning point in post-war history." He said it had become evident that freedom cannot be walled in, years on end. The present issue, he submitted, was the initiation of a step-by-step process "pursued with responsibility and moderation" that would at its end allow all Germans to live with one another in freedom and dignity.

From November 10 to 12 hundreds of thousands of East Germans visited the FRG and West Berlin. For the most part, the border guards allowed people to cross over with their identification cards. When guards insisted upon stamping visas into identification documents, additional delays resulted in already chaotic traffic conditions, as for example, at the Rudolphstein checkpoint which reported a backup of over thirty-five miles on November 11. An estimated three million East Germans visited the FRG and West Berlin in less than four days. *Neues Deutschland,* by this time almost completely adrift, proclaimed on its November 13 front page, not without an odd blustering, that over four million visa applications had already been filed; the editorial staff apparently retained its obsession with raw numbers. On the same front page mention was made of scattered "border provocations" without any clarification of who exactly was provoking whom. As border crossing points were insufficient in size to permit the outflow of people, border guards resorted to simply punching holes in the walls and chopping through the barbed wire. Presumably then, the border guards were the chief perpetrators of the "provocations."

The Glienicker Bridge, a symbol of the cold war and hitherto closed for all but official use, was opened for automobile and pedestrian traffic on November

10. To the great pleasure of crowds, on November 12 a hole was punched in the Wall at Potsdamer Square, once the busiest traffic circle in Europe, but haunted by a ghostly silence since the city's division. Also on November 12, GDR defense minister Kessler canceled the shooting order on the frontier, a ghastly provision overtaken by events anyway. Border troops were instructed to facilitate the orderly free flow of traffic in every possible way. They were to ensure that the border fortifications were not damaged or destroyed by anyone, an odd order since the guards were improvising frontier apertures, and, "under no circumstances were weapons to be used."[27] At that point it would have been difficult to imagine any purpose for the use of weapons. *Neues Deutschland* provided assurances on the front page of the November 11 edition that the border opening was not temporary, but permanent. Two days later it heralded Moscow's praise for the recent "correct and intelligent decisions" taken in the GDR.[28] The television news announced the following day that all villages, buildings, and other facilities situated in "protected border areas" would henceforth be accessible to all. The twelve nautical mile expanse of territorial sea was also opened for recreational purposes. Deutschlandpolitik had become the art of the impossible.

At one point during the weekend, Momper met with the mayor of East Berlin, Erhard Krack, directly on the sector line at the Potsdamer Square. Speaking again of an historic moment, Momper pointed out: "Potsdamer Square was once the heart of Berlin. It will beat again as before." Even Krack, who was politically close to the Honecker Politburo, and would later be forced out of office in disgrace, showed considerable pleasure. Both mayors announced their intentions to cooperate on administrative matters and to facilitate travel between the two halves of the city.

The world held its breath. This was to be the strangest week of post-war German history. It was not the least irony in a miraculous year clogged with ironies that the border was opened for the very reason it had been sealed over twenty-eight years before. Only the travel freedom East Germans had longed for could staunch the outflow of people. East Germans had long since found effective ways to breach the walls around their country: over 200,000 had availed themselves of the opportunity in the first ten months of 1989. With the borders open, the flow of refugees through Hungary and Czechoslovakia promptly stopped, to the great relief of Budapest and Prague. There was, of course, no longer a reason for East Germans to take the Hungarian or Czech roundabout.

Although the party's November decision was dramatic to say the least, in throwing open the borders Krenz and his followers rendered de jure what had become de facto. The precipitant measures bought the party a modicum of breathing space just as the situation seemed to be spinning out of control, and by permitting people to come and go as they pleased, the SED was banking on people returning. Most did, but only to return home to call for more reform.

REACTIONS ABROAD

The Soviet foreign minister described the border opening as a wise and reasonable decision that had been taken without any prodding from Moscow. He said the move had been a completely sovereign act of the GDR. Gorbachev welcomed the leadership changes and what promised to be the attendant breakthrough of *perestroika* in the GDR. Foreign ministry spokesman Gennady Gerasimov hinted that the Soviet Union could accept a noncommunist government in the GDR so long as the latter remained in the Warsaw Pact. He indicated the Soviet Union would show the same understanding for reform in the GDR as it had shown vis-à-vis Hungary and Poland. "Poland is a good member of the Warsaw Pact and in Poland there is a coalition government, not a communist one," he said. In an evident application of the new Soviet "Sinatra Doctrine" (each does it his own way), Gerasimov stated: "You see, governments may change, but international obligations remain. . . . It is their (the East Germans') decision, just like in Poland."[29]

Press secretaries of both the Czech and Hungarian foreign ministries hailed the SED's decision also. The spokeswoman of the Polish government stated that Poland, as a signatory of the 1966 Treaty on Civil and Political Rights, was very pleased that yet another country was granting freedom of travel to its citizens. On the question of German reunification, the spokeswoman said that the Polish government considered this a strictly German matter, but nonetheless one to be addressed in a European context. There would have to be guarantees for European security, she said, but of course the two German states could unify within their present borders should they so wish.

President George Bush said he was elated by the news from the GDR, calling it a "dramatic happening" and a "victory for freedom." Admitting he had been taken by surprise, Bush added that the Berlin Wall had "very little relevance," and the GDR had taken a major step toward compliance with the Helsinki Agreement. In response to a question about reunification, he said that in his view it was still too early to discuss the matter.

Western European governments generally displayed considerable satisfaction with the opening of the borders. British prime minister Margaret Thatcher expressed the hope of her government that the GDR had opened itself to the world permanently. The first priority must be the creation of a "truly democratic form of government in East Germany," she said, and Great Britain completely supported the demands of East Germans for free elections and a multi-party system. In an official statement the Belgian government called the new freedoms granted to East Germans "a victory for freedom and democratic values."[30] Belgian prime minister Wilfried Martens voiced his hope that the democratic process in the GDR would develop in a "harmonious and constructive manner." Chancellor Franz Vranitzky of Austria described the opening of the borders as "one of the most memorable events in the history of Europe." French prime minister Michel Rocard said in an interview that there could be no real peace in Europe so long as the German people were not at peace with themselves. Through most of the autumn French president François Mitterrand curtly opposed reunification. Later, bowing to what he had come to regard as the inevitable, he shrugged in a display of Gallic stateliness, and adjusted to developments that had taken on completely new dimensions.

Just prior to that unforgettable weekend the senior British EC commissioner, Leon Brittain, fueled a vital EC discussion on a united Germany when he said in a London lecture that the GDR should be welcome in the EC as part of an extended FRG or a unified Germany.[31] The only condition he laid down was that the GDR have the same liberal and democratic institutions as Western European countries. At the same time he warned:

> If Germany's partners give the impression of being opposed to reunification, this will only increase what is at present a small risk: that some in Germany may be tempted to seek reunification on the basis of doing a unilateral deal with the Soviet Union, involving the setting up of a new unified Germany outside the Community.[32]

Brittain was verbalizing what many Europeans, including not a few Germans, had secretly feared. Germany's partners had to make far-sighted responses, and face directly the German question which had for so long been on the back burner. "Opposing unification will make it more likely to occur in the form we would least want," Brittain asserted. Not surprisingly, German diplomats in Brussels called Brittain's remarks "astonishing," and the very notion of the FRG somehow going it alone caused chuckles in Bonn. Strangely, West Germans were among the last to take reunification of their country seriously; even when it was on the doorstep many intelligent West Germans still had difficulty believing it was actually happening. As late as September 1989, with the German question rising to the top of the political agenda as East Germans began forcing themselves on their wealthy neighbor, West German journalists, scholars, and politicians, supposing passivity to be a mark of statesmanship, skirted the issue as much as possible. In fairness, it should be pointed out that such an attitude was to be explained in part by the apprehension many West Germans understandably felt about the growing speculation concerning the imminence of reunification, fearing among other things that reunification talk would unduly alarm Bonn's partners. This was one reason many West Germans were indisposed to contemplate the future of Germany publicly. While there was basic agreement that the crux of the German question was national self-determination for the GDR, two fundamental questions were for the most part sidestepped in the FRG until developments necessitated dealing with them. First, what was to happen if the East Germans chose unification? Second, what if the collapse of the old regime prompted a societal collapse, leaving the FRG to pick up the pieces?

Some West Germans denied their country would be forced to choose between European integration and surmounting Germany's division, once the reunification issue was back on the political agenda.[33] Addressing French expressions of concern about Germany "wandering east," Kohl repeatedly assured Mitterrand in the eventful fall of 1989 that "for us there is no teetering or moving back and forth between different worlds. Our place is in the Western community of values, and in Europe in European integration."[34] West German EC Commissioner Martin Bangemann also disputed that such a dilemma would present itself, insisting the FRG could satisfy national aspirations, while continuing to work toward European integration. "We are striving for both of these," he said.[35]

But the combination of the German question and the time-honored perplexities of European integration seemed almost mind-boggling that fall of 1989. The EC was uncertain what to do and, accordingly, had no real policy. One commissioner, Frans Andriessen, advised a wait and see posture toward Germany. Only after the political situation became less fluid, he believed, could the EC begin negotiations on trade agreements with the GDR. Bangemann, convinced that the EC should encourage reform by providing economic incentives to the GDR, vehemently disagreed. The French, for their part, had become the leading proponents of European integration in the train of eruptions in the East Bloc. Believing that the FRG could be more firmly anchored in the West by accelerating the pace of European integration, Paris exhorted its partners to "deepen" the Community and to deal with the GDR on trade issues as well, that is, to expand the European Community. In fact, the French were using the fission in the Soviet Bloc largely as a pretense for speeding up European political integration and monetary union.[36]

With his pronouncement Brittain was joining forces with those like Bangemann who believed the EC had to take an active role in the East Bloc to induce democratization, and to chart the reform course. For them, a unified Germany was not to be the final stone but an essential foundation of the European house. In retrospect Brittain was correct in his analysis, not so much because of the problem of German "unilateralism" (this being in part for French and British domestic consumption), but rather on account of the growing political and economic chaos in the GDR that would quite quickly bring the country to the brink of lethargy and outright collapse, with its leaders discredited, and its people bolting.

NOTES

1. *The Times* (London), November 8, 1989.
2. *Neues Deutschland*, November 3, 1989.

3. Ibid.
4. *Archiv der Gegenwart*, no. 24, November 8-21, 1989.
5. *Neues Deutschland*, November 4, 1989.
6. *Frankfurter Allgemeiner Zeitung*, November 6, 1989.
7. *Neues Deutschland*, November 6, 1989.
8. *Archiv der Gegenwart*, no. 24, November 8-21, 1989.
9. *The Times* (London), November 8, 1989.
10. *Junge Welt*, November 7, 1989.
11. *The Times* (London), November 8, 1989.
12. *Archiv der Gegenwart*, no. 24, November 8-21, 1989.
13. *Frankfurter Allgemeine Zeitung*, November 9, 1989.
14. *The Times* (London), November 8, 1989.
15. *Archiv der Gegenwart*, no. 24, November 8-21, 1989.
16. *Der Spiegel*, November 20, 1989.
17. *The Economist*, October 14, 1989.
18. *Der Spiegel*, November 20, 1989.
19. *Archiv der Gegenwart*, no. 24, November 8-21, 1989.
20. *Neues Deutschland*, November 11, 1989.
21. *Süddeutsche Zeitung*, November 11, 1989.
22. *Archiv der Gegenwart*, no. 24, November 8-21, 1989.
23. Ibid.
24. *Frankfurter Allgemeine Zeitung*, November 11, 1989.
25. Ibid.
26. *Archiv der Gegenwart*, no. 24, November 8-21, 1989.
27. Ibid.
28. *Neues Deutschland*, November 13, 1989.
29. *The Independent* (London), November 10, 1989.
30. *The Times* (London), November 10, 1989.
31. *The Independent* (London), November 8, 1989.
32. *The Times* (London), November 8, 1989.
33. See the discussion in *This Week in Germany*, November 10, 1989.
34. *The Times* (London), November 8, 1989.
35. Ibid.
36. *Frankfurter Allgemeiner Zeitung*, November 20, 1989.

Part III
Why 1989?

13
Dwindlng Options

THE ISSUE IN 1989

Opening the borders was an admission of desperate weakness on the SED's part, much in the sense that the erection of a wall in 1961 represented an acknowledgment that the country's problems were acute and could not feasibly be disposed of any other way. In retrospect the move to open the borders in the interest of buying time could not even be described as a pyrrhic victory, although some SED leaders held out the hope at the time that short-term concessions could evolve into some longer-term strategy, which, if it did not preserve the party's position, would at least limit damage to the rapid political erosion threatening to sweep the SED away. Could the people be bought off with modest reforms stopping short of free elections and multi-party democracy? With their newly won travel freedom, would the people maintain the pressure for reforms? Would the opposition groups, still in fledgling stages, continue to rally the people against the SED state?

To ask these questions in the autumn of 1989 was to misunderstand the main issue. By that time regime concessions no longer served the people's purposes. The issue was freedom: East Germans, along with their East Bloc neighbors, were now determined to have it. It was not a change of administration most East Germans wanted, but of a system. Speculation in the West that righteous anger toward the SED would turn into "West Berlin chocolate" was unfounded. The life-blood of Honecker's "actually existing socialism" ran out through porous borders. The two most recurrent popular complaints about Honecker's GDR, specifically, "We are constantly lied to" and "We are treated like children," reflected an antipathy surpassing mere dislike of personalities, or disagreement on single issues. The vast majority of East Germans had had enough of what they pertly dubbed their authoritarian kindergarten.

Upheaval in the GDR involved the politics of suddenness, and events often followed one another so quickly that party officials were unable to keep up with them. As one observer so aptly put it, assessments of the situation sometimes became dated while they were still in commentators' mouths. For the GDR's rulers, the path of reform turned into a slippery slope. Compromises on their part tantalized popular political appetites; far from placating indignant people, concessions generated more demands. Once East Germans witnessed the impossible happening—the entrenched SED leadership being sacked *en masse* and the borders opening—few had much inclination to be appeased with circumscribed, party-instigated reform. Exasperated by the "authoritarian kindergarten," cognizant that they had made the great changes happen, they were now going to force a completely new order of things.

MODROW TAKES OVER

For the first time in its history, on November 13 the *Volkskammer* elected a new president in a secret election. Chosen was the DBD chairman, Günter Maleuda, who closely nudged out Manfred Gerlach. Maleuda replaced Sindermann, who in the course of events had lost all his party and state offices. Politburo member Werner Jarowinsky was elected deputy president of the *Volkskammer*.

In his initial address Jarowinsky proposed direct talks on travel matters and related issues with the FRG. Groups of experts would be formed to address all major problems facing the GDR, economic ones in particular. Jarowinsky emphasized that "revolutionary renovation," not German unification, would be the principal governmental objective. Recent developments made constitutional amendments absolutely necessary, he said, and the SED parliamentary faction would begin preparing a new election law providing for free and secret elections with multiple parties and candidates. The criminal code would be changed, he said, to delete the provisions recently identified by the populace as objectionable. There would be new media laws, as well as laws providing for freedom of speech and assembly. The government of the GDR would become a genuine coalition, as promised in the SED's Action Program.

Jarowinsky strongly criticized the ousted party bosses whose leadership style he said was characterized much more by "political arrogance and self-satisfaction" than it was by competent work.[1] The leadership perennially ignored the needs and demands of society, he said, and overcentralization and paternalism were primarily responsible for the present crisis. He spoke positively of the newly formed opposition groups, and praised New Forum for its contributions to the handling of the crisis.

In their remarks on November 13 other party representatives touched upon the same themes. The deputy chairman of the Liberal Democrats, Hans-Dieter Raspe, urged the repeal of Article 1 of the Constitution which mandated monolithic unity. The GDR must have democratic mechanisms, he insisted, that allowed citizen participation in government. In the past, parties, indeed the parliament itself, had been no more than organs of dictatorship, he observed. "None of us effected the political turnaround," he stated, "but this was forced by the people of the GDR on the streets and on the routes leading out of the country."[2] The CDU representative Christine Wienynk criticized her party for the years of docile cooperation with the SED, and underscored the necessity of independent parties and pluralism.

But the most notable addresses of the day were given by former Politburo members who had been invited by the *Volkskammer* to account for their past actions. Their speeches were broadcast live on both East and West German television. Former premier Willi Stoph began his address by admitting that the operation of the government had been considerably circumscribed by the party apparatus to which he belonged. He was right, of course. The comfortable consensus between the SED and political institutions obviated any separation of party and state. Party usurpation of power, said Stoph, prevented the Council of Ministers under his direction from assuming its constitutional function. The body continuously neglected to consult the parliament about specific problems or to solicit cooperation.[3] In the economic sphere, particularly with regard to investment decisions, the Council of Ministers kept parliamentarians in the dark, he conceded, and important investment choices were made in an authoritative fashion outside the council, often without the knowledge of the ministers. Stoph did have a point: It was odd that a cabinet with forty-one portfolios did not have an economics ministry. He emphatically shifted blame for the country's crisis upon Honecker and Mittag, but accepted some responsibility for the political dereliction. After all, he had been a member of the Politburo since 1953 and the premier of the GDR for a total of twenty-two years.

Then came the turn of Sindermann, the former president of the *Volkskammer* who had hesitated for weeks to convene the body, knowing full well that one of its initial acts would be to topple him. To the rostrum came a broken old man who shed tears and begged forgiveness. "I apologize quite openly, especially to the FDJ," he stammered.[4] Melancholy and forlorn, he was to die shortly thereafter.

Mielke, for his part, displayed the obstinacy bred from running the Ministry for State Security for decades, as well as his talent for turning the implausible into the preposterous. Unfalteringly defending the work of his ministry, he alleged it had always maintained "close and friendly contact with all working people."[5] The chamber roared with laughter. The chief task of his ministry, he said, was to uncover any threat to peace, and to that end, ministry officials provided "outstanding information." Another important ministry accomplishment, he added, was the strengthening of the economy. The problem, as he described it, was that recommendations were not followed, and significant information was disregarded. He insisted that he had identified the economic difficulties associated with mass exodus early on, only to have had his warnings ignored. "To no avail we showed how many doctors and teachers were leaving the GDR," he said.[6] Mielke closed his only speech to the *Volkskammer* with the memorable remark, "I love you all," to the whoops and derision of the entire assembly.

On a less facetious note, there followed a dreary economic discourse by the finance minister, Ernst Hofer, and the recently appointed chief of planning, Gerhard Schürer. Hofer, who had confidently presented supposedly balanced budgets before the *Volkskammer* for nine consecutive years, was now forced by parliamentarians and the pressure of events to concede that "balancing" had been possible only through large amounts of hidden red ink.[7] The GDR had in fact run up debts of over 150 billion marks, and as minister he had repeatedly cooked the books. Ambitious building programs, sinking exports, the heavy subsidization of foodstuffs and other items, and the construction of atomic energy plants all consumed enormous amounts of funds, he said. Failure to inform the parliament about huge spending and heavy indebtedness, he suggested, "involved a certain lack of courage and sometimes unreserved cover-ups." He conceded furthermore that the GDR had for years been running a relatively high inflation rate, something previously denied by officialdom, although he was unable to confirm the rumored 12 percent rate in 1989.

Schürer refused to specify how much of the public debt was owed in hard currency, claiming this was highly classified information, but admitted the percentage to have been significant. It would later be disclosed that the recurrent official refusals to provide economic figures, even when these were available, were rooted not only in a deeply ingrained propensity for secrecy. Employees of the Central Institute for Economic Research of the SED Central Committee told the Western press that the institute genuinely feared citizen reprisals, had the truth about the East German economy been revealed.[8] Schürer concluded his remarks with a scathing attack on Mittag, who, he said, continuously refused even to entertain the possibility of severe economic difficulties, much less to consider reform. The revelations were the first of a series of alarming economic signals, and furnished an initial inkling of the scandals that would surface in the following weeks.

The *Volkskammer* closed its November 13 sitting by electing Modrow as the new premier. By this time he had been recognized as the only member of the party's upper echelon who enjoyed much popular sympathy: of all the SED leaders he alone could appear before crowds without eliciting boos and catcalls. He was known to have opposed Honecker's anti-reform attitudes long before it became fashionable in the party to do so, and in fact he had had serious rows with Honecker's Politburo. In addition to endorsing Moscow's reform course, as Dresden regional party boss he often made unsolicited suggestions about economic targets to the central planners, and furthermore had the audacity at times to second-guess them. Mittag, it seemed, was particularly irked by what he perceived to be the interference of a "provincial" in his sphere. Early in 1989 Mittag dispatched a 120-member investigation committee to the Dresden region to examine alleged irregularities in Modrow's administration. *Neues Deutschland* publicly attacked the hapless party boss in June, charging his directorate with, among other things, "deficiencies in political work with the masses."[9] Such attacks might have marked the end of Modrow's career, but as it turned out, in the turbulent fall of that year nothing could have bestowed better credentials upon an SED functionary. Realizing that the fate of the regime was inextricably linked with Modrow, both Krenz and Schabowski, their fingers now constantly checking prevailing political winds, pushed to have him assume the highest state office. He was, they realized, the regime's last hope.

Delivering a blistering attack on former high officials in his first speech, Modrow seemed true to his principles. "The very existence of socialism is at stake," he said. "Many communists are bitter about the leadership's mistakes and their refusal until recently to reform."[10] Modrow promised a complete reorganization of the economy, while underscoring his commitment to political and legal reform. He proceeded to initiate coalition discussions with the parties represented in the *Volkskammer* the following day.

His position was an unenviable one, his room for maneuver limited, and many of the tasks he had set for himself mutually contradictory. Although personally squeaky clean, he belonged to a party becoming more discredited by the day. He had been appointed to maintain the SED in power, but promised free elections the party had very little chance of winning. Indeed, in a poll taken in the third week of November, less than 30 percent *of party members* believed the SED could win a fair election. Modrow was pledged to establish a multi-party system and to organize a genuine coalition government, but at the same time was expected by many SED members to preserve the leading role of the party. The party's objectives were for the most part irreconcilable with popular demands, and the lessons of the split in the Hungarian Communist party could not have been lost on Modrow.

An industrial society that had been shaken to its foundations was to be held together and revitalized without coercion. Modrow focused upon reorganizing the economy and improving its international competitiveness, but capitalism for him remained taboo. Planning and "market-orientation" were to be "bound together," he said, and the revamped economy was to be freed of the encumbrances of centralization. Market forces were to be introduced into a basically socialist economy, whose main enterprise configuration was to remain the *Kombinat*. Modrow thus set out on an exercise in squaring circles. Modrow was a communist in an era when communism as a form of social organization was rapidly being discarded. Adherence to the ideology hindered Modrow and other SED reformers from addressing fundamental questions. For starters, how could a democratic and pluralistic society be established so long as the old security apparatus was still largely in place? How could an economy with market orientation and private property operate with heavy-handed planning bureaucrats still in office? How could a veritable separation of political powers be reconciled with the retention of the SED's leading role?

On November 17 Modrow introduced his new cabinet, which was composed of twenty-eight ministers instead of the previous forty-one. The SED held seventeen portfolios, the LDPD four, the CDU three, and the DBD and the NDPD each two. Ministries for Church Affairs, for Labor and Wages, for Tourism, and for Economics were added. The latter post was filled by Christa Luft, rector of the Academy for Economics in East Berlin, and for the most part untainted by Mittag-style concepts of command economy. Lothar de Maizière, the new CDU chairman, who would later have the distinction of being the first (and last) freely elected prime minister of the GDR, held the Ministry for Church Affairs. Nine ministers were taken from the former cabinet, an inauspicious sign, and all important portfolios, interior, foreign affairs, defense, culture, finance, education and youth, and planning were held by the SED. Modrow eliminated the Ministry for State Security, replacing it with the new Ministry for National Security, whose purview was to be reduced. He justified retention of the fundaments of the ministry with public order arguments. The move hardly fostered popular trust, and maintaining the ministry in any form met with considerable resistance. Public loathing of the ministry, which was still effectively in operation, was great, and Modrow underestimated popular feeling about it more than once. He would later be forced to dissolve the ministry altogether.

In his state-of-the-nation address Modrow emphasized the irreversibility of the reform process. Calling the opening of the borders "an historic event the entire world watched," he characterized the reform process that had begun in the GDR after October 7 as "democratic and popular change in the best sense of the word."[11] He said his government would begin forthwith to draft legislation designed to strengthen the rule of law and to guarantee civil rights. A major overhaul of the criminal code would take place as well, he promised, and his cabinet would work with the parliament "to determine exactly the different legislative, executive and judicial functions, and to separate these from one another, to provide guarantees against abuse of power and office."[12] He pledged equality before the law to the people, and promised that all would at last be equally protected by it. He vowed an end to the "practical discrimination" against women in the GDR (a hitherto thoroughly taboo subject), even if quotas were necessary to accomplish this. In the economic realm, "performance principles" would be employed. Subsidies were to be pared back, and markets for the most part were to determine prices. His government would combat administrative arbitrariness and inordinate centralization. Sweeping administrative reforms would strengthen local and regional authority with the objective of reestablishing communal self-government, something that Modrow described as the crucial first step in the decentralization process. There would be an end to what he referred to as the "capricious command economy of the former member of the Central Committee, Günter Mittag."[13] He estimated that the budget deficit for the year would exceed 15 billion marks, but noted the impossibility of furnishing a budget package for the following year because of the great economic uncertainties his government faced.

With regard to foreign relations, Modrow emphasized the importance of GDR relations with the European Community, undoubtedly with an eye upon the economic difficulties he had been alluding to. "Our position toward the European Common Market must be based upon cooperation," he said. "We should recognize that it [the Common Market] is both a challenge and a chance for us. We are working to achieve more cooperative relations with the European Community as soon as possible." Modrow generally favored a deepening of relations between the two German states, but could not conceal his uneasiness about the challenge the GDR faced in the relationship.

> In opening her borders for free travel, the GDR undertook an action welcomed and supported worldwide. The reforms we are proposing and are already introducing will put the GDR on the proper path toward the realization of self-determination, whereby the legitimacy of the GDR as a sovereign socialist state, and sovereign German state, will be renewed. Not empty slogans but the reality of life in the GDR will impart a final rejection of unrealistic, indeed dangerous, speculation about reunification. Despite their different social orders the two German states have a common history that is centuries long. Both sides should now seize the opportunity to give the relationship a good neighborly character. By fully respecting one another, the German states can offer an example of cooperative coexistence. . . . We advocate transforming the community based upon accord into a fuller community of responsibility, one extending beyond mere international accords and agreements. The two German states and their mutual relations can thereby become important pillars of the framework of the common European house.[14]

As if to complement Modrow's determination to strengthen the GDR's export sector and to expand trade with the FRG, *Neues Deutschland* carried articles the following day about expressions of interest on the part of West German firms in new GDR markets.[15] One article stated that, according to the West German Federation of Industry (BDI), tens of thousands of firms were potential investors in the GDR's economy.

THE SHIP BEGINS TO SINK

Notwithstanding his good intentions and personal popularity, Modrow could not have been more than a transitional figure. As the supposed savior of a Leninist party never able to legitimize its rule, he was in no position to rescue the regime. He spoke of "a new legitimacy" in his state-of-the-nation address, but only free elections could have accomplished that. He and many other party members realized that the SED would not obtain anything like a working majority in such an election, much less a popularly sanctioned entitlement to maintain the party's leading role. A large number of East Germans continued to vote against the SED with their feet; those who did not, would settle for nothing less than a government legitimized by their ballots. And only signs of hope, beginning with popular self-determination, held out any chance of quelling the refugee tide.

The general secretary, for his part, could not even aspire to being a transitional leader. In demanding a thorough political house-cleaning, Krenz advanced the most cogent argument for his own departure. There was simply no denying that he had been as responsible for betraying the people's trust as had those he now so sternly attacked. He was as guilty as they of what Gerlach had called in speeches to the *Volkskammer* "crimes against the people" and the "perversion of power." The principal organizer of rigged elections in which the SED never received less than 95 percent of the vote now wished to preside over a parliamentary democracy. Certainly by the second week in November, few in his own party believed the SED would have any chance of acquiring credibility either at home or abroad so long as former institutions were in place, and significant vestiges of the old guard still in office. Each week brought manifestations of the sometimes frenzied endeavors to discard compromised functionaries and to jettison ideological baggage.

Setting the tone, Politburo member Wolfgang Herger, in a November 18 speech, underscored the importance in the "new" GDR of a strict separation of governmental powers and the redistribution of authority, to include the reconstitution of the former five states on the territory of the GDR. He acknowledged that a mere change in the name of the Ministry for State Security was not acceptable to the populace. The ministry had to be reconstituted and assigned new tasks, he said, correctly asserting that the people would stand for nothing less.[16]

Little time was wasted in turning at least some pledges of renewal into deeds. In the third week of November the *Volkskammer* expelled twenty-seven of its most prominent members. The roster read almost like a Who's Who list of the old regime, and included Honecker and his wife, Stoph, Sindermann, Hager, Götting, Tisch, Axen, Mielke, Mittag, Herrmann, Lange, Mückenberger, Dickel, Chemnitzer, and Krowlikowski.[17] Of the few associates of Honecker's Politburo whose names did not appear on the inventory were those formally proposing the expulsions: Krenz and Schabowski.

Also on November 18 Attorney General Günter Wendland gave an account of police and Stasi conduct during the demonstrations on October 7 and 8 to the *Volkskammer*. *Neues Deutschland*, by this time providing genuine news coverage, published his official report.[18] Wendland charged the security forces with having committed grossly illegal acts against peaceful demonstrators and handling persons in a manner incompatible with human dignity. The report stated that in East Berlin and Dresden alone 3,456 persons were taken into custody, most of them on trumped-up charges. Many were held beyond the twenty-four-hour maximum detention period specified by law. Some detainees were held in unheated vehicles and garages. The injured, which numbered as many as a thousand, were not provided with adequate medical treatment. Some demonstrators had been insulted, kicked, and ruthlessly beaten. Charges of brutality leveled by church officials at the time were in the main substantiated. The conduct of the security forces was inimical to a lawful society and, in addition, the trials of demonstrators were a travesty of justice, the report went on to say, citing an example of an individual charged with inciting to riot for having repeatedly shouted "No violence" to fellow demonstrators.[19]

What was worse, Wendland said, security forces had deliberately provoked the demonstrators in an effort to turn the assemblies violent. Innocent bystanders were attacked and on occasion seized. Children were targeted to induce reactions on the part of adults that would serve as a pretext for the use of force. Investigators had uncovered evidence indicating the Stasi had attempted to promote an escalation that would justify the use of troops. Party officials and the press at the time had labeled the demonstrators "hooligans" and "rowdies." The same *Neues Deutschland* covering Wendland's testimony in the *Volkskammer* had condemned the protest marches as "counterrevolutionary" the previous month.

SCANDALS COME TO LIGHT

"All personally-controlled hunting areas of any sort are to be closed. All special hunting areas, established by local and county organs are to be immediately closed and special hunting provision for certain persons in hunting clubs are to be eliminated." With this astounding pronouncement on the second page of the November 16 edition of *Neues Deutschland* came one of the first hints of the major scandals that would rock the GDR late in the year 1989. The average reader must have stared open-mouthed: "personally-controlled hunting areas?" Did these even exist in the workers' and farmers' state on German soil?

The next weeks were to bring disclosures about massive SED corruption even many party members would have thought unlikely. But as Wandlitz, the party bosses' settlement just outside Berlin, at last became accessible to average citizens, as the dachas and hunting lodges were opened to the press, as lesser officials began disclosing the bits and pieces of what they had gleaned over the years about foreign bank accounts controlled by upper level functionaries, the country was stunned. As *Der Morgen* so deftly described the proletarian leaders of the East German state once the immensity of the improprieties became clear,

"They advocated the virtues of tee-totaling while secretly enjoying vintage wines."[20]

In Wandlitz the bosses lived in what was by GDR standards almost unimaginable luxury. Many of the houses were outfitted with saunas and hot tubs. Most members of the Central Committee were provided with imported automobiles at nominal charge. Members of the Politburo and Council of Ministers all had a Mercedes-Benz or a Volvo, each nearly priceless in the automobile-impoverished GDR, and many chauffeur-driven. Not for nothing did Wandlitz became popularly know as "Volvograd."

A special store carried prime meats unavailable on the local market, along with cheeses and wines unknown in the GDR.[21] Not uncommon in Wandlitz homes were oriental rugs and antique furniture. A community facility contained a manmade beach, complete with solarium. Since an East Berlin newspaper ran an article on the "feudal residence" of the disgraced head of the metalworkers' trade union, Gerhard Nennsteil, in early November, crowds began snooping around formerly restricted areas where party bosses were rumored to have lived.

Honecker's hunting lodge in Drewitz near the village of Nossentiner Hütte in Mecklenburg was situated on a prohibited area of 11,500 hectares.[22] The lodge itself, replete with every conceivable creature comfort including imported furniture, floor heating, swimming pool, and saunas consisted of six attached buildings and covered an area of nearly 14 hectares. The terrace overlooked the Schwerin Lake, which was closed to visitors by officialdom so that the general secretary and his guests would have an uncluttered panorama.[23]

Mielke had at his personal disposal the ministry's hunting chateau in Wolletz near Angermunde on the Polish border. The Stasi chief, it seemed, was a man of the most fastidious tastes. Service personnel and area guards from the elite unit *Felix Dzierzynski* were outfitted in traditional German hunting raiment. Of the 15,000-hectare estate, over 3,000 hectares of land were set aside for Mielke and his immediate family. The grounds, also strictly off limits for outsiders and carefully watched by armed Stasi personnel were stocked with expensive, and in part imported, game.[24] On Mielke's orders the animals received the best nourishment money could buy. This was reported to have included 226 tons of rice, 65 tons of soy beans, 10 tons of chestnuts, 250 tons of turnips, 140 tons of assorted fruits, 66 tons of oats, and 10 tons of bran each year.[25] When these numbers were revealed, East Germans grumbled aloud that some of these products were not readily available for human consumption in food stores. Making cynical reference to Mielke's departing remarks to the *Volkskammer*, one newspaper commentary quipped: "Mielke loved not only his people, but the beasts of the forest as well."[26]

Stoph maintained his hunting retreat on the eastern side of Lake Muritz near the Honecker residence. As at the Mielke estate, the armed security guards also wore traditional green garb. An enthusiastic horticulturalist, Stoph maintained large greenhouses where he grew exotic plants and employed three professional botanists.[27] Interior Minister Dickel pursued his hunting pastime in the Harz region where he kept a chalet near Friedrichsbrunn. In the same vicinity stood at least a dozen other functionaries' hunting dachas, all paid for at state expense.[28]

Perquisites were accorded to party leaders in line with rank as entitlements were tendered the nobility in centuries past as a matter of birthright. In addition to their main lodges, Honecker, Sindermann, Mielke, Mittag, Tisch, and others also maintained private dachas in Schorfheide, of Nazi fame, just north of Berlin. An embittered society could not resist making certain associations with some of the most unsavory characters of German history when the press began publishing photographs of Honecker's Wildfang with its lovely gardens, Mittag's Trammersee with its boathouse and seven-car garage, or Sindermann's cozy getaway with tennis courts and four-car garage. *Neues Deutschland*, replete by the end of November with muck-raking editorials entitled one: "Whose Interests Did (Union Boss) Tisch Represent? Of the Hunting Lord and his 'Eixener Wald.'"[29]

The estates *pur autre vie* in a country freed of the exploitation of man by man would have rivaled in size and quality those of a feudal monarchy. According to a December 1989 parliamentary report, 20 percent of the entire Neubrandenburg region that was later to become one of five states in the GDR was inaccessible to the public, and classified as "special hunting ground," that is, for *nomenklatura* use only. Upkeep of these areas, not to include game-stocking, was estimated to have cost nearly six million marks a year, creamed off the state forestry budget by the central planners.[30]

In 1959 the Council of Ministers requisitioned for its exclusive use the Baltic Sea island of Vilm, reputed to be one of the loveliest areas of the entire coast. There Politburo candidate member Schürer acquired a "weekend retreat" commonly known as Object 86, since the structure was officially a defense facility built by the Ministry for State Security.[31] Estimated to have cost over 1.5 million marks, the villa had a two-story satellite building and a radio antenna installed by a military helicopter. The villa's interior had been finished by a vocational school for interior design and the furnishings specially built by a Rostock contractor. Axen disposed of an even more luxurious house on the island, complete with custom-made furniture, servants' quarters, and motor boat. Building costs were reported to have run into millions of marks, with the tab picked up by the Defense and Security Ministries.[32]

Disclosures of the widespread use of public funds to construct residences for SED leaders' offspring understandably nurtured impressions that actually existing socialism had the attributes of a feudal state. Indignant commentators began comparing the GDR to the Philippines, and people growled about their "socialist banana republic." The sons of Stoph, Kleiber, and Krolikowski had all acquired houses built under orders from the undersecretary of the Council of Ministers. Frank Krolikowski's house had an estimated value of over 400,000 marks; he paid none of the construction costs himself.[33]

Beginning around the middle of November, not a day passed without fresh revelations of corruption, improprieties, and outright crime. East German newspapers were in fact competing furiously to outdo one another in investigative journalism. Papers were regularly running articles on various aspects of the lives of the country's elite. *Der Morgen* published details in early December of the party's annual holiday celebrations.[34] It told of gala programs at the Grand Hotel and other facilities in East Berlin, entrance to which was denied to average citizens; it described costly shows and opulent candlelight dinners on offer for DM 500 or more. There, party members with hard currency to burn rubbed elbows with Western high society. It was a dreadful spectacle.

By early December three official investigating organs were in place to inquire into the abuse of office and to uncover corruption in high places.[35] The first of these was the parliamentary investigating committee chaired by the CDU judge Heinrich Toeplitz whose task was to examine high officials. The second was the SED investigating committee commissioned by the provisional party governing board. The committee was headed by Gregor Gysi, the SED attorney known for his contacts with opposition groups, and widely respected for defending political dissidents when this was still risky business in actually existing socialism. Its principal assignment was to investigate alleged violations of the party statute. The third organization was a joint committee consisting of government representatives and members of the various opposition groups and parties, and given the job of investigating corruption and betrayal of the public trust.

There seemed no end to the horror stories. To the parliamentary committee a former state secretary in the Ministry for Construction told how party members had pilfered funds reserved for construction firms facing financial difficulties. The money was then used for building private homes, and the records were thereafter appropriately fudged.[36] Considerable sums were siphoned off church funds, in Schildow, for example, where construction for the functionaries was done under the rubric of "church-building."[37] Of particular interest to officials was the assistance provided by West German religious communities to the churches of the GDR. Such assistance was often provided in the form of hard currency, some of which could be readily drawn off. When assistance was provided in kind, roofing shingles, copper pipes, interior wiring, lumber, and stained glass were all in great demand for outfitting private residences and SED facilities.

Most appalling to East Germans, though, were disclosures about the operations of Alexander Schalck-Golodkowski, former state secretary in the Ministry for Foreign Trade and head of the ministry's shadowy Commercial Coordination Section (KoKo), an assemblage of some three-dozen enterprises that, taken together, was the GDR's leading hard currency generator. Schalck-

Golodkowski was a highly influential personage with direct control of numerous firms and personal access to huge accounts, most of these in the West, into which he deposited tens of billions of dollars over the years. His operations reflected yet another quirk in the GDR's administrative structure in that the firms conducted business under the authority of the Central Committee's Secretariat for the Economy, whose chief, Mittag, was Schalck-Golodkowski's taskmaster.[38] This meant that the Council of Ministers had been for the most part short-circuited and provided with no effective control of the Commercial Coordination Section. Schalck-Golodkowski was his own man, whose mercantile business ran the gamut from hotels to optical equipment to art dealing and weapons trade. KoKo operated Genex, all Intershops, most tourist (hard currency) hotels in the GDR, and numerous front organizations and firms in the West. Through such enterprises and on his own authority, Schalck-Golodkowski would channel weapons of East Bloc and sometimes Western manufacture to Third World countries. Against the laws of his own and some Western countries, he transferred weaponry to crisis areas including the Persian Gulf, the Middle East, South Africa, and Central America. Even senior officials in the trade ministry could assert with complete truthfulness that they had little knowledge of Schalck-Golodkowski's operations. *Der Spiegel* suggested he might have been the second most powerful economic figure in the GDR.[39] Although he was a member of the Central Committee and had received some of the highest distinctions of the GDR, he was little known in the West prior to the fall of 1989. A former head of the FRG's Permanent Mission in East Berlin, Klaus Bölling, appropriately characterized him as the "fanatic of silence."[40]

According to East German law, citizens were forbidden to "engage in commercial activities abroad or to possess commercial property abroad."[41] This prevented East Germans from owning or controlling foreign companies, and left direct export as the only permissible type of commercial intercourse. KoKo front operations circumvented these provisions on a massive scale, however. One of its most lucrative enterprises was the West Berlin firm of Chemo-Plast, whose business, according to the trade register, was the "import and export of basic organic and inorganic chemical materials" as well as "undertaking commercial industrial representation," which could mean almost anything. "Industrial products" included GDR-manufactured machine tools, but small arms and ammunition also. Another KoKo operation was the limited liability trade firm Palast-Elast in Essen specializing in the export of chemicals. Palast-Elast was in turn under exclusive and clandestine control of the East Berlin firm AHB Chemie-Export, run directly by Schalck-Golodkowski's office. KoKo managed at least two dozen firms in the FRG, several in Switzerland and Liechtenstein, even one in Spain.

One of Schalck-Golodkowski's oldest commercial operations in the West was the firm Intrac SA located in Lugano, Switzerland. According to the Swiss trade registry, Intrac engaged in commerce of all sorts. Its principal purpose was, according to the parliamentary investigating committee, smuggling embargoed goods into the GDR, especially those of military utility. Through neutral Switzerland KoKo could evade the trade restrictions imposed upon the GDR by the Coordinating Committee for East-West Trade (Cocom). An additional task was to smuggle products like perfume, cigarettes, and alcohol, tax- and duty-free either into Western Europe or through Western Europe into Third World countries. The numerous tricks of KoKo, including false labeling and packaging usually baffled EC customs officials, who reported their suspicions at times but were unable to provide conclusive evidence of improprieties.

Intrac was headquartered in Pankow, a section of East Berlin, as was its sister firm, Zentral-Kommerz. Intrac headquarters was divided into four main branches: metals, chemicals, finance, and ecology. The latter had primary responsibility for running the GDR's "ecological" waste dumps where Western European firms could dispose of industrial byproducts, often toxic, at very reasonable prices. "Ecology" in SED Newspeak meant turning large tracts of land into Europe's waste-yard in order to acquire hard currency. Zentral-Kommerz, for its part, engaged in the import and export of grain, exported certain light industrial products of GDR origin to the West, and was a primary purchasing agent of the Intershops. It furthermore was responsible for stocking the special SED stores, in particular the exclusive shops in Wandlitz that were laden with specialty foods and beverages of Western origin.

The Schalck-Golodkowski enterprise Transinter was founded to facilitate the operations of West German firms in the GDR.[42] Over the years it acquired offices in most West German companies operating in East Berlin, and undertook to improve the market position of its clients, albeit for a handsome fee. As an intermediary with official authorization and invaluable political connections, Transinter received funds that were thinly concealed kickbacks and bribes. When, for example, Western firms were required to bid on a particular deal, Transinter would make the necessary arrangements.

Two other "private" firms operated by Schalck-Golodkowski, combined several of the less reputable functions of the firms already described, including intermediary roles and the smuggling of embargoed Western products. These two firms, Gerlach and Forgber worked primarily for the Stasi, procuring such items as laser microphones, high sensitivity listening devices, special riot control equipment, and high-speed computers, along with the prized software to run them.[43] The firm F. C. Gerlach had a history dating from before World War II and had become the chief representative in the GDR of some of the largest and most prestigious West German companies including Thyssen, Krupp, Mannesman, and Klöckner. In 1976 the firm was placed under Schalck-Golodkowski's direct control.

KoKo had in fact been granted a monopoly on foreign firm representation in the GDR. In other words, all foreign enterprises doing business in the GDR had little choice but to deal in one way or another with Schalck-Golodkowski's organization. Almost without exception, Western firms doing business in the GDR were assigned a special intermediary agent charging an average commission of 3 percent. The charges to Western companies were in the main obligatory even when services rendered were merely pro forma. This activity allowed Schalck-Golodkowski to cream off a sum amounting to several percent from inter-German trade, and the SED was reported thereby to have earned tens of millions of marks annually. Creative bookkeeping prevented the tracing of such funds, and frustrated efforts to obtain information about actual amounts. Profits accruing from intermediary commissions or other transfers from Western firms would, for example, be transferred to Chemo-Plast in West Berlin, which in turn, would channel monies into Swiss companies wholly owned by KoKo.

Within a period of several weeks the investigating commissions uncovered four methods Schalck-Golodkowski's financial empire had employed to export weaponry.[44] The East Berlin firm Imes GmbH Export dispatched small arms through a Polish shipping company for reexport to South America.[45] Weapons destined for Arab lands and the Palestine Liberation Organization (PLO) were sent through a Swiss KoKo affiliate. GDR trade representatives in several Yugoslavian ports rechanneled East Bloc weapons deliveries to African countries, including the GDR's paper enemy, South Africa. Guns destined for the Caribbean area were shipped by a Spanish branch of KoKo, whose vice-president was formerly an official of the Castro regime in Cuba. Finally, Schalck-Golodkowski used the Hamburg forwarding agency Richard Ihle which was 80 percent owned by the Liechtenstein company Unisped, a KoKo front organization. The Hamburg firm was, moreover, the principal West German representative of one of the largest East German export-import companies, the nationalized firm Deutrans.[46] To cover the tracks of large-scale weapons export, Ihle managers would at times make deposits and withdrawals from certain private accounts in order that potentially compromising entries not appear on the firm's books.[47]

Managers and sales representatives of KoKo companies in the West were often members of the local communist parties, class warriors wielding capitalism's formidable weapons to expedite its demise. To renew their ideological vigor they would be summoned to the GDR at least once a year for indoctrination sessions led by Professor Max Schmidt, director of the Institute for Politics and Economics in East Berlin or the infamous Otto Reinhold, professor at the Central Committee's Academy for the Social Sciences. What is more, these financial pillars of the proletarian vanguard showered SED functionaries with gifts from the West through procedures known as "friendship" or "comradely" services. On one of his birthdays, Honecker was reported to have received sixty-five cases of vintage port wine from the year 1912. His wife regularly received jewelry purchased in the West and worth thousands of marks. A Munich businessman testified at one point that he had received contracts from Western firms rumored to have been East German affiliates to outfit the dachas of dozens of SED party bosses.[48]

To expand the reach of Schalck-Golodkowski's financial empire even further, it had established a sort of joint venture with a department of the SED, the party's own Commerce and Communication section run by Josef ("Jupp") Steidl and Julius ("Johnny") Cebulla.[49] Together, this department and KoKo established and operated a myriad of firms in the West with an estimated annual turnover of $4 billion and a net profit of nearly $250 million. Profits of the firms, named Refinco, Rexim, Anglolux, and other innocent enough sounding designations, were deposited for the most part in Swiss and Liechtenstein banks. Unisped was one of these joint enterprises, some of which were little more than mailbox companies or straw men. The Vaduz (Liechtenstein) firm Elmsoka alone was reported to have deposited DM 200 million over a period of several years into various bank accounts, or to have transferred large sums into the KoKo firm Intrac. The Commerce and Communication section managed the East Berlin company Simplex which had a function analogous to Schalck-Golodkowski's intercessor outfits, specifically, charging fees to West German companies operating in the GDR for "consultation and arbitration." Average annual turnover: DM 60 million.[50]

Following the November resignation of the Politburo, Schalck-Golodkowski, rightly fearing that he had lost his political protectors, fled the GDR. In the first week of December he was indicted on charges of fraud and embezzlement. According to allegations made in the *Volkskammer* and by the public prosecutor's office, former Politburo members squirreled away billions of marks of public money in private Swiss bank accounts.[51] Schalck-Golodkowski himself had personal accounts containing at least hundreds of millions of marks.[52]

The disclosures of seemingly endless scandals shocked and outraged East Germans who hitherto had little or no notion of SED crime and corruption. Many, including even some regime critics, considered their leaders for the most part well-intentioned, albeit misled and imperious old men. No one doubted SED officials were dogmatic and reactionary, but few looked upon them as criminals. Suddenly in December human chains formed in East Berlin and other major cities, with participants demanding not only free elections but the prosecution of the GDR's former leaders as well. Enraged crowds increased the pressure from below to investigate and prosecute party functionaries. Police offices were inundated with telephone calls from irate citizens requesting the investigation of areas with fenced-in residences. Following the initial wave of crime and corruption exposés, the *Volkskammer*, with its majority of still nominally communist deputies, voted *unanimously* after less than fifteen minutes of discussion to abolish the SED's constitutionally mandated leading role, with Krenz himself pushing for such action as part of his desperate effort to prove a determination to reform. The party, complacently secure and seemingly unassailable less than a year before, hung onto power by a thread.

NOTES

1. *Archiv der Gegenwart,* no. 24, November 8-21, 1989.
2. Ibid.
3. *Frankfurter Allgemeine Zeitung,* November 14, 1989.
4. *Der Spiegel,* November 20, 1989.
5. *Frankfurter Allgemeine Zeitung,* November 14, 1989.
6. *Der Spiegel,* November 20, 1989.
7. *Archiv der Gegenwart,* no. 24, November 8-21, 1989.
8. Ibid.
9. *Der Spiegel,* November 20, 1989.
10. *Archiv der Gegenwart,* no. 24, November 8-21, 1989.
11. *Neues Deutschland,* November 18, 1989.
12. *Frankfurter Allgemeine Zeitung,* November 18, 1989.
13. *Archiv der Gegenwart,* no. 24, November 8-21, 1989.
14. *Neues Deutschland,* November 14, 1989.
15. *Frankfurter Allgemeiner Zeitung,* November 20, 1989.
16. *Neues Deutschland,* November 17, 1989.
17. *Neues Deutschland,* November 20, 1989.
18. *Der Spiegel,* December 18, 1989.
19. Quoted in *Der Spiegel,* December 11, 1989.
20. *Neues Deutschland,* November 29, 1989.
21. *Der Spiegel,* December 11, 1989.
22. *Neues Deutschland,* December 2, 1989.
23. *Neues Deutschland,* December 15, 1989.
24. *Der Spiegel,* December 11, 1989.
25. Ibid.
26. *Neues Deutschland,* November 29, 1989.
27. *Der Spiegel,* November 27, 1989.
28. *Neues Deutschland,* November 24, 1989.
29. *Der Spiegel,* December 11, 1989.
30. *Neues Deutschland,* December 2, 1989.
31. *Der Spiegel,* December 11, 1989.
32. *Neues Deutschland,* December 7, 1989.
33. *The German Tribune,* December 17, 1989.
34. *Der Spiegel,* December 11, 1989.
35. Ibid.
36. Ibid.
37. *Der Spiegel,* November 20, 1989.
38. *The German Tribune,* December 17, 1989.
39. *Der Spiegel,* December 11, 1989.

40. See Günter Gaus's description of Schalck-Golodkowski in *Wo Deutschland liegt Eine Ortsbestimmung* (Hamburg: Hoffman and Campe, 1963), 260-66.

41. *Frankfurter Allgemeine Zeitung*, December 8, 1989.

42. *Der Spiegel*, December 11, 1989.

43. *Der Spiegel*, July 8, 1991.

44. *Der Spiegel*, December 11, 1989.

45. *Der Spiegel*, May 13, 1991.

46. *Der Spiegel*, December 11, 1989.

47. *Der Spiegel*, July 8, 1991.

48. *Der Spiegel*, December 11, 1989.

49. Ibid.

50. *Der Spiegel*, July 8, 1991.

51. *Neues Deutschland*, December 7, 1989.

52. *Der Spiegel*, May 13, 1991.

14
The Synthesis

THE CLASS ENEMY IS WELCOME

With power concentrated in so few hands, a hallmark of highly centralized economic decision making, the mass party sackings beginning in November 1989 brought on a virtual decapitation of the planning hierarchy. Accompanying the disintegration of the SED was the debacle of a regime closely identified with heavy encroachment in the economy. And the puncturing of the border, with the ensuing direct exposure of the GDR to a modern capitalist economy, precipitated the end of central planning in the GDR. Large numbers of East Germans had come to regard the command economy as a vital component of an old regime they overwhelmingly rejected. Revelations about the widespread corruption of the former party bosses fueled popular bitterness, sharpening resolve for fundamental change. The firsthand knowledge millions of East Germans acquired of the wealthy western neighbor both before and after the opening of the border intensified the feeling many had of being deceived and cheated by their state.

As the inner German border opened wide, economic integration began growing by leaps and bounds. In many areas such consolidation represented a natural development in neighboring regions kept artificially apart by German division. Labor became increasingly mobile as underemployed human resources (long hidden from official statistics) in eastern border areas shifted to the booming West German economy. West German producers, especially farmers, gained access to nearby markets they had been excluded from since the 1940s. Stagnating regions on both sides of the border long detached from their economic hinterland witnessed much-welcome upturns in trade. And West German corporations, cash-rich after several years of strong economic growth and record export earnings, began investing in low-wage areas where there were no language barriers and the education level was high. For Volkswagen, which had been scheduled to make investments of more than DM 30 billion worldwide over a span of several years before the opening of the border, buying into the GDR represented an immediate and irresistible opportunity. Less than a month after the breaching of the Wall, VW chief Carl Hahn announced more or less out of the blue that his firm would assist the IFA *Kombinat*, at the time the largest East German producer of automobiles, with designing and building a completely new model. The joint venture, involving an investment by VW of nearly DM 5 billion, actually began before the end of the year.[1] Opel responded with multi-billion mark investments, announcing shortly thereafter that it would be manufacturing 150,000 automobiles annually in the GDR by the mid-1990s.[2] Daimler-Benz, the FRG's largest industrial group, poured several billion marks into the GDR in the first months of 1990 alone, with much of this investment going into the East German truck-manufacturing *Kombinat*. These business ventures alone signified potential West German dominance of the East German motor industry short months after the breaching of the Wall.

From a popular standpoint, there was little doubt as 1989 drew to a close that the vast majority of East Germans considered the capitalist FRG the more just, better organized, and above all, the more prosperous German state. East Germans increasingly demonstrated a braced and deep-felt sense of political purpose. As would be evidenced later in the winter election of 1990, the first (and last) free nationwide election in the GDR, the citizenry gave ringing endorsement to the market economy, or social market economy as the FRG refers to its economic order. Backlash against a corrupt former regime that preached egalitarianism and professed to speak on behalf of the working class reinforced the developing consensus. In the first days of December 1989 the SED lost over one-quarter of its cardholders, when over 600,000 members, most of them ordinary working people, tendered their resignations in disgust following the revelations of corruption in high places. The Rostock shipyard was a case in point. Over 600 of the 2,000 SED members employed there left the party in the first week of December. Illusions about the old order faded quickly, and with them lingering pretensions of communist legitimacy. In a press interview at the time, several shipyard workers, members of the industrial elite of the SED state, heartily subscribed to the repartee of one: "The class enemy is welcome here."[3]

Fervor for a much closer economic relationship with the FRG was by no means limited to the grass roots. Heinz Warzecha, the powerful general director of the machine tool *Kombinat* "7 Oktober," one of the flagships of East German industry, by late November unreservedly advocated a market economy. Warzecha was acutely aware of his firm's dependence upon the West German economy for "emergency" supplies of materials, spare parts, and investment capital. Warzecha openly scoffed at the old notion of the "socialist producer," much preferring to be called a "capitalist entrepreneur."[4] Only if his enterprise could double productivity in just a very few years, he insisted at the time, would it have much chance of survival. Such productivity increases were possible, he said, only with

West German technology and investment capital, for which reason he expressed keen interest in having his enterprise slot into the high-tech firms of Baden-Württemberg and other areas, that is, to integrate with Western Europe's economic cutting edge.

Other East German captains of industry took similar positions. Heiner Rubarth, general director of the Dresden *Kombinat* for electrical machine tools, spoke of the pressing need for reform, to include investment laws and clearly defined property rights. The only East German enterprises with much chance of being successful in the future, he insisted, would be those following the market. Rudi Rosenkranz, general director of the Chemnitz (formerly Karl-Marx Stadt) textile *Kombinat* berated central planning and statism even before the SED had departed the stage. In public statements he repeatedly underscored the importance of economic competition in providing firms and individuals with necessary performance motivation.

In their advocacy of sweeping reform, these managers spoke for many others as well. The points on which they concurred exhibited considerable prescience: all three deplored the crying want of investment capital in the GDR; all agreed on the necessity to trim unproductive human resources; all wanted market forces to operate in the economy. All granted that many of the *Kombinate* would need to be broken up or reorganized in the interest of efficiency. Beyond this, yet another common thread was unmistakable: East Germany's economic future was inextricably linked with that of West Germany.

That these views were those of the East German managerial elite running top priority enterprises under central planning was portentous. As a matter of course, the *Kombinate* suffered financial and raw material shortages far less than the second-tier producers and service enterprises. The latter felt the tight pinch of resource misallocation and investment deficiency severely. As a consequence, many smaller industries also welcomed the opportunity of closer cooperation with neighboring West German firms.

A number of East German managers attempted to turn swelling West German interest in their economy rapidly to good account. Admitting his enterprise to be a behemoth, Peter Weller, general director of the artificial materials *Kombinat* in Dresden, embarked upon dividing it into smaller, more efficient subunits before the year was out. With some initial assistance from West German commercial organizations, he submitted, several divisions of his cumbersome *Kombinat* would by virtue of the dual advantage of high technology utilization and modest wages become internationally competitive. Albert Jugel, a law professor and former chief of the high-tech *Kombinat* Robotron maneuvered investment and property rights legislation, structured closely along West German lines, through the *Volkskammer*. Forceful in his advocacy of swift economic integration, he insisted the East German economy would stand or fall on the issue of direct investment.

THE CURRENCY ISSUE

As discussed above, the East German mark was not a currency in the strictest sense of the term; outside the borders of the GDR it had little worth. Even domestically it could function as a circulating medium only so long as the borders were tightly sealed; with the frontier open, currency exchange got completely out of hand, and the GDR lost all effective control of its money. Without tight currency controls, the weak East German mark began plummeting in value.

According to official estimates, East Germans took over three billion East marks out of the GDR the week after the border was opened.[5] Export of the currency was, of course, still illegal, and newspapers carried stories of East Germans being caught by customs officials in border spot-checks with thousands of marks concealed in car trunks or glove compartments. But with tens of thousands of people crossing the borders daily, the chances of being caught with a wad of bills were low. Fearing with some justification that their currency would become completely worthless, many East Germans began converting their stock of money into West marks, putting yet more downward pressure upon the East mark's exchange value. Immensely exacerbating the exchange rate problem was the huge monetary "overhang" in the GDR, where savings were estimated to have exceeded 150 billion marks.[6]

Continued high subsidization of basic foodstuffs and other articles in the GDR encouraged West Germans living in border areas to cross the frontier to shop. Even at parity, that is, a one-to-one exchange rate, a kilogram loaf of bread cost less than one-third what it did in the FRG. At an exchange rate of twenty to one the same loaf of bread cost about one pfennig. As a consequence, smuggling basic goods out of the GDR became very lucrative, and Westerners could buy all manner of things in the GDR at absurdly low prices. Vice versa, East Germans had an insatiable desire for West marks to purchase the Western goods they had so long been deprived of. Smuggling jewelry or antiques into the West for sale on the black market became a tempting proposition. Many Poles, who rightly or wrongly enjoyed a singularly bad reputation on both sides of the inner-German border for being conversant with black market operations, were in their element. With the GDR's borders open, they would drive through, stock up on subsidized items, sell these in the West for hard currency, promptly exchange the currency on the black market, then return to the GDR, their pockets bulging with East marks, to begin the cycle yet again.[7]

Corresponding asymmetries existed, of course, in the labor markets.[8] A skilled worker earning 1,000 East marks in Plauen might have earned twice that amount working on the other side of the border. At an exchange rate of twenty to one he would be earning 40,000 East marks a month, and would thus have a powerful incentive to work in the FRG. Use of two currencies, one rock solid, the other feeble, was a formula for chaos, especially in the border regions. The situation was clearly unsustainable over time.

Many West Germans, with large sums of money to spend because of the favorable exchange rate, attempted to avail themselves of this occasion to purchase property in the GDR, often through shady deals. Two weeks after the Wall opened, advertisements began appearing in West Berlin newspapers offering to buy rental property in East Berlin from private owners. Since it was illegal for foreigners to own property in the GDR at the time, West German speculators used front men in their endeavors to acquire real estate in the East. Although the GDR authorities insisted that all contracts signed with a view of circumventing laws were invalid, the efforts continued.[9]

So long as the GDR had a currency that was, quite simply, not worth working for, difficulties would beset the country. The opening of the borders and the greatly accelerated pace of de facto economic integration necessitated an overhaul of the monetary system. Through most of December the GDR's government had no official position on the matter. Rumors abounded almost daily about an imminent currency reform, or at least the replacement of large banknotes in circulation, the idea being that new banknotes would have demonetized East marks held in the West. Such steps had actually been taken by the GDR several times in the past. But with the borders open and traffic moving relatively freely, demonetization could have been only a temporary measure since fresh notes would quickly have begun circulating back and forth. In the first week of December, Bonn agreed to establish a special fund to replace the so-called "welcome money," a one-time DM 100 payment all East Germans were entitled to. From the new fund East Germans could obtain 200 West marks at a very favorable exchange rate. This procedure treated only a symptom, however, and had the added disadvantage of entailing the subsidization of a virtually worthless currency. GDR authorities had little alternative to imposing controls and clamping down on black-market trading. Among other difficulties this caused, such action had political fallout. For example, use of roving customs squads, in particular one known as the Workers' and Peasants' Inspectorate and answerable directly to the Central Committee, put many East Germans, with their visceral mistrust of bureaucratic oversight, very ill at ease.[10] In point of fact, any sort of reform in the GDR presupposed the introduction of scarcity pricing and an end to the subsidies that furnished an incentive for smuggling. Modrow's administration had inherited a financial muddle.

In a series of meetings in December, the president of the West German Central Bank (*Bundesbank*), Karl Otto Pöhl, and his East German counterpart, Horst Kaminsky, explored possibilities for currency reform. An early and widely discussed proposal envisaged a fixed "peg," that is, an exchange rate set at a specified amount, with accompanying West German guarantees of the par value. The chief problem with such a pegging arrangement even in the short-term, Pöhl believed, was that it would encourage the East German monetary authorities to print money and spend it. Pöhl accordingly vetoed the scheme. For West German financial officials renowned for protecting the worth of their currency, the proposal was simply a "non-starter."

The logical pathway to full currency convertibility for many people in both Germanys lay in proclaiming the West mark the official currency of a country where it had for years been the unofficial one. The research section of the West German Economics Ministry published a report dated December 1989, and entitled "Political/Economic Challenges for the FRG in Its Relations with the GDR," that called for an all-German DM zone, with the attendant GDR acceptance of the West mark as the official currency. The report's central hypothesis was that only a common and stable currency would assure adequate future investment in the GDR.[11]

One *Bundesbank* official, who was amenable to the report's recommendations, stated the unspoken but barely concealed implication of the report: the DM zone was synonymous with economic anschluss.[12] An advocate on the other side of the border, a *Kombinat* director, commented to the press that the alternative for the GDR to such a currency union was social turmoil. He was in all likelihood correct: when money is no longer good, people wrestle with the approaches of despair. In fact, the report became the basis of the July 1990 currency union marking the beginning of economic and political unification.

THE MOOD SOURS

As East Germans forged ahead with the dismantling of the SED state, popular indignation about past heavy-handedness and corruption in high places became laced with a desire for revenge. By the middle of December the GDR was beset with investigation fever. In the demonstrations that continued for the most part unabated, the people's wrath became palpable. Placards called for the prosecution of party functionaries, and protest chants of "corrupt thugs behind bars" could be heard in all large cities, as the GDR experienced the emotional catharsis of reformation from below. The churches repeatedly issued public statements exhorting the populace to avoid allowing its wrath to degenerate into a thirst for vengeance and outright hate.

In every county seat and in many communities as well, angry demonstrators forced their way into the local headquarters of the hated Stasi, and demonstrations threatened to turn violent as the temptation rose to avenge past misdeeds. A group calling itself Women for Change stormed the Stasi complex in Erfurt and occupied it for several hours. Citizens wanted access to official files for reasons ranging from idle curiosity to discovering the identity of Stasi informers to obtaining evidence of alleged security force misdeeds. In many areas violence was thwarted and the personal safety of security force employees assured by New Forum activists and civil rights groups, the very people who short weeks before had been labeled "rowdies" and "enemies of the state." Throughout the GDR these people warned against violence, while organizing citizen committees and control councils to prevent documents from being destroyed or hidden. In some cases they transported documents to a central location where these would be protected, and in many areas local police forces and citizen committees joined hands to keep order. Modrow's government was pressured to decree that official documents and files not be destroyed or hidden.

In addition to averting mobocracy in those fast-paced December days, citizen committees restrained party officials from covering their tracks or stowing away their ill-gotten gains. The month before, SED leaders had commenced with a massive cover-up campaign. As the state foundered, incriminating documents were burned and shredded, and the Stasi began systematically disposing of its enormous volume of files. A plane of the GDR's national airline *Interflug* was reported to have left East Berlin's Schoenefeld airport in the first week of December headed for Romania with crateloads of documents.[13]

Following rumors that the district mayor of Berlin-Friedrichshain was destroying official documents, an angry crowd marched over to the building and forced its way into his office. Stoph was caught red-handed attempting to dispose of the trappings of a luxurious life. In the early hours of December 4, acting on a citizen tip-off, police seized a large truck filled with Stoph's personal possessions. These included expensive American-made electronic equipment, and a small tractor Stoph had used to tend his lawns and gardens.[14] On the same day it was announced that Mittag, Tisch, and former Politburo candidate-member Hans Albrecht had been arrested on corruption charges.

Later that day, the Central Committee convened for two prearranged purposes. The first was to expel twelve of the GDR's most prominent figures from the Central Committee and from the SED: Honecker, Krowlikowski, Kleiber, Mielke, Sindermann, Stoph, Tisch, Albrecht, Schalck-Golodkowski, Dieter Müller, Gerhard Müller, and Herbert Ziegenhahn.[15] The second was to resign en masse. With its announcement of these events, *Neues Deutschland* stated it was no longer to be the organ of the SED Central Committee, but instead the newspaper of the entire party. Two weeks later it would describe itself merely as a socialist daily newspaper. And it appeared to have little sympathy for its past masters: in editorials of the first and second weeks of December the paper ardently opposed an amnesty for those accused of corruption or abuse of office.

An amnesty was not in the cards. Before the week was out, Mielke, Stoph, Kleiber, Krowlikowski, and Herrmann were taken into custody and charged with corruption, abuse of office, and gross negligence. Honecker and Axen were able to avoid apprehension only for serious health reasons. Former East CDU chairman Götting was indicted for embezzlement, and sums in excess of a million marks were mentioned.[16] In response to the arrests, one West German newspaper commented that these men had extolled themselves as antifascist freedom fighters and apostles of peace, when in fact they were little better than hedonistic renaissance potentates.[17]

Krenz's political career ended on December 6, just over six weeks after his assumption of Honecker's positions. Gerlach, heading a now completely independent Liberal Democratic group with close ties to its sister party across the border, replaced him as chairman of the Council of State. Yielding to pressure from his own party and from the streets, Krenz resigned from all his state posts. In his farewell statement Krenz said:

> My lengthy membership in the Council of State and the Politburo under the leadership of Erich Honecker significantly undermined the credibility of my policies for the renewal of socialism in the eyes of many citizens. Public trust is the first condition for the exercise of the office of Chairman of the Council of State. . . . In the interest of the country's stability and of essential revolutionary change in our land, I hereby resign from my positions as Chairman of the Council of State and of the National Defense Council.[18]

Krenz's resignation came as no great surprise. There had been considerable prior speculation about the political demise of Honecker's obedient protegé, and many commentators believed his departure to have been only a matter of time. The SED's self-purification campaigns highlighted the fact that the party was disintegrating, and the country in increasing disarray. Figures released on December 12 indicated 17,000 people had already left the GDR that month, for a total of 317,548 since the beginning of the year.[19] And several dossiers in the public prosecutor's office heralded the times. Among the indictments in various cases, former officials were charged with membership in a "criminal organization known by the name of SED." "Through the systematic construction of a mafia-like association," read one report, "said organization destroyed our country, broke people's lives, and drove citizens from the land."[20]

THE PARTY REMAKES ITSELF

From the outset of the special SED party conference held on the weekend of December 9 and 10, there was a consensus to break finally with the Stalinist past. Remaining party leaders—and the ranks were depleted by that time—including Modrow, Berghofer, and Gysi, had committed themselves to the establishment of a new party.[21] What, though, was to be its purpose in a new pluralistic GDR? For four decades the SED's raison d'être had been preservation of monolithic unity and the safeguarding of Soviet hegemony in Central Europe. The mood of the conference delegates and the irresolution of the party leadership bespoke the self-doubt pervading the SED. The inability of the special conference even to decide upon a new name for the widely discredited party reflected the prevailing uncertainty. Membership was declining daily, and no one was in a position to say how many still belonged to the party. According to some estimates, more than half of the comrades had already quit the SED.

Upon his election to the chairmanship, the post of general secretary having been eliminated along with the institutions of the Politburo and the Central Committee, Gysi appeared on the speaker's platform with a large broom, promising to sweep away the party's unfortunate past. It was no secret that Gysi was not the party's first choice as leader. Following Gysi's election, *Neues Deutschland* claimed the party's overwhelming choice would have been either Modrow or Berghofer, but that both had turned down the office.[22] Berghofer left the party not long thereafter to join the Social Democrats. "There wasn't exactly a swarm of volunteers" (for the chairmanship), Gysi remarked sardonically to the delegates. Notwithstanding his willingness to defend regime dissidents when this was indisputably dangerous, Gysi was widely regarded, inside and outside the party, as being too closely affiliated with the past, among other reasons because his father, Klaus Gysi, had been one of Stoph's ministers. As if to underscore this, at one point during the conference delegates inquired what privileges he had enjoyed as a youth.[23]

In his first international press conference, Gysi depicted his still unnamed party as a "political home for all working people."[24] Speaking on behalf of the new governing committee, Gysi apologized to the East German people for the past "failures and mistakes" of SED functionaries.[25] But the party still had neither program nor statute. Gysi described the organization simply as one being founded upon grass roots socialism, and pledged that a statute would ensue from consultations within the political base of the party. Asserting that a specific program was unnecessary for the time being, Gysi said the party would make do with several general social and political themes.

At the conference, Modrow settled a few scores with Krenz, who was by this time already in the political wilderness. Honecker's successors, Modrow charged, had committed countless errors.[26] For starters, Krenz, Schabowski, and others had manipulated their election in the Politburo in the time-honored fashion. Krenz's notion of a "turnaround" in the GDR was a farce, Modrow said, tantamount to the old king crowning the new prince. He pointed out that four of those elevated to the Politburo at the time of Krenz's selection were so discredited that they had to be quickly removed from office. The hypocrisy was not to be missed, he suggested: while speaking of the need for a separation of powers, Krenz claimed three high offices for himself.

The party conference readjourned the following weekend, December 16 and 17, for more deliberations. On the first day, Honecker attended to give a short speech. He humbly acknowledged some personal responsibility for the crisis in the country, but fiercely denied having committed any wrongdoing. Most delegates listened in stunned silence. When it was his turn, Gysi the conciliator extolled the virtues of the FRG: civil liberties, pluralism, the tolerance of the society, the role of the media. But in the next breath, Gysi the class warrior lashed out, condemning the "power interests of the capitalist monopolies and the transnational corporations" which had a "decisive influence" upon the governing of the country.[27] He praised the communist ideal of the classless society, and affirmed that this ideal would remain his own. He confidently spoke of the possibility of finding comprehensive solutions to mankind's problems.

After all was said and done, though, the goals of the party remained unclear. The leadership furnished no clarification, and tendered only clichés, rejecting Stalinism and right-wing radicalism, and scorning inhumanity and intolerance. When pressed, Gysi modestly spoke of the party's desire to embrace the positive aspects of communism, social-democracy, and pacifism. In a concluding resolution party delegates agreed that administrative socialism had led to stagnation, crisis and putrefaction in the country, in stark contrast to the relevant provision of the October Action Program indicting only the former general secretary and certain former Politburo members. The conference closed with an agreement to affix the initials PDS, or Party of Democratic Socialism to name, giving the party the dual cognomen, SED-PDS. Later, the letters SED would be dropped altogether.

A SINGLE GERMANY?

Fighting an increasingly uphill battle, Modrow soldiered on. The Round Table he assembled, consisting of fourteen parties and constituting the effective government of the GDR, was faced with the pressing need in December to halt the exodus. The December 8 Round Table announcement of the scheduling of national elections for the first week in May of the following year was universally welcomed, but drew speculation in the West about whether the GDR would hold out that long. Concern in many corners was in fact growing that the GDR would begin quite literally to disintegrate. West German leaders for their part feared that economic depression would bring new waves of East German refugees the FRG could not assimilate. With 2,000 people exiting the GDR daily by the month of December, all political parties in Bonn concurred with Modrow that convincing East Germans to stay home had to be the principal short-term objective of both German states.

Prior to this, in a speech to the *Bundestag* on November 28, Chancellor Kohl seized the political initiative with his Ten Point Plan to deal with the very fluid situation. Vastly overshadowing the proposal's provisions was the larger purpose of forming a new German state, should a consensus on the matter develop, as seemed likely. Kohl appeared convinced that conditions in the GDR held out opportunities finally to overcome division. Accordingly, he gave unification new impetus by putting it squarely on the table. As the chants of demonstrators increasingly turned from *Wir sind das Volk* ("We are the people") to *Wir sind ein Volk* ("We are one people"), it became clear that large numbers of people in the GDR strongly favored unification. As nearly all were searching for signs of hope amidst the wreckage of the old regime, the moment was a propitious one to offer the first glimmers. But Kohl's plan was clearly directed to the Western powers, Great Britain, France, and the United States, as well as to the people of the GDR. In addressing all interested parties, the Ten Point Plan represented the first slash at the Gordian knot of prickly German problems. Kohl had in effect sketched the contours of a new European political order where a unified Germany could find a place. In his address, Kohl reminded the FRG's allies of their commitment to the Germans as laid down in NATO's 1967 Harmel Report:

> A final and stable settlement in Europe is impossible without a solution of the German question, which forms the nucleus of current tensions in Europe. This settlement must remove the unnatural barriers between Eastern and Western Europe that are manifested most conspicuously and most cruelly in the division of Germany.[28]

And by suggesting that the solution to division would take place not on the national but on the EC level, Kohl, as a representative of the EC's most powerful state, was extending the Community's hand to other East Bloc states freeing themselves from Leninism's grip. The message could hardly have been missed: Europe was to have no artificial rim any longer. With a national election in the FRG less than a year off, Kohl was only too pleased to come forward as a German statesman able to take the lead in time of crisis.

The path he envisaged toward a federal Germany was to begin with joint committees and a loose confederation between the two states, an arrangement which would accommodate the joint agreements Modrow had already proposed. In its essence, the Ten Point Plan envisioned the initial negotiation of a "contractual community," the *Vertragsgemeinschaft*, and provided for the founding of "structures of confederation," which would eventually evolve into a federal system.[29] Along the path, Kohl proposed, a single currency for the two states would be established. The entire process, Kohl assured the international community, would take place within the framework of existing agreements, and would in no way impinge upon the four-power status.

The plan found considerable support among the former bloc parties in the GDR, whose sway was steadily increasing. The East CDU chairman and by then Deputy Premier de Maizière initially referred to the plan as "an interesting concept containing substantial elements of our own ideas," and thereafter gave it his party's support.[30] Had not Modrow himself come out in favor of a German "confederation"? To the FRG's allies, Kohl posed the all-important question: if the majority of East Germans favored unification, could the West stand in the way? By seizing the initiative, the CDU had placed itself in a position to have the upper hand on national issues.

Kohl's program had more immediate and consequential results than he or anyone else anticipated. Brandt, troubled that the Christian Democrats were poised to reap the fruits of the Ostpolitik he had begun some twenty years before, convinced a sizeable number of West German Social Democrats to endeavor to outflank Kohl by linking forces with the fledgling East German SDP. What Kohl and Brandt thus set in motion in a matter of weeks was a process neither one of them could have braked even had he so desired. Catalyzed by political parties in the FRG, this process was appropriately described by one observer as "competitive reunification policy."[31] Against the better judgment of many in his party, including then chancellor-candidate, Oskar Lafontaine, Brandt arranged for the West SPD to provide support to its sister organization across the border, and to explore the possibilities of party union. Wary of Brandt's stature, and sensing his potential electoral appeal in the GDR where he had drawn enthusiastic crowds back in the dark days of 1970, the West German CDU, CSU, and FDP began eagerly to build bridges to the East. Before long, party mergers were on the top of the political agenda, and GDR issues were drawn into the vortex of West German domestic politics. And in a country becoming absorbed with national matters by necessity, where expressions of solidarity were potential vote-fetchers, it should have come as no great surprise that politicians began purposefully forming a consensus for unification.

To be sure, unification talk did not find a universally positive echo in the GDR. In response to Kohl's November 28 speech, Stefan Heym issued a petition formulated by Christa Wolf, and signed by thirty prominent scholars, artists, and pastors. Entitled "For Our Country," the petition rejected unification, and advocated the preservation of an autonomous GDR. Heym accused Kohl of making "overtures of annexation" with his discussion of union. Hence the resolution: "We still have a chance to develop a socialist alternative to the FRG with good neighborly relations with all European states. We can still recollect the anti-fascist and humanistic ideals that were once our point of departure."[32]

Some GDR politicians criticized reunification ideas as well. Pastor Rainer Eppelmann, a leader of Democratic Awakening and member of the Round Table, dismissed Kohl's plan as "very premature." Neues Forum, according to its own self-definition a political discussion group and not an organized party, was so divided that it had no position at all. The United Left, which was also represented at the Round Table, actually tried to organize a December demonstration against unification. Many of the former opposition groups in fact adhered to socialism even after the very notion of it had become distinctly unpopular. Lacking organizational structure, and in some cases a distinctive political identity altogether, they retained idealistic dreams at a time when the country was falling apart, and hard decisions had to be made under considerable time restraints. Many groups were apprehensive about becoming appendages of more powerful West German political organizations, should the socialist fabric of the GDR not be preserved. But obstinacy proved to be a rather grave political mistake. In stubbornly holding on to utopian schemes, in advocating socialism in a country where it had already been widely rejected, they had misjudged the country's mood, and as a result rapidly lost all political relevance. Very few people in the GDR abided anything smacking of utopian schemes; most wanted hard answers. A demonstrator's remark captured the mood. "Opposition leaders," he said, "provide only intellectual abstractions, but people think with their stomachs." Accordingly, the revolution would discharge its own children, as East German politics began to assume a West German complexion.

NOTES

1. *Der Spiegel*, December 11, 1989.
2. *The Economist*, March 31, 1990.
3. *Der Spiegel*, December 11, 1989.
4. Ibid.
5. *The German Tribune*, December 17, 1989.
6. *DDR Handbuch*, vol. 2, 1,246-47.
7. *Hannoversche Allgemeine*, November 24, 1989.
8. *Saarbrücker Zeitung*, November 28, 1989.
9. *Frankfurter Rundschau*, November 24, 1989.
10. *The German Tribune*, December 10, 1989.
11. *Der Spiegel*, December 11, 1989.
12. *Der Tagesspiegel*, December 7, 1989.
13. *Der Spiegel*, December 11, 1989.
14. *The German Tribune*, December 17, 1989.
15. *Neues Deutschland*, December 4, 1989.
16. *Neues Deutschland*, December 16, 1989.
17. *Stuttgarter Zeitung*, December 11, 1989.
18. *Neues Deutschland*, December 7, 1989.
19. *Neues Deutschland*, December 12, 1989.
20. *Der Spiegel*, December 18, 1989.
21. *Neues Deutschland*, December 9, 1989.
22. *Neues Deutschland*, December 13, 1989.
23. *Der Spiegel*, December 18, 1989.
24. *Neues Deutschland*, December 11, 1989.
25. *Der Tagesspiegel*, December 10, 1989.
26. *Der Spiegel*, December 18, 1989.
27. Ibid.
28. *Frankfurter Allgemeine Zeitung*, November 29, 1989.
29. Josef Joffe, "Once More: The German Question," *Survival* 32, no. 2 (March-April 1990), 134.

30. *Der Spiegel*, December 4, 1989.
31. Joffe, "Once More: The German Question," 134.
32. *Der Spiegel*, December 4, 1989.

15
Into the Dustbin

ELEVENTH HOUR

The convergence of several factors was instrumental to the collapse of East German communism in 1989. First, the unity of Honecker's Politburo, so conducive to the pursuit of key policies in the 1980s, and which conveyed the impression of considerable regime stability, communicated a deception. Mistrust of the aging leadership was widespread in the country at large and support for the SED elite within the party rank-and-file was ebbing. Second, Moscow imparted for the first time that year its unwillingness to employ its own troops for domestic crackdowns in the satellite states, depriving the local regimes of their ultimate security guarantee. Third, Gorbachev's encouragement of reform initially proved counterproductive in the GDR, as the Central Committee rallied around Honecker in an effort to resist the reform course, even to set back the clock. Then the foot-dragging backfired on the SED as the citizenry began demanding that the GDR take Gorbachev's advice. Fourth, and closely related to the third, a multi-year curve of rising expectations started to crest in 1989. East Germans, closely following reform discussions outside the GDR, were eager for change and bitterly disillusioned when the SED demurred.

It is to be noted that this last factor represented a classical precondition for revolution. Revolutions tend to occur not when things are getting worse, but paradoxically, when they are getting better. The people's political as well as material expectations had been rising for years in the GDR, and the SED would not or could not deliver on these. Predicated on the eradication of alternative political actors, and intolerant of all group interest articulation, the political system of the GDR was designed to enforce social uniformity. New thinking, new ideas, new political and economic demands inevitably brought to the fore new actors the regime in its own self-interest could not accommodate. Revolution often follows an outpouring of political demands and the sudden eruption of popular participation. "The political essence of revolution," Huntington observed, "is the rapid expansion of political consciousness and the rapid mobilization of new groups into politics at a speed which makes it impossible for existing political institutions to assimilate them."[1]

The torrent of participatory demands elevated in significance the coercive power of the police and the military to regime stability. Security forces, ultimately backed by the Soviet Army, had of course always constituted the main buttress of the politbureacratic dictatorship. Yet, in another of a long string of ironies, one of the East Bloc's most efficient and feared security apparatuses balked at the critical moment. At a time of crisis, the security apparatus in this highly militarized country, renowned for its almost ubiquitous police and paramilitary forces, became increasingly inconsequential. The SED failed to order the army to carry through a "Tiananmen Square solution" and the police for their part often preferred to avoid confrontation.

WHY WASN'T FORCE USED?

Though all the particulars might never be known, the November 9 "Monday demonstration" in Leipzig, coming on the heels of the GDR's dreary anniversary celebrations, almost became a bloodbath. On that evening the nascent German revolution might in fact have turned into a tragedy. In anticipation of the protest march, security forces were at the ready in key locations around the city. Hundreds of police with complements of trucks and other vehicles had assembled. Heavily armed riot squads had ringed the main train station and the regional headquarters of the Ministry for State Security. Contingents of the *Kampfgruppen* stood stationed in front of the Hotel Stadt Leipzig. Stasi toughs were menacingly located around the city, in the parks, in the churches, wherever crowds might have gathered. Outside the city, armored and airborne units of the NVA had been placed on alert. According to reports, the airborne troops had been instructed to land in the city by helicopter to seize or protect selected sites where they would be provided with additional support from the *Kampfgruppen*. Local hospitals had been furnished with extra blood supplies. In short, the signs in Leipzig on October 9 were ominous, and on preceding days the SED had provided sufficient examples of real existing socialism's iron fist. The Politburo, it seemed, had decided upon confrontation.

Hours before the demonstration, an eerie atmosphere pervaded a city rife with rumors, the most incessant of which, as might have been expected, was that the forces had received shooting orders. Some demonstrators later told the press they almost expected to be shot at that evening.[2] Then, soon after the demonstration began, the police and troops were suddenly withdrawn. The few police remaining on duty cleared busy intersections for the demonstrators and showed no enmity whatsoever. The apparent recall of the security forces invariably prompted the question: Who had ordered this? Had the Politburo decided upon a Tiananmen Square solution, only to have changed its mind? Shortly thereafter allegations were made that Honecker had indeed issued a shooting order for October 9. Gerlach claimed in November to have seen written orders to that effect, and Gysi announced at the huge demonstration in East Berlin on November 4 that he had evidence of the existence of such orders.[3] But since he had no official post at the time, and was in fact very much an outsider, Gysi's assertion was subject to some doubt. Both Gysi and Gerlach, along with physicist Manfred von Ardenne, said Krenz had withdrawn the order and issued a new one prohibiting the use of force. According to Gysi's November statement: "Many heard several months ago what Egon Krenz said about China [justifying Tiananmen Square brutality]. But I also know that Krenz was responsible for the decision on October 9 in Leipzig: 'Chinese solution' or democratic one. He chose the latter."[4]

Krenz unhesitantly suggested that it was he who had withdrawn the shooting order, first mentioning the order's retraction to Bishop Leich and other religious leaders the day after Honecker's resignation. On November 17, in response to *Volkskammer* queries about his policy role, Krenz alleged that his actions had been crucial in preventing violence. At the time Krenz stated: "I was in Leipzig [on October 9] and declared there: we advocate only political solutions to political conflicts. I helped in so arranging matters."[5] Krenz failed to explain whom exactly he was referring to with the plural, "we," but one can suppose he meant the anti-Honecker putschists. On the same day, however, the muck-raking East German media caught the general secretary in a lie. As it turned out, Krenz was not in Leipzig on October 9, had traveled there only a few days afterward, and hence could hardly have been on the spot averting a bloodbath. Besides, he had quite plainly been unwilling or unable to prevent police and Stasi action against demonstrators during the anniversary celebrations. Confronted with these ambiguities in a live television interview, Krenz backed off, saying merely that his efforts to prevent brutality had been "done together with other comrades."[6] This was scarcely a satisfactory explanation, though, and with the media in hot pursuit, Krenz was not about to get off easily. On November 23 Krenz acquiesced when a West German television reporter pressed the issue: "I must decisively reject that there was any shooting order." Then, equivocating, he added that he had not yet been appointed general secretary the second week in October.[7] The latter observation, while factually true, was irrelevant since Krenz had for years been the highest official for security affairs in the country. That he would not have known about the existence of such an order had one been given was unthinkable. What then, he was asked, about the shooting order that Gerlach and others claimed to have seen? Had Honecker not issued such an order? Krenz replied: "I do not think so."[8]

With certainty, dealing with a free press was not Krenz's strong suit. SED experience in such matters was limited. In a later clarification, Krenz explained he had gone to Leipzig several days after the watershed Monday demonstration with an order drafted by him and signed by Honecker in his capacity as chairman of the National Defense Council giving word that state organs were to refrain from violence or provocations of any sort. Krenz claimed to have held personal consultations on this matter with local officials.[9] What exactly had transpired on October 9?

Kurt Masur, director of the Leipzig Gewandhaus orchestra, came forward at the time to deny that Krenz or any Politburo official had acted to prevent bloodshed, insisting instead that intercession had taken place only at the local level. Regional party secretaries, he said, having been furnished with orders for a crackdown in Leipzig, not only ignored these, but withdrew the security forces at the crucial moment.[10] That Masur sympathized with the demonstrations is beyond doubt, as is the notion that he did his utmost to avert violence. On the afternoon of October 9, Masur received three regional party officials, Kurt Meyer, Roland Wötzel, and Jochim Pommert, in his Leipzig residence, and there agreement was reached that no force should be employed against demonstrators.[11] A joint statement to this effect was issued and read in the church services preceding the protest march. The three party secretaries acknowledged the occurrence of the meeting and the nature of the agreement concluded there. All said, perhaps not unsurprisingly, that they refused to undertake any action against the demonstrations.[12]

Pommert testified in November that he and his two colleagues acted on their own initiative that October afternoon in calling for peaceful dialogue and ordering the security forces to withdraw. He claimed to have been afforded no directions from East Berlin, but to have received a telephone call from Krenz later that evening in which the latter expressed his personal support for peaceful dialogue.[13] Masur and Pommert both maintained that the joint appeal and subsequent action of the regional secretaries were effectual in hindering brutality. Following his resignation as general secretary in December, Krenz confirmed having made the call to Pommert welcoming the unhostile attitude, but continued to insist that no explicit shooting order had been issued.

There is reason not to totally discount Krenz's role, his verbal flipflops notwithstanding. The initial prevarications were those of a man desperately struggling for his political life, who would be compelled by pressure from the streets and party colleagues to resign short weeks thereafter. A command for the concurrent mobilization of police, army, *Kampfgruppen*, and Stasi units must have originated in the Politburo, since no official below this level would have possessed the necessary authority. The same is true for the withdrawal of the security forces. Local party secretaries in Honecker's GDR would not have been in a position to call back NVA troops, let alone members of the Stasi who belonged to an organization constituting a veritable state within a state.[14] Only four officials in the GDR would in fact have been authorized to effect such a measure: Honecker himself, Krenz as head of all security forces, Mielke as minister of state security, and Krenz's deputy, Wolfgang Herger, chief of the Central Committee's Department of Security and chair of the *Volkskammer* Committee for National Defense.[15] Since Krenz and Mielke had by October 9 already set the stage for Honecker's resignation, it follows that they might indeed have rescinded a shooting order, lest they later be held responsible for a cruelty perpetrated by Honecker. Aware of the directive to mobilize forces in the Leipzig area, Krenz in all likelihood became alarmed at the prospect of a large-scale confrontation, with or without a shooting order, for he of all people knew that Gorbachev opposed the use of force. The October 9 Monday demonstration was the last time large contingents of troops and police appeared at any protest, which suggests that Krenz, upon assuming power, if not wholly committed to dialogue, was at least unwilling to use brute force against his people. In point of fact, there were no repeats of October 6 and 7.

Attention here must be paid to two central features of the upheaval in East Germany. The first was the attitude of the Soviet Union. Commenting upon the contingency of employing troops against the fall demonstrations in the GDR, Soviet officials have since said unequivocally that Soviet military commanders in the GDR were instructed not to use force against civilians.[16] Assuming this to have been the case, had it ordered the police or the military to fire upon demonstrators, the GDR's Politburo would have been acting in a manner inimical to Soviet policy. If one further assumes that Krenz and several other members of the Politburo had received a green light from Gorbachev to topple Honecker, it is highly improbable these same leaders would have chosen deliberately to offend Moscow, much less have undertaken an action likely to lead to civil war. The risk of the latter would have been too great. What sane East German leader would have gambled with civil war knowing in advance that the Soviet Army would not stand behind him?

Not a one. In 1989 the refusal of the Soviet Union to employ its forces as it had done in the past to quell East Bloc uprisings, either aboveboard or in a disguised mode, became what the historian would refer to as a direct (or efficient) cause of the SED regime's end. In their practice of nonviolence, the East German people, of course, deserve much credit as well. By their enormous self-discipline, they scrupulously avoided giving the authorities any pretext to deal a blow. Had there been a crackdown, responsibility would have lain exclusively with the SED. Surely one of the last things a reform-minded Kremlin wanted in 1989 was the world witnessing harsh repression in the GDR. The last drop of Gorbachev's credibility abroad would have run out with the blood flowing on East German streets.

The second feature was the faltering of the GDR's security apparatus. During the second week in October a sizeable number (how many is not known) of police personnel were sitting in jails for refusing to use force against peaceful demonstrators on October 6 and 7.[17] Members of the *Kampfgruppen*, an arm of the party with a primary mission to subdue domestic unrest, had refused in large numbers to train for street fighting.[18] Indisposed to fire upon their fellow citizens, units began to melt away even as early as October.

Beginning that month there was considerable discussion of industrial strike action, especially in the large enterprises of the south. The *Kampfgruppen* were organized at the factory level, and the possibility of their use against demonstrating citizens fueled strike talk. Meanwhile, the FDGB faced mass resignations and former union members in industrial areas began setting up their own local branches. Union members were regularly marching in the protest demonstrations, as presumably, were some of the *Kampfgruppen* personnel. Compliance with orders, had these involved bloodshed, could not have been taken for granted by the party.

The same hesitancy to use force against the citizenry presented itself within the NVA's officer corps as well, particularly in the face of Soviet opposition. Many NVA officers took offense at the supplanting of their external security duties with ones of internal security, especially if bloodshed was likely to have ensued. Quashing domestic unrest is usually regarded with aversion by the professional soldier, and in the case of the NVA, officers harbored considerable misgivings about the reliability of a conscript army ordered to fire upon citizens. Some anticipated serious morale problems and were even concerned about the eventuality of civil war should NVA units have become involved in clashes with state security forces. One officer stated categorically in December 1989: "The National People's Army and the border troops . . . will use no force against the people, and we do not want any to be used against us."[19] That Stasi units would have attacked demonstrators unfalteringly had they been ordered to do so is highly likely, but under the circumstances, they might have found themselves acting alone. How, if at all, would the NVA have responded to massive Stasi brutalities? If the December events in Romania are any guide, the outbreak of civil war in the GDR was a plausible scenario. Had this occurred at any point to Krenz and other GDR officials?

Many questions will remain open, though the deeper meaning of the week October 9 to 13 cannot escape notice. The events of that week suggest that Krenz and the majority of SED leaders, however strong their desire to retain power, had grudgingly accepted as basic facts that social problems are not solved by sending in troops, that ordering out the army or the security forces against the people results in more problems. There is much to be said for the proposition that the Kremlin arrived at this conclusion some years before. Although there is adequate reason to doubt the strict veracity of Krenz's statements about October events, he was quite evidently reluctant to use force once he became general secretary. Those SED leaders harboring anxieties about the possibility of rampant violence and disorder in 1989, were vindicated when Romania exploded in the last days of the most remarkable year since World War II.

EPILOGUE

A cardinal element of the GDR's enduring and ultimately irresolvable dilemma was the absence of an established civic culture, the gradual and fusioned development of which has taken place historically in those states whose difficulties have been spread over considerable spans of time, allowing for the resolution of each in its turn. In this sense the GDR contrasted sharply with nations like Great Britain and the United States, but also with many nations of continental Europe as well. In the GDR the problems of centralization of authority, integration into the East Bloc, social mobilization, economic rebuilding, and modernization arose not sequentially but concurrently.[20] When it came to power, the SED had to face an array of problems and contradictions all at once, beginning with the most basic issues of national consciousness. In a mere four decades the SED did not succeed in fostering a separate political or social identity, and as a consequence, an underlying difficulty of the state was never resolved. At the root of this difficulty was the popular identification with the larger German nation rather than with a separate East German nation-state.

"Political socialization" is a term used to refer to the developmental process through which people gain political orientation and fashion patterns of behavior.[21] The overriding objective of the political socialization process in the GDR was to instill socialist political culture into the citizenry. This political culture had not only to be uniform with ideological imperatives and aspirations, but also had to stand on its own because of the absence of a broader based national culture. Given the newness of the state and its political institutions, the attendant lack of traditions, along with the continual challenge on the national question, the SED always faced an uphill task. To develop the proper orientation and attitudes, the GDR concentrated upon the consciousness of youth: through the younger generation political culture via political socialization was to be transmitted.

Such a political culture failed to emerge in the GDR; legitimacy and a national consciousness (*Nationalbewusstsein*) were perpetually lacking. Identification with the state (*Staatsbewusstsein*), the extent of which was sometimes overestimated, was perceived by average citizens in terms of tangible social and economic benefits, and in some measure, vague notions of social justice. But the SED proved unable to transform these into broader, more durable, support for the leading role of the party or into popular sentiments that the regime spoke with authority, and accordingly deserved to be obeyed.

In the fall of 1989 German questions were increasingly being posed by East Germans, to be addressed by West Germans.[22] Once it became evident that East Germans would hasten the pace of change and thrust themselves upon the FRG, West German leaders had little alternative to developing programs for unification. As one observer suggested, anschluss was foisted on the stronger country by the weaker one. Once they were provided a choice, few East Germans showed much inclination for compromise between the ancien régime and a completely new ordering of things. SED rule represented "the days that are no more," and for many, unification could not come quickly enough. The rapidity of change itself in 1989 increased East German impatience.

Once the withering away of the SED state had begun its inexorable course in 1989, the main driving force behind German unification was not nationalistic but rather economic, in a manner not unlike the unification process early in the last century. Beginning in the 1820s, it should be remembered, economic forces also drove German unification. The gradual merging of the various German states resulted far less from a desire for close union than from economic, and later political, necessity. Even the deep mistrust of Prussian power did not thwart the process. Although German "particularist" sensitivities could be assuaged initially by the notion that union of coinage, weights, measures, and tariffs would by themselves suffice for the needs of modernization, in the longer term this belief proved naive. The German Customs Union (*Zollverein*) was a cornerstone of a later united Germany, and served in this century as a model for the EEC, established by the Treaty of Rome in 1957. The Customs Union reduced the localism so characteristic of Germany, helped integrate disparate German-speaking areas and stimulated industrial production, even in less developed regions, some of which were three-quarters agricultural in character. Thus, it strongly encouraged national feelings not confined to trade. Then, as now, economic developments tended to generate a political dynamic of their own.[23]

At the end of the eventful year of 1989, where this analysis ends, movement toward unification of the Germanys could be considered under several keynotes. First, change throughout the East Bloc was characterized not by gradual evolution but by suddenness. Second, the GDR, already profoundly influenced by its wealthy neighbor, was especially affected by such change. Third, and closely related to the second, with the breaching of the inner German border, the East German economy rapidly began to integrate with the FRG's. Fourth, concomitant with the outset of this integration process, there emerged a partial political vacuum in the GDR, the result of the SED's downfall.

As Thomas Baylis has pointed out, past instances of change in communist systems resulted from "restiveness over economic failures, cultural ferment provoked by ill-timed censorship or repression or even insufficiently rapid liberalization, resurgent nationalism or regional particularism, disputes and rivalries among Communist leaders, or some combination of these."[24] All these conditions obtained in the GDR in 1989 and interacted in sometimes unforeseen ways. Throughout, one of the purposes of this book has been to give the reader a sense of how these conditions were linked. Nevertheless, even some combination of all of them would probably not have been sufficient to bring revolutionary change to the GDR. Skepticism about the possibility of revolution in Germany has been perennial, and it was the communists, after all, who lamented at the end of World War I that revolutions do not occur in Germany because the people are hesitant even to walk across the grass without permission.

Revolution in the GDR involved more than the concurrence of these conditions. What rendered the events of that year different from so many other past changes in regime was that the people themselves (Germans at that) successfully carried out revolutionary transformation. To the above conditions and causes must be added the component of "people power," the midwife of revolutionary change in the GDR. It was not only the peacefulness itself (for the most part at least) of the East Bloc revolutions that was so remarkable, but also the replacement of war by "people power" as the revolutionary midwife. In communist thinking there was no place for such an eventuality, and it was for this reason above all others that the aging SED leaders were so ill-prepared for what was to befall them. The upheavals of 1989 all had a certain cohesion which was logically attributable to Gorbachev's programs. His ideas fomented what communists regarded as impossible: a revolution on German soil. In Greek mythology the gods were known to punish man by fulfilling all his desires. But wasn't it Gorbachev who advocated *demokratizatsiya*?

NOTES

1. Samuel P. Huntington, *Political Order in Changing Societies* (New Haven, Conn.: Yale University Press, 1968), 266.

2. *Frankfurter Allgemeiner Zeitung*, October 10, 1989.

3. *Der Spiegel*, November 27, 1989.

4. Ibid.

5. *Neues Deutschland*, November 18, 1989.

6. *Der Spiegel*, November 27, 1989.

7. *Frankfurter Allgemeiner Zeitung*, November 24, 1989.

8. *Der Spiegel*, November 27, 1989.

9. *This Week in Germany*, October 20, 1989.

10. *Der Spiegel*, November 27, 1989.

11. Ibid.

12. *Neues Deutschland*, November 21, 1989.

13. *Der Tagesspiegel*, December 9, 1989.

14. See *Der Spiegel* series entitled "Schild und Schwert der Partei," February 5 and February 12, 1990.

15. *Die DDR* (Bonn: Informationen zur politischen Bildung, 1984), 14-15.

16. Josef Joffe, "Once More: The German Question," *Survival* 32, no. 2 (March-April 1990), 139.

17. *Der Spiegel*, October 30, 1989.

18. *Der Spiegel*, October 16, 1989.

19. Joseph S. Gordon, "The GDR: From Volksarmee to Bundeswehr," in Jeffrey Simon, *European Security Policy after the Revolutions of 1989* (Washington, D.C.: National Defense University Press, 1991), 161.

20. Huntington identifies this dilemma as a frequent one among new nations. Huntington, *Political Order in Changing Societies*, 46.

21. David Easton and Jack Dennis, *Children in the Political System* (New York: McGraw-Hill, 1969), 17.

22. *The Economist,* December 9, 1989.

23. Michael Howard, "The Springtime of Nations," *Foreign Affairs* 69, no. 1 (Spring 1990): 18.

24. Thomas Baylis, *The Technical Intelligentsia* (Berkeley: University of California Press, 1974), 276.

Bibliography

BOOKS AND ARTICLES

Adomeit, Hannes. "Gorbachev and German Unification: Revision of Thinking, Realignment of Power." *Problems of Communism* 39, no. 4 (July-August 1990): 1-23.

Almond, Gabriel A., and Sidney Verba. *The Civic Culture*. Boston: Little, Brown, 1965.

Almond, Gabriel A., and G. Bingham Powell, Jr. *Comparative Politics: A Developmental Approach*. Boston: Little, Brown, 1966.

Apter, David. *The Politics of Modernization*. Chicago: University of Chicago Press, 1965.

Aristotle. *The Politics of Aristotle*. London: Oxford University Press, 1974.

Ash, Timothy Garton. *The Magic Lantern: The Revolution of 1989*. New York: Random House, 1990.

———. "Mitteleuropa?" *Daedalus* 119, no. 1 (Winter 1990): 1-21.

———. *Polish Revolution: Solidarity*. New York: Scribner's, 1983.

Axen, Hermann. *Zur Entwicklung der Sozialistischen Nation in der DDR*. East Berlin: Dietz, 1973.

Bahr, Egon. *Zum europäischen Frieden*. Berlin (West): Siedler, 1988.

Bahro, Rudolf. *Die Alternative: Zur Kritik des real existierenden Sozialismus*. Cologne: Europaische Verlagsanstalt, 1977.

Bahry, Donna, and Brian D. Silver. "Soviet Citizen Participation on the Eve of Democratization." *The American Political Science Review* 84, no. 3 (September 1990): 821-48.

Bark, Dennis L., and David R. Gress. *A History of West Germany*. 2 vols. Oxford: Basil Blackwell, 1989.

Baylis, Thomas A. "East Germany: In Quest of Legitimacy." *Problems of Communism* 21, no. 2 (March-April 1972): 46-55.

———. *The Technical Intelligentsia and the East German Elite*. Berkeley: University of California Press, 1974.

Bender, Peter. *Das Ende des ideologischen Zeitalters Die Europäisierung Europas*. Berlin

(West): Severin und Siedler, 1981.

————. *Offensive Entspannung.* Cologne: Kiepenheuer und Witsch, 1965.

————. "The Superpower Squeeze." *Foreign Policy* 65 (Winter 1986-87): 98-113.

Berger, Wolfgang, and Otto Reinhold. *Zu den wissenschaftlichen Grundlagen des neuen ökonomischen Systems der Planung und Leitung: Das neue ökonomische System— ein wichtiger Beitrag der Sozialistischen Einheitspartei Deutschlands zur marxistisch-leninistischen Theorie.* East Berlin: Dietz, 1966.

Brandt, Peter, and Herbert Ammon, eds. *Die Linke und die nationale Frage.* Reinbek: Rowohlt, 1981.

Bryson, Phillip J. *The Consumer under Socialist Planning.* New York: Praeger, 1984.

Brzezinski, Zbigniew, and Samuel Huntington. *Political Power: USA/USSR.* New York: Viking, 1965.

Bühr, M., and A. Kosing. *Kleines Wörterbuch der marxistisch-leninistischen Philosophie.* East Berlin: Dietz, 1975.

Childs, David. *The GDR: Moscow's German Ally,* 2d ed. London: Unwin Hyman, 1988.

————, ed. *Honecker's Germany.* London: Allen and Unwin, 1985.

The Constitution of the German Democratic Republic. East Berlin: Staatsverlag der DDR, 1974.

Croan, Melvin. *East Germany: The Soviet Connection.* Beverly Hills: Sage, 1976.

Dahrendorf, Ralf. *Essays in the Theory of Society.* Stanford: Stanford University Press, 1968.

DDR Handbuch. 3rd ed. 2 vols. Cologne: Verlag Wissenschaft und Politik, 1985.

Dennis, Mike. *German Democratic Republic Politics, Economics and Society.* London: Pinter, 1988.

Deutsch, Karl. "Social Mobilization and Political Development." *American Political Science Review* 55, no. 3 (September 1961): 493-514.

DiFranceisco, Wayne, and Zvi Gitelman. "Soviet Political Culture and Covert Participation in Policy Implementation." *American Political Science Review* 78, no. 1 (March 1989): 603-21.

Dougherty, James E., and Robert L. Pfaltzgraff, Jr. *Contending Theories of International Relations.* 2d ed. New York: Harper and Row, 1981.

Duve, Freimut, Heinrich Böll, and Klaus Staeck, eds. *Kämpfe für die Sanfte Republik.* Reinbek: Rowohlt, 1980.

Easton, David. *A Systems Analysis of Political Life.* Chicago: University of Chicago Press, 1979.

Easton, David, and Jack Dennis. *Children in the Political System.* New York: McGraw-Hill, 1969.

Fischer, Fritz. *Germany's Aims in the First World War.* London: Chatto and Windus, 1967.

————. *Juli 1914: Wir sind nicht hineingeschlittert.* Reinbek: Rowohlt, 1983.

————. *War of Illusions.* New York: W. W. Norton, 1967.

Fricke, K. W. *Politik und Justiz in der DDR Zur Geschichte der politischen Verfolgung 1945-1968.* Cologne: Verlag Wissenschaft und Politik, 1979.

Gamson, William. *Power and Discontent.* Homewood, Ill.: The Dorsey Press, 1968.

Gaus, Günter. *Wo Deutschland liegt Eine Ortsbestimmung.* Hamburg: Hoffmann und Campe, 1983.

Gesetzblatt der DDR, Berlin (East), various years.

Glotz, Peter. *Die Arbeit der Zuspitzung*. Berlin (West): Siedler, 1984.

Grass, Günter. *Two States—One Nation?* San Diego: Harcourt Brace Jovanovich, 1990.

Gress. David. *Peace and Survival*. Stanford: Hoover Institute Press, 1985.

————. "The Politics of German Unification." *Proceedings of the Academy of Political Science* 38, no. 1 (1991): 140-52.

Gurr, Ted Robert. *Why Men Rebel*. Princeton: Princeton University Press, 1970.

Gwertzman, Berhard, and Michael T. Kaufman, eds. *The Collapse of Communism*. New York: Random House, 1990.

Hamilton, Daniel. "Dateline East Germany: The Wall Behind the Wall." *Foreign Policy* 76 (Fall 1989): 176-97.

Hanhardt, Arthur M., Jr. *The German Democratic Republic*. Baltimore: Johns Hopkins University Press, 1968.

Hanke, Irma. "Sozialistischer Neohistorismus?" *Deutschland Archiv* 21, no. 9 (September 1988): 980-95.

Havemann, Robert. *Dialektik ohne Dogma? Naturwissenschaft und Weltanschauung*. Reinbek: Rowohlt, 1964.

Heck, Bruno. "Vaterland und Nation Heute." *Die Politische Meinung* 29, no. 214 (May-June 1984): 28-40.

Heidenheimer, Arnold J., and Donald Kommers. *The Governments of Germany*. 4th ed. New York: Harper and Row, 1975.

Henrich, Rolf. *Der vormundschaftliche Staat Vom Versagen des real existierenden Sozialismus*. Reinbek: Rowohlt, 1989.

Herspring, Dale Roy. *East German Civil Military Relations: The Impact of Technology 1949-1972*. New York: Praeger, 1973.

Honecker, Erich. *From My Life*. New York: Pergamon, 1981.

————. *Reden und Aufsätze*. East Berlin: Dietz, 1976.

————. *Die Rolle der Arbeiterklasse und ihrer Partei in der sozialistischen Gesellschaft*. East Berlin: Dietz, 1974.

Howorth, Jolyon. "The Third Way." *Foreign Policy* 65 (Winter 1986-87): 114-34.

Hudson, Michael. *Arab Politics, The Search for Legitimacy*. New Haven, Conn.: Yale University Press, 1977.

Huntington, Samuel. *Political Order in Changing Societies*. New Haven, Conn.: Yale University Press, 1968.

Hutten, Kurt. *Christen hinter dem eisernen Vorhang*. Stuttgart: Quell-Verlag, 1963.

Joffe, Josef. "Once More: The German Question." *Survival* 32, no. 2 (March-April 1990): 127-40.

Kaiser, Karl. "Germany's Unification." *Foreign Affairs America and the World 1990/91* 70, no. 1: 179-205.

Keithly, David M. "The GDR and Reform." *Politics and Society in Germany Austria and Switzerland* 2, no. 1/2 (Spring 1990): 80-87.

Kirkpatrick, Jeane. *Dictatorships and Double Standards: Rationalism and Realism in Politics*. New York: Simon and Schuster, 1982.

Kovrig, Bennett. *Of Walls and Bridges*. New York: New York University Press, 1991.

Kuhlbach, Rodrich, and Helmut Weber. *Parteien im Blocksystem der DDR*. Cologne: Verlag Wissenschaft und Politik, 1969.

Langguth, Gerd. "Neuer Kurs in der Nationalen Frage?" *Die Politische Meinung* 33, no. 241 (November-December, 1988): 15-21.

Larrabee, Stephen F., ed. *The Two German States and European Security*. New York: St. Martin's Press, 1989.

Leenen, Wolf-Rainer. *Zur Frage der Wachstumsorientierung der marxistisch-leninistischen Sozialpolitik in der DDR*. West Berlin: Duncker und Humblot, 1977.

Lippmann, Heinz. *Honecker and the New Politics of Europe*. New York: Macmillan, 1972.

Lipset, Seymour Martin. *Political Man*. Garden City, N.Y.: Doubleday, 1960.

Lubbe, Peter. *Der staatlich etablierte Sozialismus: Zur Kritik des staatsmonopolistischen Sozialismus*. Hamburg: Hoffmann und Campe, 1975.

Ludz, Peter Christian. *Parteielite im Wandel*. 3rd ed. Cologne: Westdeutscher Verlag, 1970.

McAdams, A. James. *East Germany and Detente, Building Authority After the Wall*. Cambridge: Cambridge University Press, 1985.

———. "Inter-German Detente: A New Balance." *Foreign Affairs* 65, no. 1 (Fall 1986): 136-53.

———. "The New Logic in Soviet-GDR Relations." *Problems of Communism* 37, no. 6 (September-October 1988): 48-62.

McCardle, Arthur W., and A. Bruce Boenau, eds. *East Germany: A New Nation Under Socialism?* Lanham, Md: University Press of America, 1984.

McCauley, Martin. *The German Democratic Republic Since 1945*. New York: St. Martin's Press, 1983.

———. *Marxism-Leninism in the German Democratic Republic*. London: Macmillan, 1979.

Melzer, Manfred. "The GDR Housing Construction Program: Problems and Successes." *East Central Europe* 11, nos. 1-2 (1984): 78-96.

Meyer, Gerd, and Jurgen Schroder. *DDR Heute Wandlungstendenzen und Widersprüche einer sozialistischen Industriegesellschaft*. Tübingen: Günter Narr, 1988.

Mittag, Günter. *Probleme der Wirtschaftspolitik der Partei bei der Gestaltung der entwickelten gesellschaftlichen Systems des Sozialismus in der DDR*. East Berlin: Dietz, 1968.

Moreton, Edwina. *East Germany in the Warsaw Alliance: The Politics of Detente*. Boulder: Westview, 1978.

Müller-Römer, Dietrich. *Die Neue Verfassung der DDR*. Cologne: Verlag Wissenschaft und Politik, 1974.

Mut zur Einheit. Festschift für Johann Baptist Gradl. Cologne: Verlag Wissenschaft und Politik, 1984.

Nawrocki, Joachim. *Bewaffnete Organe in der DDR*. Berlin (West): Holzapfel, 1979.

Neugebauer, Gero. *Partei-und Staatsapparat in der DDR: Zu einigen Aspekte der Instrumentalisierung des Staatsapparats durch die SED*. Opladen: Westdeutscher Verlag, 1978.

Norden, Alfred. *Ein freies Deutschland entsteht*. Berlin: Dietz, 1963.

Nove, Alec, Hans-Herrmann Hohmann, and Gertrud Seidenstecker, eds. *The East European Economies in the 1970s*. London: Butterworths, 1982.

Pfeiler, Wolfgang. "Intra-German Relations in a Period of East-West Tensions." CISA

Working Paper No. 50, Center for International and Strategic Affairs (June 1985).

Ritter, Gerhard, *The German Problem*. Columbus: Ohio State University Press, 1965.

Roeder, Philip. "Modernization and Participation in the Leninist Development Strategy." *American Political Science Review* 83, no. 2 (June 1990): 859-84.

Rudolph, Hermann. "Die Getrennten Brüder." *Die Politische Meinung*, 31, no. 227 (July-August 1986): 22-31.

Sachs, Jeffrey, and David Lipton. "Poland's Economic Reform." *Foreign Affairs* 69, no. 3 (Summer 1990): 48-64.

Scharf, C. Bradley. *Politics and Change in East Germany*. Boulder: Westview, 1984.

Schneider, Peter. *Deutsche Ängste*. Darmstadt: Luchterhand, 1988.

Schulz, Eberhard, and Peter Danylow. *Bewegung in der deutsche Frage?* Bonn: Deutsche Gesellschaft für Auswärtige Politik, 1985.

Schöpflin, George. "The End of Communism in Eastern Europe." *International Affairs* 66, no. 1 (1990): 3-16.

Schwarz, Hans-Peter. *Die gezähmten Deutschen Von der Machtbessenheit zur Machtvergessenheit*. Stuttgart: Deutsche Verlags-Anstalt, 1985.

―――. "Der Vergessene Staat." *Die Politische Meinung* 32, no. 232 (May-June 1987): 24-32.

Schweigler, Gebhard. *National Consciousness in Divided Germany*. London: Sage, 1975.

Seiffert, Wolfgang. *Das Ganze Deutschland Perspektiven der Wiedervereinigung*. Munich: Piper, 1986.

―――. "Die Deutsche Frage nach dem Honecker-Besuch." *Deutschland Archiv* 20, no. 12 (December 1987): 1,252-57.

―――. "Die Natur des Konflikts zwischen der SED-Führung und Moskau." *Deutschland Archiv* 17, no. 10 (October 1984): 1,043-59.

―――. "Grundgesetz und Deutschlandpolitik." *Deutschland Archiv* 18, no. 10 (October 1985): 1,056-65.

―――. "Ist die DDR ein Modell?" *Deutschland Archiv* 20, no. 5 (May 1987): 470-74.

Selznick, Philip. *The Organizational Weapon*. New York: McGraw-Hill, 1952.

Simon, Jeffrey, ed. *European Security Policy after the Revolutions of 1989*. Washington, D.C.: National Defense University Press, 1991.

Smyser, W. R. *German-American Relations*. Beverly Hills: Sage, 1980.

Starrels, John M., and Anita M. Mallinckrodt. *Politics in the German Democratic Republic*. New York: Praeger, 1975.

Statistical Pocket Book of the German Democratic Republic. East Berlin: Staatsverlag der DDR, various years.

Statistisches Jahrbuch der DDR. East Berlin: Dietz, various years.

Statut der Sozialistischen Einheitspartei Deutschlands. East Berlin: Dietz, 1988.

Steele, Jonathan. *Socialism with a German Face: The State that Came in from the Cold*. London: Jonathan Cape, 1977.

Steiniger, Rolf. *Eine vertane Chance Die Stalin-Note vom 10. März 1952 und die Wiedervereinigung*. Bonn: J. H. W. Dietz, 1986.

Stürmer, Michael. "Nation und Demokratie." *Die Politische Meinung* 32, no. 230 (January-February 1987): 15-27.

Terry, Sarah Meiklejohn, ed. *Soviet Policy in Eastern Europe*. New Haven: Yale University Press, 1984.

Tucker, Robert C. *Philosophy and Myth in Karl Marx*. Cambridge: Cambridge University Press, 1972.

Ulbricht, Walter. *Die Entwicklung des deutschen volksdemokratischen Staates 1945-58*. East Berlin: Dietz, 1959.

Weber, Max. *The Theory of Economic and Social Organization*. New York: Oxford University Press, 1947.

Wettig, Gerhard. *Die Sowjetunion, die DDR und die Deutschlandfrage 1965-1976: Einvernehmen und Konflikt im sozialistischen Lager*. Stuttgart: Verlag Bonn Aktuell, 1976.

Whetten, Lawrence L. *Germany East and West*. New York: New York University Press, 1980.

Wintrobe, Ronald. "The Tinpot and the Totalitarian: An Economic Theory of Dictatorship." *American Political Science Review* 84, no. 3 (September 1990): 849-72.

Das Wissenschaftssystem in der DDR. 2d ed. Frankfurt: Campus Verlag, 1979.

Wrong, Dennis H. *Power, Its Forms, Bases and Uses*. New York: Harper and Row, 1979.

Wuthe, Gerhard. "Zur Identität in Deutschland." *Politische Vierteljahresschrift* 28, Special Edition 18 (1987): 86-93.

Zaslavsky, Victor. *The Neo-Stalinist State: Class, Ethnicity, and Consensus in Soviet Society*. Armonk: Sharpe, 1982.

Zimmermann, Hartmut. "The GDR in the 1970s." *Problems of Communism* 27, no. 2 (March-April 1978): 1-40.

PERIODICALS

Archiv der Gegenwart
Business Eastern Europe
Business Outlook
The Daily Telegraph (London)
Deutschland Archiv
Deutschland Nachrichten
Economic Bulletin
The Economist
Frankfurter Allgemeine Zeitung
Frankfurter Rundschau
The German Tribune
Hannoversche Allgemeine
Horizont
The Independent (London)
Intereconomics
Junge Welt
Mitgliederinformation
Der Morgen
Neues Deutschland
Neue Zeit

New York Review of Books
The New York Times
Der Tagesspiegel
Saarbrücker Zeitung
Stuttgarter Zeitung
Süddeutsche Zeitung
Tribüne
The Times (London)
Das Volk
The Washington Post
Die Welt
Wochenbericht
Die Zeit

Index

About the Author

David M. Keithly is a university professor and a consultant. He has taught at Lynchburg College, Claremont McKenna College, Troy State University, Embry-Riddle Aeronautical University, and Old Dominion University. He has published two books, *Nuclear Strategy, Arms Control, and the Future* and *Breakthrough in the Ostpolitik*, as well as numerous articles.